THE TEN THINGS YOU CAN'T SAY IN AMERICA

Larry Elder

ST. MARTIN'S GRIFFIN ⚕ NEW YORK

To Viola and Randolph, my mom and dad

www.stmartins.com

ISBN 0-312-28465-9

10 9 8 7 6 5 4 3 2

ACKNOWLEDGMENTS

So many people to thank, so little time.

I wish to thank Paul Cox, who first saw my potential in radio. Radio executive George Green defied conventional wisdom and hired a radio personality with virtually no experience. And I'd like to thank my radio colleague Dennis Prager, who recognized my ability and introduced me to KABC. Dennis pounded on management to give me a shot, and they listened.

I want to thank Dennis Goulden, who first saw my potential in television and hired me as a coanchor in Cleveland on WVIZ-TV's *Fabric*. Mr. Goulden encouraged me during my early days in television and saw talent in this raw, untrained future host.

I want to thank Gwen L. Deegan, my longtime partner and assistant at Elder and Associates, the executive search firm I ran in Cleveland for nearly fifteen years. She stood next to me at the beginning and through the sale of the business.

This book could not have been written without the advice, guidance, and wisdom of Alan Schonberg, the chairman of Management Recruiters International.

I wish to thank the Center for the Study of Popular Culture's David Horowitz, who rallied behind me when I most needed it.

My editor, Elizabeth Beier, remained enthusiastic about the book from the first day we met. Her suggestions made the book better.

Attorney James Wilcox, among others, read the draft manuscript and made numerous sound suggestions.

Thanks to Les Siegel for weekends diligently spent fact-checking.

To Pinky Winters-Hardaway and Jennifer Hardaway for tireless hours spent helping to type and proof the manuscript.

And thanks to my assistant, Dana Riley, for suggestions, feedback, and criticism, as well as the countless late nights, early mornings, and weekends she worked on this book to ensure that a quality manuscript was finished on time. I don't know how I could have done it without you. Now get back to work.

CONTENTS

PREFACE

Bad schools, crime, drugs, high taxes, the social security mess, "racism," the health-care "crisis," unemployment, welfare state dependency, illegitimacy, the gap between the rich and the poor. What do these issues have in common? Politicians, the media, and our so-called "leaders" lie to us about them. They lie about the cause. They lie about the effect. They lie about the solutions.

The Ten Things You Can't Say in America shows how the media, politicians (both Democrats and Republicans), schools, universities, and churches have ignored these problems—or often made them worse.

The well-intentioned though wrong-headed "war against poverty," for example, actually *encourages* poverty. The "war on drugs" makes casualties of innocent citizens, making them increasingly vulnerable to gang and drug-related violence.

"Race stories" fill our newspapers. Police brutality. Racial profiling. DWB (driving while black). "Cultural bias" in standardized testing. Minority "underrepresentation" in colleges and universities. Different perceptions of the O. J. Simpson case along racial lines. The truth is, "race relations" in America have never been more cohesive. Considering the staggering diversity of its people, racism in today's America approaches insignificance. But if you are white and say this, you're a bigot. If you're black and say it, you're an Uncle Tom. Besides, there's good money in yelling "racism."

"Leaders" fight crime by urging more gun control. To the "anti-gun" media, the "gun lobby" is not simply wrong when it says, "more guns, less crime." They are evil, out-of-control cowboys responsible for the deaths of innocent handgun victims. Never mind that armed citizens thwart hundreds of thousands, if not millions, of crimes and assaults each year, often by simply brandishing a gun. "Gun control" laws mean innocents get controlled while the bad guys get the guns.

This book rips off the cover of political correctness. *The Ten Things You Can't Say in America* says out loud what most say across the kitchen table, shop floor, and at the water cooler. Something is wrong. We've become a nation of "victicrats." We demand government handouts, bailouts, loans, tax breaks, subsidies, special protections, and guaranties while refusing to accept responsibility for our own actions. We expect the government to do that which we could and should do ourselves.

The "glass ceiling"? Nonsense. Democrats vs. Republicans? Little difference between them. Hate crimes? All crimes are hateful. O. J. Simpson? He did it, and his defense team shamelessly used the black victicrat mentality to escape conviction.

The book speaks out against self-defeating and destructive political correctness, the liberal media, the phony health-care "crisis," the job-destroying stupidity of minimum wage laws, the unconstitutional attack against smoking, and the blood on the hands of the "good guys" who want more and more gun control.

The Ten Things You Can't Say in America sets the record straight with facts, anecdotes, and common sense. It names names, corrects the record, and offers solutions.

The goal is simple. As Americans, we must refocus our energies. We must face and defeat the twin villains—a dependency-creating government and our refusal to accept responsibility for our own lives.

This book questions why the government takes so much of our money. It illustrates the damage to our national psyche when politicians pit group against group by giving some "set-asides" and other special privileges. It shows how the private, charitable sector can better address the needs of the poor and the sick than government.

Imagine a country where people who commit crimes actually get punished, where those who behave badly must own up to the consequences of their actions, and where a small and decent government allows citizens maximum personal and financial freedom. Imagine an America of the next century—a happier, fairer, more productive society.

We can get there, but not if we remain a country with "ten things you can't say in America."

1

BLACKS ARE MORE RACIST
THAN WHITES

Make no mistake about it. The Klan is alive and well in Southern California and there is a good chance that many of the CEOs who sit in powerful positions could either be Klan members or Klan sympathizers.[1]

—Columnist for the black news weekly
Los Angeles Sentinel

Racism Is Racism

"Larry Elder, is there a connection between your beliefs and the house and the white woman you have waiting for you in the hills?"

A black man asked me that during a debate over whether Hollywood conspires to shut out blacks. I called the notion paranoid and was greeted with that rather charming question.

Unfortunately, the questioner was typical. Many American blacks falsely and unfairly accuse whites for black America's "plight." Bad schools? White racism. Crime? White racism. Underperformance on standardized tests? Racist or "culturally biased" tests. Can't get a loan for a home or a new business? Racist lending officers, who would rather reject profit than give a black man a loan. Disproportionately high arrest rates? Racial profiling by racist cops.

To put it more bluntly, many blacks simply despise whites. They assume white bigotry and hostility toward blacks, and feel—against all evidence—that "white racism" remains an intense and formidable obstacle. What nonsense. So convinced that white racism stops black progress, many blacks not only ignore obvious signs of progress, but viciously attack anyone—especially someone black—who dares challenge the "they're-out-to-get-us" point of view. To hold the view—as I do—that racism no longer represents a serious threat to black upward mobility, to feel confident and positive about "race relations" in America—that makes me a "sell-out." Thus, the questioner's attack, not on my views, philosophy, or ideology, but on me personally.

I take three positions, earning the wrath of blacks. First, I repudiate the "Johnnie Cochran doctrine." Recall that during the O. J. Simpson trial, defense attorney Cochran voiced the mantra of many "black leaders" when he said, "Race plays a part of everything in America." Second, I oppose race- and gender-based affirmative action. And, third, I believe O. J. Simpson butchered two innocent human beings. For this, "my people" have called me the following:

Oreo. Uncle Tom. Boot-licking Uncle Tom. Straight-up Uncle Tom. Judas. Boy. Bug-eyed. Foot-shuffling. Sugarcane Negro. Handkerchief head. Trojan Horse. Anti-black. Pro-white. Remus. Sambo. Sambo-Tom. The Anti-Christ. Clarence Thomas supporter. Sniveling weasel. Evil. Ass-kisser. Coconut. Wannabe white. Nickering nabob of negativity. And this is just an abbreviated list.

How dare I suggest that the fate of blacks is, well, in the hands of blacks!

Many blacks, encouraged by the so-called "black leadership," view life starkly. Us against them. Black versus white. Rich versus poor. Key is the following assumption: that whites encourage, endorse, perpetuate, welcome, are happy about, and take pride in the oppression of blacks. Challenge the traditional white-man-done-me-wrong-and-continues-to-do-so mentality, and some blacks go absolutely crazy.

What about black Atlanta mayor Bill Campbell's over-the-top defense of affirmative action? "Everybody who is a person of color in this country has benefited from affirmative action. There's not been anybody who has gotten into college on their own, nobody who's gotten a job on their own, no one who's prospered as a businessman or businesswoman on their own without affirmative action."[2]

Hysterical. How else to describe how some blacks reacted to the California debate on affirmative action? Students at a local college there, Cal State Northridge, decided to host a debate over Proposition 209, a ballot initiative to exclude race and gender as a consideration in public hiring, public contracting, and admissions into state colleges and universities. For the pro-affirmative-action side, they selected a black veteran civil rights activist in Los Angeles. To defend the anti-affirmative-action position, they invited . . . David Duke! That's right. David Duke. See, anyone opposing affirmative action therefore supports racism, Jim Crow, lynchings, hangings, police brutality, and the Klan. Why, if the anti-affirmative-action folks could, they would reenact slavery, take away the women's vote, and deregulate cable. Quick, somebody stop them! Is this not racist?

Influential black congresswoman Maxine Waters, former head of the Black Congressional Caucus, once called President George Bush "racist."[3] Why? He differed with her on policy. That's enough. And Waters routinely refers to Republicans as "the enemy." Blatant bigotry against whites, for many blacks, resembles a badge of honor. Many blacks feel they can, with impunity, make utterly racist statements.

Vice President Al Gore's presidential campaign manager, a

black woman named Donna Brazile, once talked about the importance of defeating the Republicans. We must, she said, defeat the "white boys." "White boys," she said, has nothing to do with "gender or race, it's an attitude. A white boy attitude is 'I must exclude, denigrate, and leave behind.' They don't see it or think about it. It's a culture."[4] A "white boy attitude"? She also attacked black Republicans General Colin Powell and Oklahoma congressman J. C. Watts: "The Republicans bring out Colin Powell and J. C. Watts because they have no program, no policy. They play that game because they have no other game. They have no love and no joy. They'd rather take pictures with black children than feed them."[5]

Colin Powell, perhaps the most respected American public figure, would "rather take pictures with black children than feed them"? Colin Powell, who spends considerable time and energy in promoting volunteerism, would "rather take pictures with black children than feed them"? Powell, mind you, supports affirmative action, favors gun control legislation, once called the Newt Gingrich Republican "Contract with America" too harsh, and is pro-choice. But he has "no love and no joy." Hey, a statement like that gets a "white boy" campaign manager canned. But Ms. Brazile remains in charge, with virtually no one making an issue out of her blatantly bigoted statements.

Influential black director Spike Lee made a movie, *Jungle Fever*, about an interracial black-white romance. Lee, however, publicly stated his contempt for interracial relationships. In an October 1992 *Esquire* interview, Lee said, "I give interracial couples a look. Daggers. They get uncomfortable when they see me on the street." Charming.

In the Spike Lee movie *Malcolm X*, Lee depicts an actual incident where a white teenager approaches the angry activist. "Excuse me, Mr. X. Hi, I've read some of your speeches, and I honestly believe that a lot of what you have to say is true, and I'm a good person, in spite of what my ancestors did, and I just, I wanted to ask you, what can a white person like myself who isn't prejudiced, what can I do to help you . . . further your cause?" she asks plaintively. He stares sternly and replies, "Nothing."

When I gave a speech at a local high school, the front row featured several young black men wearing Malcolm X T-shirts. The picture on the T-shirts was that of "Malcolm-as-firebrand," with his finger thrust in the air circa his "white-man-is-the-devil" period.

"Do you know what happened to Malcolm X late in his life?" I asked the students. Two of the three said, "No." But the third said, "Yes. After he visited Mecca, where he saw people of all colors worshiping together, he changed the way he thought."

"Yes," I said. "Malcolm repudiated his 'white man as devil' anger and found that people had more in common than apart."

In Alex Haley's *The Autobiography of Malcolm X*, Malcolm X later reflects and regrets his response to the white coed.

"Well, I've lived to regret that incident. In many parts of the African continent I saw white students helping black people. Something like this kills a lot of argument. I did many things as a Muslim that I'm sorry for now. I was a zombie then—like all Muslims—I was hypnotized, pointed in a certain direction and told to march. Well, I guess a man's entitled to make a fool of himself if he's ready to pay the cost. It cost me twelve years."[6]

Yet many blacks prefer to freeze their notion of Malcolm X in time, leaving him at the "white-man-is-devil-and-done-me-wrong-and-he's-gonna-get-his" stage. Never mind that Malcolm later renounced this blanket hatred of whites.

Suppose hypothetically, that director Martin Scorsese, in a television interview, says, "You know, whenever I see a black guy with a white woman, I give 'em a look like someone just expelled gas." Quicker than you can say "Arnold Schwarzenegger," Scorsese's publicist holds a press conference, issues a heartfelt and sincere apology, and explains that someone took the director's remarks out of context. Scorsese then steps up and announces the establishment of a "minority outreach fund" to develop screenwriters, directors, and producers. We all, says a tearful Scorsese, must become more sensitive to the concerns of the downtrodden and the "under-represented." Now Scorsese's back in business.

But what of Spike Lee? Perhaps someone should remind Lee of the 1970 Supreme Court decision that struck down laws against interracial marriage. Does Lee wish to reenact them? Does he agree with Chief Justice Taney, of Dred Scott fame, who deemed blacks to be sub-citizens without full rights, including the right to marry whomever they wish? Lee thus insults NAACP chairman Julian Bond, who married a white woman, as well as millions of other Americans in "interracial relationships." But did anyone, whether a black leader, editorial writer, political pundit, or movie reviewer demand an apology, or at least an explanation, from Spike Lee? Did anyone boycott his movies the way Catholics, blacks, Hispanics, and other groups target "offensive" movies? No, an unbelievably and blatant racist statement made by influential public figure Lee just floated right on by.

South Carolina's Bob Jones University lost its tax exempt status for refusing to admit blacks. While the university today admits blacks, it refused to allow interracial dating until recently. Critics blasted Republican presidential candidate George W. Bush for giving a speech there. "Racism," screamed critics who blasted Bush for his racial insensitivity in daring to give a speech at such a repulsive institution.

But is Bob Jones's anti-interracial dating policy any less offensive than a position taken by the National Association of Black Social Workers? That organization opposes "trans-racial" adoptions. According to that organization, blacks and whites have vast cultural differences. A white couple should not, therefore, adopt a black child.

In 1992, the National Association of Black Social Workers drafted a position paper, calling white adoptions of black children "cultural genocide." The group warned against "transcultura-tion . . . when one dominant culture overpowers and forces another culture to accept a foreign form of existence."[7] A foreign form of existence?

Furthermore, many blacks, like whites, flatly oppose interracial dating and interracial marriage. In 1994, 65 percent of whites approved of interracial dating versus only 43 percent in 1987. Among young whites, 85 percent approved of interracial dating.

The majority of blacks, too, approved of interracial dating, with 88 percent giving approval in 1994. Among blacks, however, approval for mixed marriages fell from 76 percent in 1983 to 68 percent six years later. Among whites, though, those accepting mixed marriages continued to grow.[8]

Black Racism and Black Myopia

When Julian Bond became NAACP chairman, he declared his intention to wage war on the number one problem facing blacks: "the new racists."

The new racists? Care to name names, Mr. Bond?

Examine Bond's mind-set. America is a battlefield. Good versus evil. Us versus them.

During the Second World War, Japanese fighters in Burma continued fighting long after the warring parties negotiated peace. Their remote location prevented them from learning the news, so they continued fighting. Similarly, many blacks continue "fighting the struggle" long after the declaration of peace. By nearly any measure—the right to vote, to use public accommodations, to attend a state college or university if qualified—the "civil rights" struggle, thank God, is over. The black leadership should stick the pole in the ground, raise the flag, salute, and convert the troops to civilian duty. Instead, they continue fighting a war long since won while ignoring far more pressing issues. The black leadership is in Burma.

In 1977, I accepted a job as an associate attorney with an old-line, silk-stocking Cleveland law firm. The firm, now more than a hundred years old, had, in its history, hired just a handful of blacks. My uncle, a thirty-year auto machinist with General Motors, sat me down to "caution" me about white treachery. "Larry, let me tell you something. You know I grew up on a farm in Alabama. My brothers and sisters and neighbors and I would walk, barefoot, five miles to the nearby schoolhouse. The white kids got bused to a school three miles away. And, as the bus drove by us black kids walking in single file, the white kids would curse at us, call us niggers, spit at us, and throw eggs and tomatoes. And this is how white folks can be, and I want you to—"

I cut him off. "Thurman," I said, "you know I love you. But, what happened to you has never happened to me. Nor will it. Today is today."

The real danger lies with the NAACP, not the KKK. Racism exists, and treachery always lurks. But the vision my uncle painted—however burnished in his own mind—bears little resemblance to contemporary America.

Hard memories. Tough, quite understandable, hard memories. In Florida, the public school system, with the support of the NAACP, seeks to end decades-long court-ordered desegregation. But one of the original litigants, Charles Rutledge, now 75 years old, denounces the proposed end to forced desegregation. Never mind that the lifting of the court order is supported by the NAACP, an organization whose chairman declared as his number one agenda to go after "the new racist." Say what you will about the NAACP, they are not soft on racism.

But Rutledge says, "If the court order is rescinded, they'll do what they want. America is still a racist nation. Hearts of men haven't changed that much."[9]

Hard memories. But these memories do not reflect the memories of today's America. No one says forget, but we should recognize obvious progress, and maintain perspective.

My mother also grew up in the South, on a farm near Huntsville, Alabama. When my grandfather took my mom and her sister to the department store downtown, they entered through a separate door. And when my mom put on a dress, once the garment touched her skin, she owned it. The store made my grandfather purchase the item, no matter how ill fitting or unattractive. Black skin tainted the garments.

When my mom finished that story, I turned to my father. "Dad, was it like that with you, too?" My father, a man of few words, simply said, "Hats, too."

In the early 1950s, my mom took a plane ride. While pregnant with me, she carried my infant brother in her arms. Few blacks, in those days, traveled by air. So, no separate facilities—waiting rooms, bathrooms—yet existed in airports for blacks. So where was my mother to sit in the airport?

My mom said a sheepish airport worker asked her to stand to the side, and he brought her coffee. My mom said she felt almost sorry for this young white man, who saw the absurdity in forcing a paying customer to stand apart because of her skin color.

My parents told us these stories to show how far America has come, not to create anger, to divide, or to poison us. That America, my mom and dad told my brothers and me, no longer exists. So work hard, they said, and success follows.

We need historical perspective. Yes, slavery is America's horror and shame. But slavery, unfortunately, appears throughout the whole of human history. Europeans enslaved Europeans. Asians enslaved Asians. Those we refer to as Native Americans enslaved other Native Americans. Black Africans enslaved other black Africans. Slave traders brought more African slaves to the Middle East and to South America than to Colonial America. Yet this country fought a civil war that resulted in the eradication of slavery. No other nation can say that.

But the black leadership in the United States remains dreary and pessimistic. Members of the Black Congressional Caucus introduced legislation for reparations for slavery.

Do wealthy blacks get a check? Should descendants of those who came to America after slavery pay up? Should descendants of those who fought and died on the Union side pay up? Should we make deductions for the trillions of dollars spent by the government on social programs from which blacks have benefited? What about people of mixed race? Should the payment correspond only to the percentage of a given citizen's "black blood"? Should we get a contribution from the African nations? After all, some black Africans assisted in the slave trade. And what about another question? Suppose the slave trade never happened, and today's thirty million American blacks instead live in Africa. Would they be better off?

Reparations, indeed! What a waste of time and energy. For all a country can be is just in its own time.

Illegitimacy, poor schools, drug abuse, crime—you name it—get blamed on white racism. This insults generations of black men and women who worked, survived, and thrived under unimaginably inhumane conditions. Today, many blacks ignore the meteoric progress of blacks, a success under way well before anyone heard of the expression "affirmative action."

In high school, my class read a poem:

While riding through old Baltimore, so small and full of glee,
I saw a young Baltimorean keep a-lookin' straight at me.
Now, I was young and very small, and he was no whit bigger
And so I smiled, but he poked out his tongue and called me "nigger."
I saw the whole of Baltimore from May until September,
Of all the things that happened there, that's all that I remember.

The teacher talked about the permanent damage done to this little boy's psyche. The permanent stain of racism. The denial of the little boy's dignity. The boy, said the teacher, will never be the same. By the time the bell sounded, everybody left angry.

I went home and repeated the poem to my mom. When I

came to the last stanza: "Of all the things that happened there, that's all that I remember," she took a spoon out of the pot she was stirring, rapped it on the side, turned to me and said, "Larry, it's too bad he let *that* spoil his vacation."

Pre–affirmative action, pre–Civil Rights Act of 1964, pre–Voting Rights Act of 1965, pre–Open Housing Act of 1968, Supreme Court justice Robert Jackson wrote in an unpublished 1954 Brown vs. Board of Education draft concurrence, "Negro progress under segregation has been spectacular and, tested by the pace of history, his rise is one of the swiftest and most dramatic advances in the annals of man."[10] Hear, hear!

And today, taxpayers provide state-funded education. Blacks can rely, for the most part, on the police to do their jobs without violating human rights. The unemployment rate stands at a thirty-year low, with black unemployment falling faster than white joblessness. A black with the same years of experience and quality of education can expect to earn what a white man earns. America's computer age rapidly increases productivity, and our nation's standard of living rises at a pace unknown in all of human history.

Midtown Los Angeles is an area largely populated with Hispanics and Asians. At the corner of Olympic and Vermont there once stood a small dingy, library.

"Larry," said my friend, Frank, who lives in midtown, "I want to show you something." About 3:30 P.M., I met Frank in front of the library. "Look at this," Frank said.

In front of the building, which stood on a slight incline, a half-dozen Hispanic kids rode skateboards. They did impressive tricks, including spins, flips, and other almost gravity-defying, Michael Jordan–esque moves.

"Now," Frank said, "come on inside."

We entered the library. Standing room only. Every chair and desk was occupied . . . by Korean-American kids and their mothers. Not a single Hispanic in the building.

Now, fast-forward ten or twenty years later. Which group will likely generate the senior vice president of sales and marketing at Merck, and which group will likely spawn lesser achievers?

Politicians can scream all they want about the "digital divide," the allegation that the computer era leaves many behind through no fault of their own. But the bottom line, ground zero, remains the little library at the corner of Olympic and Vermont. The library shows that affirmative action remains alive and well in our country. Only some call it homework.

So, today's challenge is not black versus white. It is prepared versus unprepared. This means making schools work, holding parents and students to high standards, and shaming those who irresponsibly breed and then abandon their children. The "black leaders'" almost pathological search for the Great White Bigot does not address these problems.

Black Harvard sociologist Orlando Patterson said, "The sociological truths are that America, while still flawed in its race relations . . . is now the least racist white-majority society in the world; has a better record of legal protection of minorities than any other society, white or black; offers more opportunities to a greater number of black persons than any other society, including all those of Africa. . . ."

The editor of the *National Review*, John O. Sullivan, put it this way, "White racism exists. But its social power is weak, the social power against it overwhelming."

Would the Last Black Republican/Conservative Please Turn Out the Light?

Blacks hate Republicans.

Bill Maxwell, black editorial writer and columnist for the *St. Petersburg Times*, wrote a column called "Black Republicans: Self-Loathers."[11] Some choice excerpts:

- Some creatures are just plain strange, making us do double takes because their compositions or habits or appearances defy our sense of logic and our way of viewing reality.

- Take the wildebeest, warthog, hyena, brown pelican, the Shar-Pei. These animals, seemingly wrought by committee make us laugh. Another such creature, of the human kind—and perhaps the strangest of all—is the black Republican.

- Black Republicans fail to understand that few white Republicans will accept them as equals. Although they will not acknowledge the truth, most white Republicans, like most other whites, view black Republicans as strange creatures.

- White Republicans feign consternation that most blacks find them contemptible, arguing that those mean old Democrats have been black people's real enemy all along. Keyes and others, such as U.S. Supreme Court Justice Clarence Thomas, Oklahoma Rep. J. C. Watts and California businessman Ward Connerly, also spout this nonsense.

- Some blacks like [Colin] Powell become Republicans because they see clear political advantage or because they work for Republicans.

  Most others, however, are mean-spirited self-loathers who rarely find anything positive to say about fellow blacks.

  They out-nasty the worst white racist, calling the likes of Jesse Jackson, the NAACP's Kweisi Mfume, and the Urban League's Hugh Price evil men hell-bent on destroying America.

  White Republicans love this kind of stuff. They wink and nod each time black Republicans claim that racism is a thing of the past, that whites and blacks are free to compete equally. Black Republicans have fooled themselves into believing that white Republicans are their brethren.

And, of course, black Republicans delude themselves into believing that they alone are responsible for their success.

Other than that, Mr. Maxwell, how do you really feel?

New York congressman Charles Rangel said of the 1994 Republican Congress, "It's not 'spic' or 'nigger' any more. They say 'let's cut taxes.' "[12] How bad is it? Well, nearly everybody loves Colin Powell. Except blacks. According to a 1995 poll,[13] Powell enjoyed a 73 percent popularity rating among whites. Among blacks, however, he registered only 57 percent. Think about that. A Newt Gingrich clone, he ain't. As mentioned earlier, Powell is a social moderate, perhaps truly more comfortable in the Democratic Party than in the Republican. And he made the country proud by kicking Saddam Hussein's butt.

So for a black voter, what's not to like? Yeah, blacks say, but he's . . . a Republican.

To many black people, Republicans don't simply represent a different point of view. They represent "racism," "back-of-the-busism," and, if they could get away with it, a reversal in fundamental civil rights. When congresswoman Maxine Waters calls the Republicans "the enemy," this suits most blacks just fine. Obviously, Republicans want blacks at the back of the bus and, if possible, back on the plantation.

How warranted is this black hatred of Republicans? Abraham Lincoln became the first nationally elected candidate from the newly formed Republican Party. The party platform that year sought to prevent the spread of slavery.

Because "Lincoln freed the slaves," black voters supported the Republican Party for years. Even as late as the 1956 race between Dwight Eisenhower and Adlai Stevenson, blacks gave Republicans nearly 35 percent of the vote.

This allegiance switched in the 1960 Kennedy-Nixon presidential race, when a southern sheriff arrested Dr. Martin Luther King. King's aides sent identically worded letters to both John F.

Kennedy and Richard Nixon. Kennedy responded. Nixon did not. Because of Kennedy's intervention and the public light it shed, the Southern jailers quickly released King. For this important symbolic and meaningful gesture, blacks rewarded John F. Kennedy in the voting booth, putting him over the top in this extremely close election with 70 percent of their vote.

But it was southern *Democrats* who formed the line to defend Jim Crow. Georgia governor Lester Maddox famously brandished ax handles to prevent blacks from patronizing his restaurant. He was a Democrat. Alabama governor George Wallace stood in front of the Alabama schoolhouse in 1963 and thundered, "Segregation now, segregation tomorrow, segregation forever." He was a Democrat. Birmingham Public Safety commissioner Eugene "Bull" Connor sicced dogs and turned fire hoses on black civil rights demonstrators. He was a Democrat. In 1954, Arkansas governor Orville Faubus tried to prevent the desegregation of a Little Rock public high school. He was a Democrat. President Eisenhower, a Republican, sent in federal troops to prevent violence and enforce a court order desegregating the school.

As a percentage of their respective parties, more Republicans voted for the passage of the Civil Rights Act of 1964 than did Democrats!

A Republican president, Richard Nixon, not John F. Kennedy or Lyndon B. Johnson, instituted the first affirmative action program with goals and timetables.

On the mantels of black homes, you often find pictures of Martin Luther King, Jr., and the slain Kennedy brothers. But, near the end of the Kennedy presidency, black leaders seethed over his failure to push for major civil rights legislation. Kennedy, ever the pragmatist, wanted to wait until after the 1964 election, fearing a civil rights push could alienate the important southern vote. Not exactly the credentials of a civil rights warrior.

And, it was during the Kennedy administration that FBI head J. Edgar Hoover sought and received permission to wiretap Martin

Luther King. The person granting him permission? Attorney General Robert F. Kennedy.

Want to start a fight? Walk into a black barbershop and praise Ronald Reagan.

Blacks simply do not know that blacks prospered greatly under Reagan. But black adult unemployment fell faster during his presidency than did white adult unemployment. Black teenage unemployment fell faster than did white teenage unemployment.

But Reagan, according to Black Entertainment Television commentator Tavis Smiley, "tortured" blacks. Tortured? Yet, despite popular misconception, Reagan did not shut down any significant poverty program. In fact social spending under Ronald Reagan actually grew! Reagan did not "roll back the social safety net." He preserved it, and, in many cases, expanded it.

Still, no pictures of Ronald Reagan on the mantel of blacks.

Earlier we discussed Proposition 209, California's initiative to remove race- and gender-based affirmative action. Ward Connerly, a successful black contractor, led California's grassroots effort to repeal race- and gender-based preferences. Connerly felt demeaned that the state assumed he needed a boost and believed that the affirmative action mentality creates a dependent mind-set that robs people of self-sufficiency and the willingness to assume personal responsibility.

Even affirmative action supporter Arthur Ashe, in *Days of Grace*, spoke of affirmative action's entitlement mentality: "Affirmative action tends to undermine the spirit of individual initiative. Such is human nature; why struggle to succeed when you can have something for nothing?"[14]

But Connerly clashed with black leaders, who accused him of selling out. Black California State senator Diane Watson, a staunch proponent of affirmative action, viciously attacked Connerly, "He's married a white woman. He wants to be white. He wants a colorless society. He has no ethnic pride. He doesn't want to be black."[15] What? Yet another attack from a black person about the race of another black person's spouse! Afterward, a heartfelt apology? Not on your life. When reporters later asked Senator Watson about the remark, she defiantly stated, "That's right. I said that." Spike Lee would be proud.

Suppose, during the 1996 race for the Republican nomination for the presidency, Senator Bob Dole attacked rival Senator Phil Gramm because Gramm married a Korean-American. Are you kidding? The Dole campaign goes supernova. Lights out. Case closed.

But Senator Diane Watson? Well, Clinton later nominated her as U.S. ambassador to Micronesia.

USA Today columnist Julianne Malveaux said that she hoped conservative black Supreme Court justice Thomas's wife would feed him "lots of eggs and butter and he dies early . . . of heart disease."[16]

Justice Thomas serves as poster boy for the wrath of the black left. And many blacks simply cannot rationally discuss Clarence Thomas. Equally conservative Supreme Court Justice Antonin Scalia—no problem. Many blacks can rationally discuss the politics of John Wayne, Newt Gingrich, Pat Buchanan, and even Ronald Reagan. But Clarence Thomas?

The black monthly magazine *Emerge*, with a circulation of 162,000, featured a cover on Justice Thomas. The magazine depicted a cartoonish Thomas dressed as a lawn jockey, holding a lantern and sporting a broad grin. The cover caption? "Uncle Thomas, Lawn Jockey to the Far Right." And, inside the cover, we see another cartoon picture, this time of Clarence Thomas, on his knees, shining the shoes of fellow Supreme Court Justice Antonin Scalia, another despicable "conservative."

Emerge magazine calls itself a "black news monthly." News monthly? Imagine a *Time* magazine cover story showing an obese Ted Kennedy stuffed into a jockey suit and holding a lantern with the headline reading, "Uncle Ted, Lawn Jockey to the Far Left." Recall the infamous *Time* magazine's O. J. Simpson cover. For what it thought of as dramatic effect, *Time* darkened Simpson's features. "Racism," hollered black leaders. *Time* quickly apologized. But a "news monthly" like *Emerge* can caricature a black Supreme Court justice as a shoeshine boy without fear of criticism.

Black publisher Emanuel McLittle produced a now-defunct monthly publication called *Destiny*. *Destiny*'s message: work hard, stop blaming "the White Man," and let's have a little perspective. Prominent writers such as Walter Williams sat on *Destiny*'s board and contributed columns. But *Destiny* folded, citing an inability to attract mainstream, national advertisers. The shrill, angry *Emerge* magazine faces no such problem. Chrysler, G.E., and AT&T all advertise in this magazine despite its constant attack on "racist" corporate America. What is *that* all about?

Diversity of thought simply does not exist, especially not in the black media.

Several black conservatives syndicate their columns all across the country. Professor Walter Williams's column appears in 400 newspapers, and conservative economist Thomas Sowell's appears in 150. And there are other gifted conservative black columnists in local newspapers all around the country. Donald Adderton of the *Sun Herald*, in Gulfport, Mississippi. Michael Meyers of the *New York Post*. Joe Stewart of the *San Diego Tribune*. Deroy Murdock, who has written for the *Washington Times*, the *Wall Street Journal*, the *New York Post*, the *Orange County Register*, the *San Francisco Examiner*, the *Miami Herald*, and others. Yet, the typical black weekly newspaper, the ones screaming for multiculturalism, inclusion, and diversity, completely shut these minds and thinkers out. Even most big city liberal mainstream newspapers give black conservatives more respect, carrying the occasional column by a conservative and even setting aside some space for a conservative point of view. Not so with black newspapers.

When It Comes to Shameless Demagoguery, Overheated Rhetoric, and Outright Lies, Black Leaders Shine

Many black leaders and other prominent public figures say the dumbest, damndest, and most insulting things. For example, the venerable Bill Cosby once suggested that AIDS was a plot against blacks. The entertainer said he believed AIDS was developed "to get after certain people." Admitting he had no proof, he said, "I just have a feeling."[17]

Similarly, Will Smith, in an interview with Barbara Walters, suggested that scientists conceived AIDS to retaliate against blacks.

"Ethnic cleansing," cried Jesse Jackson, following a Supreme Court decision striking down Southern Congressional districts drawn up to create minority congresspersons.[18] Along with Jackson, Elaine Jones of the NAACP Legal Defense Fund denounced the decision, saying, "The noose is tightening."[19] Her colleague, Theodore Shaw, warned that once this decision goes through, the Black Congressional Caucus "could meet in the back seat of a taxicab."[20] Well, the blacks who decided to run for reelection in now-majority-white southern districts all won! Did Jackson, who once called Jews "Hymies" and New York City "Hymie Town," apologize for his unfair and pessimistic expectations of white voters? David Duke will join the Harlem Globetrotters before that happens.

Some of the most successful, wealthiest blacks nevertheless whine about the racism. Whoopi Goldberg, the comedian-actress, complained about Hollywood, even though, at the time, she earned more money than *any* actress. "The one thing I've learned is that you're black forever in Hollywood. Your color never dissipates. It never becomes about: you're this actor. You're always: this actor who is this . . . And so I suspect that somewhat begrudgingly I sit atop that little miniskyscraper. But it's a very precarious situation always because people don't want to pay you that money."[21]

Meaning what? That studios willingly open their pocketbooks for white actresses but hold their nose when doing it for black ones?

Black baseball player Gary Sheffield, who in 1998 earned a record $14.9 million, complained about racism, noting, "You see racism [in baseball] every single minute of every day."[22] Jeez. Even during the National Anthem?

Nearly all mainstream newspapers have the obligatory angry black leftist columnist, and Julianne Malveaux serves this function for *USA Today*. When Malveaux and I appeared on a national television show, I accused her of obsessing over "the great white bigot." To this, she incredibly fired back, "There is no one 'great white bigot.' There are about 200 million little white ones!" That pretty much covers every white man, woman, and child in America and, perhaps, even a few of the unborn.

Denzel Washington reportedly refused to kiss his white female costar in the movie *Virtuosity* because he feared the reaction from the targeted white male audience. However, Kelly Lynch, his female costar, *wanted* to kiss Washington. But Washington, despite a green light from the filmmakers, said no. Lynch explained, "He felt very strongly about it. I felt there is no problem with interracial romance. But Denzel felt strongly that the white males, who were the target audience of this movie, would not want to see him kiss a white woman."[23] Think about this. Doesn't Washington's white female costar know a thing or two about white males? Presumably, her parents are white. She likely has lots of white friends. She probably, therefore, knows something about the "white male mind-set." But, Washington, obviously the expert here, knows far more about the inner bigotry of white men than his white costar. His pessimism trumps her optimism. Another victory for race relations!

How crazy does it get? Real crazy. Some black leaders even *create* racial incidents. In Beverly Hills, on June 3, 1998, the police pulled over black California State senator Kevin Murray. Police later said they had run his plates, getting back a "no access" response. Officers thought this odd, and asked Murray to pull over.

Well, the "fit hit the shan." Murray screamed "racism." Another victim of "DWB—driving while black." Had it not been a black man in Beverly Hills, claimed Murray, you guys would not have stopped me.

But a reporter for *New Times,* a Los Angeles alternative weekly newspaper, wrote that Murray intentionally blew up the incident. Murray, the reporter wrote, bragged to his neighbors that he intended to "milk this thing for as far as I can go." His neighbor claimed that Murray laughed at the incident and admitted that it had little, if anything, to do with race. "Kevin has really been enjoying the publicity from being pulled over, and I mean *really* been enjoying it," said the neighbor. "He's going for big mileage on it, and he's loving it. Don't you just love that? When it's just talk between friends, he never says it's about race. He says it's because this woman cop had a snotty tone with him, and nobody can treat [him] with disrespect."[24]

"No justice, no peace," bellowed Congresswoman Maxine Waters during the 1992 Los Angeles riots.[25] Following the "not guilty" verdict against four cops who beat black motorist Rodney King, rioters set fire to more than two thousand businesses, causing billions of dollars in damage. Koreans owned most of the businesses that were torched.

Yet, black leaders like Waters described the riots as a "rebellion"[26] or an "uprising." A rebellion or uprising against *Korean* store owners? No one calls for reparations for the Korean shopkeepers who saw their life savings and means of income wiped out in a matter of a few hours. Indeed, for allegedly failing to keep dollars within the black community, Nation of Islam Minister Louis Farrakhan calls these hardworking Los Angeles Korean store owners "bloodsuckers."

Black "Victicrats"

A "victicrat" blames all ills, problems, concerns, and unhappiness on others. This black victicrat mentality emerges in strange, unpredictable, confusing, and frequently inconsistent ways.

One summer during high school, I applied for a job with the County of Los Angeles. To qualify for the job, hundreds of students gathered downtown to take an aptitude test. If you scored below a certain level, the county deemed you unqualified, and you had to leave. After the three- or four-hour exam, we waited in the hall as the instructors graded the exams. Gilbert, a fellow student, approached me.

"Watch out, Larry, they're gonna get us."

"Who's gonna get us, Gilbert?"

Gilbert sighed and rolled his eyes knowingly. "You know, the white people, that's who."

"But, Gilbert, you think they're gonna 'punish' the blacks by flunking us?"

"Larry, you got a lot to learn."

Well, they announced the results of the exam. I passed, as did many other minorities. But Gilbert did not. He got up to leave, looked me in the eyes as he walked by, and said, "What did I tell you?"

The *Washington Post*, in 1995, wrote about black, white, Hispanic, and Asian views on race. Pollsters asked middle-income blacks whether "past and present discrimination" is responsible for your group's problems, and 84 percent of blacks answered yes. When middle-income whites were asked whether "past and present discrimination" holds blacks back, only 30 percent said yes.[27] This is no surprise. It mirrors the attitudes of blacks and whites during the O.J. Simpson case, where a majority of blacks felt Simpson innocent, while the overwhelming majority of whites felt the opposite.

Here's where things get interesting. The pollster[28] asked Hispanics whether they find "past and present discrimination" to be responsible for holding them back and 43 percent said yes. But when blacks were asked whether "past or present discrimination" holds *Hispanics* back, 58 percent said yes. In other words, *30 percent more blacks perceived discrimination against Hispanics than did Hispanics themselves.*

Similarly, Asians were asked whether "past or present discrimination" holds Asians back. Thirty-one percent said yes. But when pollsters asked blacks if "past or present discrimination" holds Asians back, 41 percent said yes.[29] Again, *30 percent more blacks perceived racism against Asians, than did Asians themselves.*

On my Los Angeles radio show, I asked people to explain why blacks saw more racism against Hispanics and Asians than did Hispanics and Asians themselves. A black caller said, "We're experts in perceiving racism." Oh. Astute and hardworking Japanese-Americans and Chinese-Americans manage to earn more money, per capita, than virtually any other group in America. Yet the very same people are too stupid to realize the white race continues to hold them back.

Despite little evidence, nearly one-third of blacks believe the CIA played a major role in the inner-city drug epidemic, and nearly that many believe, as entertainers Bill Cosby and Will Smith once suggested, that scientists concocted AIDS to further black genocide.

Many blacks blame substandard urban schools' performance on racism, claiming that urban districts get less money for schools than suburban and rural districts. So, then, it's about the money? But, in districts like Washington, D.C., New York, and Los Angeles, districts spend upwards of $9,000 per child, far more than the average tuition for private and parochial schools.

Furthermore, black superintendents run many urban districts, often with substantial black membership. Many of these troubled districts reside in cities run by black mayors and where the city council is substantially, if not majority, black. Despite the money, despite black management, all too often, the results are lousy.

Journalist David Beard, writing for the *Sun-Sentinel, South Florida* noted that a Barbadian SAT score of 1345 was "about average for the students of . . . secondary school in this Caribbean nation." The teachers in Barbados earn less money than their U.S. counterparts. A substantial number, over 50%, of the students come from single-parent households. Yet, said former Boston University chancellor John Silber, "They defy all of the expectations and all of the clichés passed off as excuses for the poor quality of primary and secondary education in the United States."[30]

Why do black students in Barbados perform so well on the "culturally biased" SAT? And, if the SAT is "culturally biased," wouldn't the test handicap students from the "Barbadian culture" more than students from the "black American experience"? An educator working for a pre-university school in Barbados said, "The parents expect the kids to do well. Barbados parents as a whole hold education to be Number One."[31]

The teachers in Barbados are not applying rocket science. Hard work, lots of homework, rote, grammar skills, high teacher expectations, and high parental expectations, accompanied by parental involvement. Computers are few, and the classes are dramatically sub-high-tech. Said U.S. educator Charles Glenn of the Barbadian education system, "In Barbados, there's no culture saying, 'The schools are racist. The tests are racist. I'm a victim.' In Britain or the United States, many kids are convinced there is nothing they can do to succeed.' "[32]

Yet when an American black kid graduates from high school and underperforms on standardized tests, black leaders urge the student's acceptance into competitive universities, anyway. Because of poorly managed schools, black kids get shafted in grades K through 12, but the civil rights establishment resists reforms. Angry black parents demand vouchers, so they can place their children in better schools. But the Democratic Party, the NAACP, and Jesse Jackson all oppose vouchers, arguing they stand to destroy public schools—the very public schools depriving urban parents of a decent education for their children!

John Stossel, commentator for ABC News, hosted a special on myths widely believed by blacks. Some blacks, he found, accuse Church's Fried Chicken of putting something in the meat to render black men impotent. And some accuse Snapple natural beverages of being manufactured by the Ku Klux Klan. Why? Well, the label featured a ship that many blacks called a "slave ship." (Actually, the bottle shows a replica of the Boston Tea Party ship.) The upper left-hand corner of the Snapple label, said many blacks, depicts a "K"—a clear-cut reference to the Klan. In actuality, Snapple was founded by a Jewish family, and the "K" on their label stands for "Kosher." But then, why let the truth get in the way of a good victicrat story?

The chairman of the African-American studies department at Harvard University, Henry Louis Gates, complains about racism by giving a personal example. He says that even though he is a learned man who has published many books, whites nevertheless see him first and foremost as a black man. He said, "When I walk into a room, people still see my blackness, more than my Gates-ness, or my literary-ness."[33] It insults him that people see his race. (How does he know what they see or think? Doesn't this "racial profiling" actually insult whites?)

Karen Russell, the daughter of black basketball great Bill Russell, writes, too, of her anger. In a *New York Times Magazine* cover story, she complains of racism. She says her white friends say things like, "Karen, we don't understand the problem [with racism]. We don't think of you as black." How dare they, writes Russell, accept me only after "denying my ethnicity." This insults her, the fact that people *don't* see her race.

So, whites piss Gates off because they see him as a black person. And whites piss Karen Russell off because they don't. Scotty, beam me up.

Remember the black man dragged by white racists in Jasper, Texas? Justifiably, this became an international story. Three white men in Jasper saw a black man, James Byrd, walking down the road. They offered him a ride, then assaulted him, chained him to the truck, and drove him several miles, scattering his body parts all over the countryside. Black victicrats, citing horrific crimes like this, call for enhanced "hate crime" legislation. The FBI recently recorded about eight thousand annual hate crimes. Of those, nearly half involved race, a substantial percentage of which consisted merely of verbal intimidation. This leaves only a handful of alleged serious "hate crimes."

But, look deeper. Americans commit nearly nine million violent crimes each year, and an additional thirty million nonviolent crimes. Thus, the several thousand "hate crimes" per year represent a tiny fraction of 1 percent.

Are blacks more likely to be victims of "hate crimes" than whites? No. Americans commit around 1.7 million *interracial* crimes each year, of which about 1.2 million involve blacks and whites. Nearly 90 percent of these involve a black perpetrator and a white victim. Ninety percent. Thus, assuming blacks commit a small percentage of these racial crimes *because* of the victim's race, then hate crime legislation, *if* applied evenly, would ensnare more blacks than whites!

The media seem to think blacks incapable of committing hate crime. In 1989, several young black teenagers raped and assaulted a Central Park jogger. The crime made headlines, but no one suggested a racial motive. Tell me, if a black woman jogged through Central Park only to be grabbed, raped, and beaten by several white youths, wouldn't *someone* wonder aloud whether race might have prompted this act of violence and vulgarity? Under the definition of a race-based "hate crime," a perpetrator need act only in part out of racial animus.

Black youths stoned and nearly killed white truck driver Reginald Denny during the 1992 riots in South Central L.A. Hate crime? Apparently not. And in 1997, three white teens from northern Michigan hopped a train that landed them in a predominantly black area of Flint, Michigan. Several black youths brutally attacked them, beating, then shooting the two white boys in the head, killing one. The white girl was forced to perform oral sex, after which she was pistol-whipped, robbed of ten dollars, shot in the face, and left for dead.[34] "Hate crime"? Apparently not.

Many newspapers and magazines wrote about the Flint crime, but no one raised the question of whether the perpetrators might have been motivated because they found some white kids in a black neighborhood. No one called it a "hate crime."

In March 2000 a black man shot five whites, killing three in a Pittsburgh suburb. A black neighbor quoted the suspect, Ronald Taylor, as saying, "I'm gonna kill all the white people." A white maintenance man, who worked at Taylor's apartment building, complained, "Whenever he saw me, he called me a racist pig, or white trash. Or he'd make a point of walking past and brushing up against me. He just didn't like me."[35]

Yet, television news anchors tiptoed around whether to accuse the suspect of a "hate crime"! Suddenly, anchors advised that we don't know whether Taylor's alleged hate crime against whites was the "primary" or "sole" reason for the shootings. Pardon me? Suddenly, somehow a new requirement got added. When did they make *that* change?

Even the local police avoided any appearance of a rush to judgment. "There's a lot of hostility in this individual," said Wilkinsburg, Pennsylvania's police chief Gerald Brewer, "so I think it's a little premature to simply define this as a racist event." A little premature?

In August 1999, white supremacist Buford Furrow gunned down several people at a Jewish Community Center in Los Angeles. He later shot and killed a Filipino letter carrier. During the first three days of the shooting, how many newspapers carried the story? Over 150. They wrote nearly 200 articles.

But, in November 1999, an Ethiopian man in Kansas City shot and killed two coworkers. The shooter, who shot and killed himself, left a letter referring to "blood sucker" whites. Over the next full year, how many newspapers carried the story of this hideous, apparently race-based shooting? Eleven.

In April 1999, teenagers Eric Harris and Dylan Klebold shot and killed several classmates, before killing themselves. The shooters had written about their hatred for blacks, athletes, and others. What do you tell the parents of a slain, white male teenager? Well, the state provides a lesser punishment for your child's killers, since your child is white. Never mind that the white teenager's body lay only feet from a slain black teenager's body, for whose killers the government provides stronger punishment. What nonsense.

And, in any case, why do we need "hate crime legislation"? Didn't Clinton supporter James Carville assert that he "hated" independent counsel Ken Starr? This is America, thundered Carville, and you don't have to like somebody if you don't want to. And isn't it racist to place one victim ahead of another, based on ethnicity, religion, gender, sexual orientation, or disability? Aren't all crimes really hate crimes in the sense that the bad guy wanted to do harm to the innocent? Hate crime legislation forces us to place greater value on some victims because of race. By all means, we should prosecute bad conduct. But if I'm standing at an ATM machine and a Ku Klux Klansman hits me in the back of the head with a brick, the operative word is not "Klansman." It is "brick."

For a 1997 PBS special, *Redefining Racism*, I interviewed George Curry, editor of the aforementioned *Emerge* magazine. I consistently challenged his facts, conclusions, and overall pessimism. He got angrier and angrier. No doubt, he disagreed with much of what I said. But, his anger, I think, comes from another place. The *Emerge* victicrat mind-set says this: "The Man rigged the game. He's stacked the odds. But, subscribe to *my* magazine, and we will show you the way. We show how to navigate the treacherous waters of racism and discrimination." Racism sells.

Publisher Curry's victicrat worldview *requires* enemies, and this makes truth tellers and falsehood shredders so dangerous. Take away "us versus them," and you remove a huge incentive to buy his magazine. A recent and typical *Emerge* article asked, "Has the Economic Boom Bypassed Black America?" Open the magazine. A woman and a man are sitting in a Jaguar, in Mitchellville, Maryland, a predominantly black Washington, D.C., suburb of sumptuous houses, lush, manicured green lawns, colorful flowerbeds, huge picture windows, and Mercedes and BMWs parked in driveways. The article tells us that "68 percent, or more than 8,000 of Mitchellville's 12,593 residents, are black. Initially, their affluence stemmed from high-paying government jobs. College degrees and entrepreneurships later fueled the movement of blacks to the suburbs."[36]

But even here, says the article, the system screws blacks. "And for all that a Mitchellville has to offer, it is equally striking for what's missing. The Starbucks coffee shops, Barnes & Noble bookstores and even bagel shops that are ubiquitous in most trendy neighborhoods are nowhere to be found. Much like poor inner-city areas, Prince George's County has more liquor stores than jewelry stores, more used merchandise stores than department stores. There are similar issues in wealthy black communities in areas such as Atlanta, Chicago, and suburban Los Angeles."[37]

Hold the phone. Assuming these neighborhoods lack these desirable businesses, how about, like, *starting* them? After all, didn't "entrepreneurship" fuel the suburban boom? Don't entrepreneurs recognize entrepreneurial opportunities?

Hollywood also finds itself in the crosshairs. According to the NAACP, the industry excludes blacks. But, as mentioned earlier, didn't Al Gore's campaign manager claim that Republicans "exclude" blacks? Name an industry more identifiably liberal than Hollywood. Marlon Brando talked about the heavy Jewish influence in Hollywood. Few groups retain their Democratic affiliation more fervently than Jews. For the most part, Jews, like blacks, do not abandon the Democratic Party for the Republican Party as they grow wealthier. Outside of Rupert Murdoch of the News Corporation (which also owns Twentieth Century Fox) one would be hard-pressed to name a Republican force in Hollywood.

Blacks watch television at least as often as do whites. Among young blacks, according to the National Center for Education Statistics, nearly half of black fourth-graders, in a 1994 survey, watched at least six hours of television a day. This is three times the rate at which white fourth-graders watched television.[38]

Washington Post writer Jon Jeter interviewed Sherri Parks, who teaches American studies at the University of Maryland. Parks, according to Jeter, says, "Marketing studies have shown that although middle-class black families typically watch less television than poorer black families, they still watch more than their white neighbors."[39]

If the industry's alleged black exclusion produces such an unappealing product, why do blacks so enthusiastically patronize the fare created by Hollywood?

Victicrats protested that NBC, CBS, ABC, and Fox discriminated against blacks by failing to include more of them in the fall 1999 new-show lineup. A black author, Dr. Earl Ofari Hutchinson, wrote a book called *The Assassination of the Black Male Image*,[40] arguing that the media intentionally depict blacks demeaningly in order to further their racist agenda.

NAACP president Kweisi Mfume blasted the networks for failing to include more minority characters. A "whiteout!" critics charged. "Ethnic cleansing," said others. Mfume threatened a boycott. But a study[41] by Linda and S. Robert Lichter of the Center for Media and Public Affairs in Washington, D.C., paints a very different picture. After studying hundreds of hours of television, the Lichters showed that prime time television depicted blacks as doctors, lawyers, dentists, or other professionals far more than their numbers in real life. And TV depicts blacks as criminals far less frequently than in real life.

It's nearly impossible to turn on your television set without seeing blacks, whether in commercials, dramas, comedies, or anchoring the news, participating in sports, hosting religious programs, on shopping networks and infomercials, or "TV-courtroom" shows. Former heavyweight champion George Foreman pushes his "George Foreman Grill" in front of predominantly white studio audiences to the tune of nearly $40 million a year. Black television fitness guru Billy Blanks, the "Elvis of Exercise," sold more than five million copies of his Tae Bo video in the first year of its release.[42]

Consider the plight of the hapless network executive: In the last few years, executives have green-lighted *The PJs*, an animated series cocreated by Eddie Murphy, and *The Secret Diary of Desmond Pfeiffer*, a spoof on Abraham Lincoln and the Civil War, with a black character in the lead. Yet some blacks protested both shows. *The PJs*, black activists screamed, "demeans" blacks through using "stereotypical characters," including a recovering crack addict. And, said the activists, *The Secret Diary of Desmond Pfeiffer* makes light of slavery, even though the show revolves around a central black character who happens to be the only sane, rational, and intelligent person in the show.

And, some years before, Fox canceled a black action show called *M.A.N.T.I.S.* Protesters considered the canceling racist, even though Fox programming featured more shows with primary black characters than network rivals.

Just how racist is television? Jesse Jackson, as mentioned, angered many by referring to Jews as "Hymies" and New York as "Hymie Town." Yet, Jackson has a television show, *Both Sides with Jesse Jackson*, on CNN, a subsidiary of Time-Warner. Time-Warner's CEO is Gerald Levin, a Jew. And, during the O. J. Simpson trial, defense attorney Johnnie Cochran likened Mark Fuhrman to

Adolf Hitler, angering many Jews. Yet, Cochran, too, has a television show on Court TV, which was founded by Steve Brill, a Jew, and is now part of Time-Warner. According to an Anti-Defamation League study, anti-Semitism in America is at an all-time low, except in the black community, where anti-Semitism is three times the national average.

The Screen Actors Guild, in 1996, reported that 12 percent of all film and TV jobs went to blacks. This happened to be the same percentage of the population of blacks in America in 1996. The Screen Directors Guild, in 1995, said 3.9 percent of all jobs went to black directors. By 1996, the figure rose to 5.2 percent. As for commercials, the Screen Actors Guild 1996 report showed that Hispanics, Asians, Native Americans, and blacks perform 21 percent of all commercial jobs, with blacks landing nearly 12 percent of the total.

"Minority Markets Alert," a New York City–based newsletter, reported that in 1995, blacks appeared in nearly 40 percent of commercials in New York, where blacks comprise about 16 percent of the state's population. Black hiring is up at the actor, director, and producer levels. A recent cover of *Ebony* magazine, a black entertainment monthly, featured "A Year of Black Women Producers," discussing the growing success of black female producers.

So, no, Hollywood is not racist. Hollywood is rough, perhaps one of the purest examples of "no holds barred," "grab 'em by the throat until they holler" capitalism.

A friend, an Asian woman, graduated from USC film school. Her class consisted of thirty students. After a couple of years of hustle, she raised financing for a film.

"Of the thirty grads in your class," I asked, "how many of them wanted to make a movie?" She said, "Why, everybody."

"How many did?" I said.

"One," she said. "Me."

Many of her classmates knew people and had relatives in Hollywood. The class consisted of mostly white males. Yet, only one managed to make a film. The point? Entertainment success is a difficult process, even when you know people. And if you're not prepared to borrow, steal, and sacrifice to make a film, it ain't gonna happen. No matter your race or gender. No matter your talent. Victicrats need not apply.

Victicrats Should Take Economics 101

David Duke starts a company. Duke Enterprises manufactures widgets. A bigot who prefers his own race, Duke hires five hundred white male workers at $5.00 an hour.

Along comes Harry Headhunter, who offers CEO Duke five hundred *black* workers at $4.75 an hour. Headhunter tells Duke that 25 cents per hour times the number of hours worked, times five hundred workers, nets Duke Enterprises an additional quarter of a million dollars in annual profits. It takes a lot of bigotry to leave a quarter of a million dollars on the table. But David Duke, being David Duke, tells the recruiter to get lost.

So that night, Mr. Duke goes home, and as Mrs. Duke serves dinner, she says, "Honey, how did it go today?" Duke tells her the story of how he protected the white race from the scourge of would-be black workers by refusing Headhunter's deal. His wife says, "You left a quarter of a million dollars on the table?" David Duke sleeps on the couch that night.

So David Duke does not take the offer, but Randy Redneck, who operates a similar widget factory down the road, does. And, if Randy Redneck does not, Consolidated Confederates, across the river, seeking to cut costs and boost profit margins, will. David Duke Enterprises then faces some financial problems and has two options, neither one pleasant. Black workers or Chapter 11. This hypothetical, conceived by Pepperdine University economist George Reisman,[43] shows how the marketplace punishes racism because racism is against the economic interests of the practitioner.

Marge Schott formerly owned the Cincinnati Reds. She is an avowed racist who collects Nazi memorabilia. She makes racist remarks, and referred to Dave Parker and Eric Davis as her "million-dollar niggers."[44] Yet, pick up the sports page and take a look at the Cincinnati Reds box score. Chock-full of black and Latino ballplayers. Why? Certainly not because Schott invites them in for high tea. Black and Latino ballplayers exist in her lineup because she has no choice. Schott's motivation for her integrated lineup was the same as that motivating Brooklyn Dodgers general manager Branch Rickey when he hired Jackie Robinson. Winning. And, to put booties in the seats in order to make money, she'd better have people who can play.

In the early seventies, USC faced the University of Alabama's still lily-white squad. USC coach John McKay's team soundly beat Bear Bryant's squad. At the end of the game, Bryant, in his trademark rumbly southern drawl, said to Coach McKay, "Where do y'all get such wonderful guards and tackles?" Said McKay, "We get them from Alabama."

Jesse Jackson frequently attacks banks for denying blacks "access to capital." But blacks collectively have a gross domestic product of $500 billion annually, enough to make blacks among the fifteenth wealthiest nations were they an independent state. Still, bankers stand accused of refusing profit earned from the interest in granting a black a loan. Does this make any sense? Think about it. "Redlining" means banks leave profits on the table. But banks make money by lending to borrowers at a higher rate than the banks' cost. Thus, to survive, thrive, and profit, banks must push its product—lending money to credit-worthy borrowers. Similarly, fast food places like Burger King, Wendy's, and McDonalds, with outlets all over the inner city, must push their products to their customers—those with the money to pay for a burger, fries, and a shake. Entrepreneurs are somehow attracted to the profits made by selling hamburgers, but profits to be made by selling money somehow repel. Sorry, you just flunked Economics 101.

Asians enjoy an even higher loan acceptance rate than whites. So the "black leaders" who say, "Banks refuse to lend to blacks" must, therefore, conclude that white lenders tilt toward Asians. This makes lenders anti-black, neutral toward their own race, but pro-Asian. Really. A white suburban friend recently complained about the "excessively competitive" nature of Asian kids who dominate the top academic spots, that, complained my friend, "crowds-out" admission slots for their kids at elite schools. So, how likely is it that their banker spouses would then favor Asians in lending, while the children of these Asian borrowers out-compete the children of the white lenders.

Similarly, insurance companies stand accused of refusing to insure black urban businesses. But, when black leaders such as Congresswoman Maxine Waters minimize and dismiss riots as "rebellions,"[45] what should an insurance company do?

For all the justified black anger against Jim Crow laws, private bus companies initially refused to enforce them. They wanted black trade and for their black customers to be comfortable. Only after authorities boarded buses and began arresting bus drivers did private carriers start enforcing racist Jim Crow laws.

In 1930, when willing workers faced a scarcity of jobs, Congress passed the Davis-Bacon Act, precisely because white workers felt threatened by skillful black labor! The Davis-Bacon Act prevented private contractors with government contracts from hiring the best at the least cost. It required payment of "prevailing union wages." The law, thus, effectively shut out hiring most skilled blacks.

Many economically illiterate black leaders push for things like minimum wage laws. But, as Nobel laureate economist Milton Friedman writes, before the imposition of minimum wage laws, black teens were *more* likely to be employed than white teens. After the imposition of minimum wage laws, an employment gap emerged between white and black teens, with black teens becoming increasingly less employed. Friedman finds "the minimum wage law to be one of the most, if not *the* most anti-black law on the statute books." The government says to someone willing to hire a teen, "You must pay at this level, no matter the willingness of the worker to work for less." This insidious law hurts the very people supporters purport to help—blacks, teens, and secondary wage earners. During the civil unrest of the fifties and sixties, southern businesspeople frequently served as voices of reason. Why? Money, baby.

Writing in the *Virginia Law Review*, Michael J. Klarman discusses the efforts of businesspeople to defuse the 1957 Little Rock school desegregation crisis. Businesspeople feared catastrophe if Little Rock became known as a place of intolerance. They were correct. Klarman writes, "The city, having attracted eight new industrial plants in 1957 and an average of five major new plants a year between 1950 and 1957, failed to secure a single new industrial relocation in the four years following the school desegregation crisis. New investment in Arkansas between 1956 and 1958 declined from $131 million to $25.4 million."[46] Racism is bad for business.

In 1901, Booker T. Washington, a former slave, said this: "When a Negro girl learns to cook, to wash dishes, to sew, to write a book, or a Negro boy learns to groom horses, or to grow sweet potatoes, or to produce butter, or to build a house, or to be able to practise [sic] medicine, as well or better than someone else, they will be rewarded regardless of race or colour [sic]. In the long run, the world is going to have the best, and any difference in race, religion, or previous history will not long keep the world from what it wants.

"I think that the whole future of my race hinges on the question as to whether or not it can make itself of such indispensable value that the people in the town and the state where we reside will feel that our presence is necessary to the happiness and well-being of the community. No man who continues to add something to the material, intellectual, and moral well-being of the place in which he lives is long left without proper reward. This is a great human law which cannot be permanently nullified."[47]

Washington wrote that book in 1901. Think about it. Slavery ended in 1865, a mere thirty-six years earlier. It is as though slavery ended in 1964, and Washington published *Up from Slavery* today. Interesting how Washington's 1901 enthusiasm shines brighter than the "black leadership's" 2000 pessimism.

A few years ago, black Secret Service agents accused Denny's of racism for failing to seat them in a timely fashion. The "fit hit the shan." To stem the loss of goodwill and market share, Denny's offered cash to any black customer complaining of discrimination. Denny's then aggressively pursued awarding franchise opportunities for minorities. They did not do this to win the Albert Schweitzer Humanitarian Award. They recognize that racism, even its appearance, is bad for business.

Some Texaco executives, caught on tape, demeaned fellow black employees. Texaco's CEO appeared on ABC's *Nightline*, to apologize to black workers, in particular, and to blacks, in general. He offered automatic raises to many black employees and publicly promised to settle the lawsuit. Why? Texaco lost $1 billion in shareholder value in two days, with many irate customers—black and non-black—preparing to cut up their credit cards unless and until Texaco did something. They did. Fast. Real fast.

Blacks and O. J. Simpson

In the O. J. Simpson case, defense attorney Johnnie Cochran accused the cops of racism. But Willie Williams, the black LAPD chief, conducted an extensive internal investigation to determine whether cops planted evidence in this case. His conclusion? No evidence was planted. Williams called the accusation of racism against O. J. Simpson preposterous. No matter that Williams is black. No matter that the criminologist who came under a great deal of heat, Dennis Fung, is Asian. No matter that Marcia Clark is a Jew, a group that remains one of the most liberal and "pro-black" in the country. Never mind that O. J. Simpson had police officer friends, and that he frequently allowed cops to use his mansion for fun and frolic. His close friend and former cop, Ron Shipp, says, "Man, the cops loved O. J."

Simpson did everything but leave his business card at the scene of the crime. Why would cops want to "get" Simpson? He posed about as great a threat to the "white power structure" as Urkel from *Family Matters*.

Former prosecutor Vincent Bugliosi said that he has "never seen a case where guilt is more obvious." Yet a rich man's clever lawyers turned a double murder trial into a referendum on race. Defense lawyers accused decent, hardworking men and women in blue of stupidity, conspiracy, racism, and evil.

After the O. J. Simpson acquittal, prosecutor Marcia Clark accused the predominantly black jury of refusing to engage in critical thinking. She's right.

Take the *New Republic* article[48] written by Mark Gerson, a white inner-city New Jersey high school teacher, during the O. J. Simpson case. Of his 110 students, mostly black, nearly all refused to believe O. J. could have killed his wife and Ron Goldman. He describes their thought processes.

> One student suggested that Ron Goldman killed Nicole before killing himself and then throwing away the knife. Another believes the dog did it. Shenia suggested that Al Cowlings, Simpson's best buddy, did it. Bryant believes the killer is O. J.'s son. Philip blames "that fag dude who wants to marry O. J."; that would be Kato Kaelin, Simpson's house-guest. Even the smartest students are willing to give more credence to the most outlandish theories than to the prosecution's.

Jon, a bright student, had his own scenario: O. J. was shaving and cut himself. Kato took the blood from the shaving cut, brought it to the crime scene and dumped it. Why, I asked, did O. J. collect his blood after he cut himself shaving? Jon called me a racist, and that was that. . . .

Eunicia said that Nicole got what she deserved as a result of messing with a black man. Wait, I said, if you think that it is wrong for O. J. to marry a white woman, doesn't he deserve some of the fault? No, Eunicia added. Women control these types of situations, and Nicole roped O. J. in to get his money. If it weren't for Nicole, O. J. would have stayed with his first wife, Marguerite, who, of course, was black. . . .

Sholanda: "Nicole was a slut. She gave some other guy oral sex in O. J.'s house. She had many lovers—even before she and O. J. married! It is only right that he became very jealous and took out his jealousy in some way."

Scary, isn't it?

The "race card" attack against the police does not go without consequences. The national acquittal rate in criminal trials stands at approximately 15 percent. But certain minority areas—the Bronx, downtown Los Angeles, Washington, D.C., Wayne County (Detroit, Michigan)—see acquittal rates of nearly two to three times the national average.

George Washington University black law professor Paul Butler takes the criminal justice system's racist argument one huge step further. He urges black jurors to acquit black defendants, *even when they know they are guilty,* if accused of nonviolent crime! He feels this protects the black community against the war declared on it by the racist criminal justice system. Never mind that the victims of black criminals are likely to be black, and that by cutting these black suspects loose, they are now free to continue preying on other blacks.

Of all the comments, columns, and commentary about the

O. J. Simpson case, a short letter to the editor[49] written by Craig Darian, CEO of Tricor Entertainment, put it best:

I watched with interest a CBS report and interview with O. J. Simpson which aired recently. I would like to offer Simpson a point of view which I believe to be shared by a majority of us so-called "white folks" who believe this case has nothing to do with racism.

When I watched you play football for USC, and later, with the Buffalo Bills, I didn't see a black man, I saw a great athlete. And I admired you.

When I watched you broadcast football games with great personality and a player's zest for the game, I didn't see a black man, I saw a competent sportscaster. And I liked you.

When I watched you run and jump for cars in Hertz commercials, and play various bit movie parts, I didn't see a black man, I saw a funny actor. And I laughed with you.

When I watched your trial for the murders of your ex-wife, Nicole Brown, and another innocent victim, Ronald Goldman, I didn't see a black man, I saw a remorseless murderer. And I despised you.

When I listened to you speak about your hitting Nicole, and she hitting you, and then rationalizing that the public's condemnation was simply a matter of "a black man being ridiculed while a white woman is revered," I didn't see a black man, I saw a violent and incessant excuse-maker. And I wanted to tell you that the issue isn't about a black person hitting a white person, it's about a man hitting a woman.

And when I saw you stand in church with an apparently loving and sincere black congregation, one to which you had been a stranger until your recent acquittal, and I heard you preach before God, I didn't see a black man, I saw a phony. And I pitied you.

This isn't about black or white, Mr. Simpson, it's about right and wrong.

To blacks, O. J. Simpson represented one thing: payback. Simple, pure, unadulterated payback. Many blacks, for reasons explained here, simply believe the criminal justice system racist. In 1965, we called what happened in Watts a street riot. Call the black reaction to O. J. Simpson an emotional riot.

For many blacks, the O. J. Simpson acquittal represents a payback for all the real and perceived slights, irritations, indignities, and put-downs experienced by blacks at the hands of whites. O. J. Simpson was about every black guy who felt passed up by cabdrivers; about the couple who feel they get the worst table in the best restaurants; about the college kid who feels less accepted by classmates; about the motorist gruffly spoken to by a cop who never explains why he stopped him. It is about every black salesman who feels shut out by racist or hostile secretaries, assistants, purchasers, human resource personnel, and about every young black kid you see on television being led away in handcuffs, and above all, it is about the enduring legacy of a people subjugated by a majority class and a country made great by the slave efforts of others. That's what the O. J. Simpson case was all about. The evidence was secondary.

Defense attorney Johnnie Cochran tells us, "Race plays a part of everything in America." Whites, guilty. Blacks, innocent. Whites, bad. Blacks, good. A white woman clutches her purse when a black guy gets on an elevator. Racism! As a black lawyer enters a courtroom, someone mistakes him for a defendant. Racism! Cochran tells blacks, "Remain hyper-sensitive. Turn these slights into assaults."

Cochran, of all people, should know that blacks commit half of all street crime in America. Twenty-five percent of young black men are in jail, on parole, or on probation. A black man is ten times more likely to rape a white woman than a white man is to rape a black woman. Blacks account for 50 percent of the nation's prisoners. Gang-bangers are almost inevitably black or Latino. Hurts the image, you know.

Don't think the young white woman in that elevator is oblivious. Don't think that a white woman living in a city hasn't seen, experienced, or had friends who experienced crime at the hands of black thugs . . . If Jesse Jackson himself says he's relieved when the late-night footsteps on the street behind him belong to white rather than black feet, all bets are off.[50]

But whites who think O. J. guilty? Racists. Defenders of the corrupt system. Blacks who think so? Uncle Toms. Traitors carrying the white man's water. Black attorneys who defend black criminals? Civil rights warriors. Black prosecutors? Lackeys. Sugar cane Negroes. Pass the Advil, please.

Prosecutor Christopher Darden said the Simpson case had "shaken his faith in the system." Meanwhile, in a near-empty courtroom, another mother cries because a thug cut short her son's life. Somebody has to put his arm around that mother. Someone must tell her that, no, we cannot bring your child back, but we can nail the S.O.B. who killed him. That someone is someone like Christopher Darden.

Racial Profiling, "Poverty Causing Crime," and Other Myths

The governor of New Jersey recently fired her state police superintendent because, according to the *Newark Star-Ledger*, he had said that certain crimes were associated with certain ethnic groups and that it would be naïve to think that race was not an issue in drug trafficking. "Two weeks ago," he allegedly said, "the president . . . went to Mexico to talk . . . about drugs. He didn't go to Ireland. He didn't go to England."[51] Civil rights leaders accuse the New Jersey cops of engaging in a form of harassment called DWB (Driving While Black) because cops stop a disproportionately high number of motorists allegedly just because they are black.

But as to the percentage of those stopped versus those arrested, whites have more to complain about. Why? True, the police stop more cars driven by black motorists. But when the police stop whites, they are *less* likely than black motorists to have drugs in the car. And so, as a percentage, whites actually have *more* to complain about than do blacks. After all, when a white is stopped, he or she is more likely to be innocent than when a black is stopped! Where are the "white leaders" screaming about DWW—Driving While White"!

New Jersey just announced it intends to stop "racial profiling" and to record each stop by race. If, as likely, cops still continue to stop a "disproportionate" number of blacks, how will "black leaders" explain this? Stay tuned.

Here are the ugly facts. Blacks, usually young black men, commit nearly half of all street crime, and most of certain other categories of crime such as robbery.

How do we know victims do not falsely accuse blacks? The FBI keeps annual victims-of-crime surveys. They ask victims of crime, whether solved or unsolved, to describe the race of the assailant. Nearly 40 percent of victims describe their assailant as black. This is the identical percentage of blacks arrested. Did those who accused blacks lie? Only if you assume that a white victim, particularly of an unsolved crime, does not care whether the police ever apprehend the actual suspect. In other words, to practice a racist agenda, white victims must lie to incarcerate a black man, while allowing the white attacker to go free! That's some racism.

Urban residents do not have burglar bars on every other home to keep out Mark Fuhrman. Rather, they place these bars there to keep out that punk or thug who lives down the street. The fact remains that nearly 40 percent of violent crimes—murder, attempted murder, nonnegligent manslaughter, and aggravated assault—are committed by young black men, who account for no more than 3 percent of the nation's population. The police would be foolish, and applying limited resources inefficiently, if they ignore race as a variable. Note that the police do not racially profile elderly black men, nor do the civil rights activists accuse the police of racially profiling black women.

The first rule of duck hunting is: go where the ducks are.

During the Million Man March in Washington, civil rights activist Al Sharpton thundered, "O. J. is home, but Mumia Abu Jamal ain't home. And we won't stop till all our people that need a chance in an awkward and unbalanced criminal justice system can come home."

The NAACP and the ACLU demand that the police record the race of any stopped motorists. This, presumably, would document the unfair and disproportionate stops. But many departments already do this. Fine. As taxpayers, and as the police's bosses, we may demand greater record keeping. A recent study of Miami Dade County police showed black cops *more* likely to shoot a black suspect than a white cop. And the reverse was true. A white cop was more likely than a black cop to shoot a white suspect.[52] And black judges sentence black criminal defendants to the same, if not longer, sentences than meted out by white judges.[53]

In 1998, over 26 percent of blacks lived below the federally defined level of poverty, as opposed to about 10 percent of whites.[54] This disparity allows some black leaders to blame crime on poverty, or even better, "root causes" of poverty, stemming, of course, from racism. While superficially appealing, it is quite wrong.

Poverty causes crime? According to James Q. Wilson and Richard Herrnstein, "During the 1960s, one neighborhood in San Francisco had the lowest income, the highest unemployment rate, the highest proportion of families with incomes under four thousand dollars a year, the least educational attainment, the highest tuberculosis rate, and the highest proportion of substandard housing. . . . That neighborhood was called Chinatown. Yet, in 1965, there were only five persons of Chinese ancestry committed to prison in the *entire* [emphasis added] state of California."[55]

Roxbury, Massachusetts, a predominantly black and impoverished area, sits next to South Boston, a predominantly white and impoverished area. Both contain the same percentage of single parent households, and public housing accounts for the same percentage of the population. Yet, the violent crime rate in Roxbury, the black area, is four times the rate of that in South Boston. If poverty caused crime, one would expect the numbers to be closer to equal.

No, the formula is more likely the other way around: crime causes poverty. The more crime, the less incentive for business-people to locate businesses in that area. Store owners must charge consumers more to offset losses caused by theft and higher insurance premiums. Homeowners, apartment dwellers, and business-people pay increased security costs to combat the ever-present threat of theft or violent crime. *This* impoverishes neighborhoods.

Blacks and Affirmative Action

"Our problem with you, Larry, is that you've benefited from affirmative action. Now you want to change the rules for everybody else."

I'm in a flower shop, and a black guy recognizes me and hits me with that.

"I went to Loyola Law School under a special minority program," he said, "and if it hadn't been for that, I wouldn't be here."

"No," I said, "you act as if your choices were Loyola Law School under affirmative action, or welding courses at Trade Tech. What nonsense."

If it hadn't been for affirmative action, this guy would likely have gone to some other law school (there are over 170) many with admissions standards consistent with his test scores, grade point average, and other criteria. This "but-for-affirmative-action-I'd-be-driving-a-truck" mentality is yet another unintended consequence of preferences. The "beneficiary" demeans and cheapens his own achievement by overestimating the impact of affirmative action on his own life. Without drive, study, and sense of purpose, all the preferential programs in the world wouldn't have helped this guy.

An affirmative action beneficiary is not the same thing as an affirmative action recipient. The credentials of affirmative action recipients are always suspect, always subject to second-guessing. Would he have made it "on his own"? Could he have "measured up" without a boost?

Why can't black recipients question affirmative action? Look at the "you got yours, so why can't I get mine" argument. Following a shipwreck, you're bobbing up and down in the sea, nearly dead from exhaustion and exposure. Someone pulls you into a life raft. Fifteen minutes later, they pull another guy in, then another, then another. One more guy and the life raft capsizes. Are you, as a "beneficiary" of your rescuers' generosity, now and forever foreclosed from saying, "Excuse me, fellows, I think you'd better think this through." Does that make you a hypocrite? Does that make you someone who benefited and now wishes to "close the door" on everybody else?

Besides, the unspoken assumption is that an affirmative action-driven education, one that puts the student in a more "elite" category of school, is simply a better education. Getting in to College A versus College A-minus, or B-plus versus B, clearly means that the graduate from the better school will, necessarily, have a better life.

But, as economist Robert J. Samuelson writes, "The trouble is that what everyone knows isn't true. Going to Harvard or Duke won't automatically produce a better job and higher pay. Graduates of these schools generally do well. But they do well because they're talented. Had they chosen colleges with lesser nameplates, they would (on average) have done just as well. The conclusion is that the Ivy League—a metaphor for all elite schools—has little comparative advantage."[56]

Researchers at Princeton and at the Andrew W. Mellon Foundation, writes Samuelson, looked at students with credentials to enter "elite schools" versus students with credentials to enter the same caliber of school but who chose not to. The results, researchers concluded, are "that students who attend more elite colleges may have greater earnings capacity regardless of where they attend school." Samuelson explains their findings: "Suppose that Princeton and Podunk accept you and me; but you go to Princeton and I go to Podunk. On average, we will still make the same. (The result held for blacks and whites, further weakening the case for race-based admission preferences.)"[57]

"Beneficiaries" of affirmative action like to point out that they were "qualified." No doubt. Beneficiaries of affirmative action still met a standard, even if that standard varied from the traditional one. This means that affirmative action "beneficiaries" were good candidates to begin with. I would like to ask affirmative action proponents and beneficiaries this question. Assume your life without affirmative action. What would have happened? How would it have turned out? Would you have been happier? Would you have been less happy? Would you have made less money? Would you have developed fewer social and business contacts, becoming, therefore, less successful?

Just a few stories from my own life. When in law school, my roommate and I got into a dispute with the landlord over deductions from our security deposit. The landlord claimed damages that exceeded what we felt we had caused. So I took the landlord to mediation. He and I screamed at each other, and I won nearly every point, substantially reducing his deduction from our security deposit. The landlord owned several buildings in Ann Arbor, Michigan. He walked up to me after the mediation, and calmly offered me a job. "You were something," he said. "How would you like to work for me?" The man later became quite wealthy. A road not taken?

While still in high school, I urged my mother to purchase a

multi-unit apartment building as an investment. This was nearly thirty years ago, well before the phenomenal California real estate boom, when nearly all real estate properties increased substantially in value. My mother resisted, primarily because of the huge college tuition costs we were about to face even with a financial aid package that included some grant money. Suppose I had deferred college, or attended a much less expensive one, and used the savings to buy that building. What kind of life then?

My dad started a restaurant in the Pico-Union district of Los Angeles. He ran it successfully for nearly thirty years, building a large, loyal clientele. When the father of Ted Turner, a major shareholder of Time Warner, committed suicide, he left Ted a tiny, near-bankrupt small outdoor billboard company, probably not much more valuable than my dad's café. Suppose I had stayed in my dad's business, where I did work for several years during high school?

Shortly after I left the practice of law and started a business recruiting lawyers, a major executive recruiting firm approached me and offered me a position leading to partnership. They came calling not because of my resumé, but because of the two years of good will I built during the start-up phase of my company.

The great jazz pianist Thelonius Monk put it this way: "There's no such thing as a bad note," he said. "If a note starts out bad, I figure out a way of turning it into something good."

And so, I told my flower shop friend, forgive me for my "insensitivity" for failing to see the negative consequences of ending affirmative action. But the evidence does not support this "Big Bang Theory of the Black Middle Class," with affirmative action serving as the catalyst.

How do you think it feels to have worked hard, and studied long hours, only to have someone say, "Hey, if it weren't for affirmative action, you wouldn't have your job." I'm a talk show host. Let's compare my credentials to other talk show hosts. Where did Rush Limbaugh go to school? Howard Stern? Dr. Laura Schlessinger? Few know, or care. What about network anchors? Where did Tom Brokaw go to college? How about Dan Rather? What about ABC's Peter Jennings? (Hint: He didn't.)

And what of all the Internet millionaires today? Many never attended college or, if so, dropped out, as Bill Gates did.

A talk show host's job is ratings. A *summa cum laude*, Phi Beta Kappa degree from Harvard does not guarantee a four share. A successful salesperson must generate revenues. A teacher's job is to motivate and educate students.

"Once you're in the job market," said Samuelson, "where you went to college may matter for a few years, early in your career. Companies don't know much about young employment candidates. A shiny credential (an Ivy League degree) may impress. But after that, what people can or can't do counts for more. Skills grow. Reputations emerge. Companies prefer the competent from Podunk to the incompetent from Princeton."[58]

"No affirmative action, no job"? No thanks.

Yet many blacks, like Atlanta mayor Bill Campbell, subscribe to the "Big Bang Theory of the Black Middle Class." If no affirmative action, then no black progress, no black businesses, no black income growth, no black middle class.

But the black middle class began long before Martin Luther King marched. And many contemporary leaders, as well as leaders before King, never wanted—let alone demanded—affirmative action.

Whitney Young, the founder of the Urban League, was one of the first blacks to push for an affirmative action plan. In *Ending Affirmative Action*,[59] writer Terry Eastland says that Young called for a "compensatory, preferential Marshall Plan for black America." In 1963, Young urged a "decade" of preferences to level the playing field. A decade! That would have ended affirmative action back in 1973! Young's board of directors, however, revolted. The president of the Urban League in Pittsburgh said the demand for affirmative action would cause the public to quite properly ask, "What in blazes are these guys up to? They tell us for years that we must buy [non-discrimination] and then they say, 'It isn't what we want.' " A member of the Urban League in New York objected to what he called "the heart of it—the business of employing Negroes [because they are Negroes]." Famed civil rights leader Bayard Rustin, the deputy director of the 1963 Washington, D.C., Jobs and Freedom March, also opposed affirmative action.

In 1963, *Ebony* magazine ran a series called "If I Were Young Today." The magazine asked prominent black achievers to give advice to the black youth of the day. What did they say? The "Architect for the Stars," Paul R. Williams, who, in addition to luxury homes, also designed the Los Angeles International Airport Theme Building said, "Whatever one does as a profession or livelihood, he should endeavor to read the current magazines pertaining to his work. One must keep pace with progress and what the other fellow is thinking and doing. In order to do this he must read— read—read!!! He should strive to become a specialist and not just *another* architect, engineer, or salesman."[60] Anything missing?

The magazine asked federal district judge Herman C. Moore to comment. He said, "Broader opportunities are opening today for Negro youth in fields which have been previously closed to them such as engineering and science. There are also wider opportunities to be lawyers, diplomats, judges, economists, organization leaders. Negroes have greater chances at apprenticeships in the skilled trades as well. At the same time, the young Negro must prepare himself to be part of an expanding world and by accomplishment to lead in its expanding progress. Performance is the key."[61] Anything missing?

Union leader A. Philip Randolph, who founded the Brotherhood of Sleeping Car Porters, said, "Negro youth must offer the future the same things that white youth offer and they must have the faith that there is no basic racial difference in potential for achievement—moral, intellectual, or spiritual. The future holds great opportunity for those who are prepared to meet and face the challenge of this age of science, technology, and industrialism, and social, economic, and political change."[62] Anything missing?

None of these leaders, all high achievers in their fields, suggested, called for, urged or even mentioned anything resembling affirmative action. Their message: Work hard, stay focused, no gain without pain.

President John F. Kennedy, revered by blacks, expressed skepticism about preferential treatment. In a 1963 interview in *U.S. News & World Report*,[63] Kennedy expected blacks *themselves* to resist a call for preferential treatment.

"The Negro community," Kennedy said, "did not want job quotas to compensate for past discrimination. What I think they would like is to see their children well educated, so that they could hold jobs . . . and have themselves accepted as equal members of the community." But what about, call it, compensatory preferential treatment? "No," said Kennedy. "I don't think we can undo the past. In fact, the past is going to be with us for a good many years in uneducated men and women who missed their chance for a decent education. We have to do the best we can now. That is what we are trying to do."

Kennedy objected to quotas: "I don't think quotas are a good idea. I think it is a mistake to begin to assign quotas on the basis of religion or race—color—nationality. . . . On the other hand, I do think that we ought to make an effort to give a fair chance to everyone who is qualified—not through a quota—but just look over our employment rolls, look over our areas where we are hiring people and at least make sure we are giving everyone a fair chance.

"But not hard and fast quotas. . . . We are too mixed, this society of ours, to begin to divide ourselves on the basis of race or color."

Even Democrat Hubert Humphrey, who helped spearhead the passage of the Civil Rights Act, said the bill did not endorse racial preferences. Humphrey pledged that if critics of the Civil Rights

Act could find any language permitting racial preferences, "I will start eating the pages one after another, because it is not in there."[64]

Nelson Mandela, imprisoned in South Africa for nearly thirty years, expressed reservations about affirmative action, warning that his government did not possess "a big bag full of money" to meet the needs of the poor. And he spoke out against what he called a "culture of entitlement." "It is important," Mandela said, "that we rid ourselves of the 'culture of entitlement,' which leads to the expectation that government must promptly deliver whatever it is that we demand."

In their important book, *America in Black and White*, Stephen and Abigail Thernstrom show that the black middle class grew well before affirmative action. Moreover, they demonstrate that affirmative action did not accelerate the pace of the black middle class and may even have contributed to a slowdown! The Thernstroms said, "the growth of the black middle class long predates the adoption of race-conscious social policies. In some ways, indeed, the black middle class was expanding more rapidly before 1970 than after. . . . Many of the advances black Americans have made since the Great Depression occurred before anything that can be termed 'affirmative action' existed. . . . In the years since affirmative action [the black middle class] has continued to grow, *but not at a more rapid pace* than in the preceding three decades, despite a common impression to the contrary."[65]

Black economist and former Federal Reserve Board member Arthur Brimmer studied the effect of affirmative action on black unemployment and concluded, "I would say that most blacks I know did not get [their jobs] because of affirmative action, but it's impossible [to determine the exact number]." Similarly, black professor Ella Edmondson Bell, who taught organizational studies at the MIT business school, says that most blacks get hired through "determination [and] perseverance."

The Industrial Revolution, and the aftermath of the the Second World War, created a huge need for workers to run northern factories. This created the largest voluntary migration in the history of the world. Nearly one million blacks moved from the South to the North in just a few years.

Northern blacks grew increasingly more prosperous and, therefore, more politically powerful. Blacks formed fraternal organizations. In cities like Chicago and Philadelphia, black families, because of these lodges, were more likely than white families to have someone in the household with medical insurance! And black segregated schools competed academically against whites of the same economic level.

Well before affirmative action, black women out-earned white women. Black females were in the job market longer, acquired more skills, and, therefore, saw increased earning power. By the 1950s, the overall black-white wage gap narrowed considerably, even in the South. And although the South lagged behind, it, too, eventually caught up.

But things are changing. For the "no affirmative action–no peace" crowd, Rene Redwood represents a major threat. Who is Rene Redwood? She formerly served as executive director of President George Bush's Glass Ceiling Commission. But she recently resigned her latest post as executive director of an organization called Americans for a Fair Chance, a group fighting for the retention of affirmative action.

Redwood quit because she grew to see the folly of blaming "racist institutions" for the inadequacies of the K–12 inner city education, a substandard education that created the need for lowering standards in the first place.

She said, "Some time in the 1980s, a sense of entitlement began to replace blacks' sense of doing things for ourselves. We started getting away from the values I was raised with—you should not bring a child into the world unless you are prepared to care for it; you had to be twice as good as whites; nothing less than an

'A' was good enough. I believe that you should not expect anyone to help you until you've done everything you can to help yourself."[66]

The *Wall Street Journal* recently published a story about the astonishing pace at which blacks, Hispanics, Asians, and other minorities now own homes, enter college, and begin businesses. If the pace continues, according to a minority marketing and demographic research company, the percentage of minority college students, homeowners, and owners of businesses will, by 2007, equal that of whites! "In terms of absolute numbers," said the head of the study, "ethnic Americans have not reached overall parity yet, but the speed at which growth rates have advanced, almost doubling over the last ten years, is phenomenal."[67] Salute affirmative action? Remember the Thernstroms' admonition: Before affirmative action, the middle class grew, a process that continues, but "not at a more rapid pace" than pre-affirmative action. So, salute the drive, energy, and work ethic of millions of black men and women—hard workers who pulled it off without affirmative action.

Victicrat Mentality and the Quest for a Level Playing Field

Affirmative action proponents insist that preferences must remain "until the playing field is level."

Pray tell, when in human history did we have a "level playing field"? In what country? Among what peoples? During the 2000 election year, Al Gore, Jr., and George W. Bush campaigned for their party's nomination. Let's see. Do you think that George W. Bush received an assist from the fact that his dad, George Herbert Walker Bush, *used to be* president? And that George Herbert Walker's father, Prescott, used to be a senator from Connecticut? Do you think that Al Gore, Jr., became *Senator* Al Gore, Jr., without some assistance from the fact that his father, Al Gore, Sr., also used to be a senator from Tennessee? Who are we kidding?

A just government attempts to ensure equal rights. But how can we possibly pretend that people are born with equal abilities, resources, quality of parenting, aptitude, drive, work ethic, etc.? And how can government "level the playing field"—beyond equal protection of the law—without creating still more unfairness? Is it fair to take from descendents of the "oppressor group," as the reparations-for-slavery crowd insist, and give to descendents of the aggrieved group?

Besides, "good circumstances" do not guarantee success, any more than the poor are destined to remain eternally poor. And wealth does not guarantee success. Billionaire Steve Forbes competed twice for the presidency, spending nearly seventy million dollars of his own money. He lost both times, quite soundly.

In politics, money helps, but it certainly doesn't guarantee victory. Just ask failed presidential aspirants like former senator Ed Muskie (D-Maine), Senator Ted Kennedy (D-Mass.), Senator Phil Gramm (R-Texas)—the list is endless.

Most wealthy people did not start out that way. For the most part, people of wealth didn't marry it, or win it in the lottery, or steal it, or inherit it. They earned it.

The question comes down to this: Do we live in a society where the rule of law, economic freedom, and limited government interference produce conditions allowing one to apply one's self and get somewhere? That's all a society can hope for, and that is quite good enough.

Level playing field? In presidential contests, the taller candidate usually wins. Fair? The average male CEO is taller than the average male non-CEO. Apparently, something about large physical stature—think of John Wayne—gives people the feeling of an authority figure confidently in control. Fair?

Attractive people have more options than non-attractive people. Heavy people are less likely to be hired than thin ones. But, in a free society, the single greatest variable, the single biggest factor in realizing goals and dreams is: hard work!

Former Los Angeles Rams and Washington Redskins coach George Allen once said, "I used to call the opposing coach's office at one o'clock on Wednesday night. If nobody answered, I knew we would win the game."

In his book, *The Millionaire Mind*,[68] Thomas Stanley discovered that the average millionaire made mediocre grades, did not attend an Ivy League college, and did not consider himself or herself to be particularly smart or visionary. They found something they enjoyed doing, and spent long hours doing it. They discovered a passion out of which they built a career or business. The goal, therefore, is a society that allows effort, drive, and energy to flourish. This means a government that stays out of the way. This means a government that does not impose minimum wage laws, that does not excessively tax, that does not excessively regulate, that does not mandate or dictate.

Reverend Jesse Jackson points out that, while blacks comprise 12 percent of the population, they own but a fraction of the country's wealth. Blacks also enjoy a lower rate of suicide than whites. Why doesn't the "white advantage" translate into a lower rate of suicide?

On standardized tests, Japanese outperform whites. Yet, in Japan, the Japanese rate of suicide exceeds that of America. If the results of an IQ test dictate happiness, why doesn't Japan have a *lower* rate of suicide?

Is the playing field level? My dad taught me about the counterproductive nature of whining about conditions over which you have no control. "Ninety percent of people don't want to hear about your problems," he said, "and the other ten percent are glad it's you."

Why It Is Important to Fight the Victicrat Mentality

Optimism. It's not just a mind-set, it is behavior.

A few years ago, *Time* magazine did a cover story called the "E.Q. Factor," meaning the emotional quotient.[69]

Among other things, the article discussed University of Pennsylvania Professor Martin Seligman's work on the importance of optimism and emotional intelligence. He defines it as a kind of self-awareness, an ability to adjust to one's circumstances, and a belief that one has the power to make one's own life better.

Intrigued by Professor Seligman's work, Metropolitan Life Insurance Company contacted him. Help us, Metropolitan Life said, to more successfully identify good salespeople. For years, Metropolitan Life gave prospective hires a kind of intelligence test. Still, many new hires failed. We wonder, said Metropolitan Life, whether the professor might design a test to identify "optimists," since Seligman argues optimists do better in life than pessimists.

So Seligman designed a test to measure the level of the applicant's optimism. The test further identified "super-optimists." And Metropolitan Life hired these super-optimists, irrespective of how badly they did on the general aptitude tests. After one year, the optimists outsold the pessimists. But the super-optimists outperformed everybody. After one year, the sales by the super-optimists exceeded those of the pessimists—who were hired by the traditional screening exam—by 21 percent, and after two years the super-optimists outsold the pessimists by 57 percent!

When optimists fail, Seligman found, they attribute their failure to something they did or did not do. In short, they faced failure with an "I can correct this" attitude.

How does this apply to black victicrat mentality? Imagine an inner-city child raised in a home without a father, or possibly a father who plays no role in his life whatsoever. He attends a bad school; sees drug dealing around him; listens to gangsta rap, with the artist's obsession with sex, drugs, and money. Like all kids, he resists doing homework, preferring to spend time dribbling a basketball or just hangin' out.

After all, he reasons, why work hard? "Black leaders" tell him the white man intends to bring him down; that a credit-worthy black can't get a loan; that a man as prominent as Danny Glover can't get a taxicab in New York; that standardized tests like the SATs are culturally biased; that the police persecuted the innocent O. J. Simpson; that the CIA introduced crack cocaine to South Central L.A.; that some scientists invented the AIDS virus to kill blacks; that he can't get into college without affirmative action; that if you get suspended from school, it is due to a racist administration seeking to persecute black children; and that you can't get a table at Denny's. At some point, this kid says to himself, "Why bother?"

He then begins to pay less attention to academics, which after all—according to the defeatist view of the world he has been taught—leads nowhere. He stops trying, stops working, adopts negative attitudes, and begins to engage in counterproductive behavior. Sure enough, his life turns out badly. "They were right," this now cynical and self-destructive young adult says. "The system screwed me." Obviously, most young minorities escape crime and lead responsible lives. But a large number do not.

I started my executive search business in 1980. Several insurance agents dropped by, unannounced, to pitch their products. One day, a bright young black man dropped by and I gave him a few minutes. Impressed, I agreed to have lunch with him.

He told me that his business was struggling. This surprised me because he seemed so efficient, thorough, and personable. "But," he said, "blacks don't have that much money, so my potential is limited."

"Blacks?" I said. "Your clients are all black?"

He answered, "Yes."

"Did your company tell you to concentrate on a black market?" I asked.

"No," he said.

"Did your company imply they wanted you to target a black market?"

"No," he replied.

Turns out he simply felt more comfortable with black clients and thought that prospective white clients would somehow not respond to him, no matter how sound his presentation.

"But why?" I said. "Out of all the insurance agents who called on me, you were the only black one. Do you think the white ones ran away after seeing me, a black man, running this company? Why have you engaged in this self-limiting behavior?"

He had no answer.

Another true story. I worked out at an athletic club in downtown Cleveland. One day, a black man and I began speaking while changing in the locker room. "What do you do for a living?" I asked.

He said he was a computer consultant, but complained about his client base. He said he worked for cities with black mayors. "But," he said, "the shelf life of a mayor is short and unpredictable. And when the mayor decides not to run for office or gets defeated, I have to try and start a new relationship." He further complained about the government's below-private-industry fees, and that government industries seldom pay on time.

"What do you do for a living?" he asked.

I told him that I placed lawyers with law firms and corporations.

"Oh," he said, "I didn't know there was an agency specializing in placing minority lawyers."

"Who said minority lawyers?" I said. "In fact," I told him, "my client base consists primarily of Fortune 1000 companies and major law firms—all 'mainstream' businesses."

"Wow," he said. "It's amazing that you were able to make that leap."

" 'That leap' ?" I said. "What do you mean, 'that leap'? I have a service, and I simply market my service to whomever I think should use me. Period. End of statement."

Again I asked, "Why do you self-limit to a market that, by your own admission, is shaky?"

Again, no answer. Just an assumption that whites would not be hospitable. His attitude, therefore, was "why try?"

Black victicrat leaders do a great deal of damage. People like Johnnie Cochran don't preach what they practice. Writer Jonathan Wilcox calls it the "Willie Brown paradox." Willie Brown, currently the mayor of San Francisco, the black son of a sharecropper, dominated California politics for nearly fifteen years as a powerful state assembly speaker. Yet, during a press conference where he defended affirmative action, Brown said to a group of white reporters, "I'm telling you; you've got no clue what it is like . . . every day in your life to know that this is the system you are in . . . it gnaws at you day in and day out."[70]

So, why didn't this "gnawing" stop Brown? Brown is a shrewd, cunning, street smart, charismatic politician. Willie Brown would have been Willie Brown, brown (pardon the pun) or not.

What Cochran preaches is that "race plays a part of everything in America." What he practices, however, is something very different. By all accounts, he rises early, works hard, and stays late. A driven man, Cochran stayed focused and is now one of America's most prominent criminal defense lawyers. This cannot happen with a negative, pessimistic attitude. Cochran does not preach what he practices.

What he preaches is "they're out to get you, cops want to brutalize you, the system hates you." Like Teflon, this nonsense slides right off the skin of a child brought up in a home with strong parental role models, where dad gets up and goes to work even when he doesn't feel like it. No, the victicrat mentality hurts the child with little or no guidance, who puts on the television and hears leader after leader blame slavery, the dastardly white man, the great white pumpkin, for our "plight."

UCLA psychologist Shelley Taylor calls optimism an "under-rated resource. It gives you," she said, "much more than people imagine it does."[71] Or, as a baseball coach once said, "A negative attitude doesn't *affect* a team. It *infects* it."

Let's Replace Affirmative Action with Affirmative Attitude

A poll in the *Los Angeles Times* asked whether, in America, "every-one has the power to succeed." Low-income whites were more likely to say yes to that statement than blacks earning $50,000 or more![72]

At American dinner tables all across the country, most parents urge their children to work hard, study hard, and prepare. But in black households, how much dinner table talk revolves around "the white man done me wrong," rather than focuses on grit, hard work, and preparation?

The formula for success is simple. Implementation is hard. As a high school friend put it, "Anybody can talk the talk. But it takes a whole other set of nuts to walk the walk."

So regardless of your race, gender, or circumstance, get ahead and stay ahead by following these thirty-two things—my Personal Pledge 32.

Personal Pledge 32

1. There is no excuse for lack of effort.

2. Although I may be unhappy with my circumstances, and although racism and sexism and other "isms" exist, I know that things are better now than ever, and the future is even brighter.

3. While I may be unhappy with my circumstances, I have the power to change and improve my life. I refuse to be a victim.

4. Others may have been blessed with more money, better connections, a better home environment, and even better looks, but I can succeed through hard work, perseverance, and education.

5. I may be a product of a single- or no-parent household, but I will not hold anyone responsible for my present or allow anyone to interfere with my future. Others succeed under conditions far worse than mine.

6. Some schools and teachers are better than others, but my level of effort, dedication, curiosity, and willingness to grow determine what I learn.

7. Ambition is the key to growth.

8. I will set apart some time each day to think about where I want to go and how I intend to get there. A goal without a plan is just a wish.

9. "Luck" is what happens when preparation meets opportunity.

10. If suitable role models are not nearby, I will seek them out.

11. A role model is someone who, through hard work and a positive outlook, has achieved.

12. A role model may be a parent, relative, friend, church member, judge, doctor, attorney, businessperson, or someone I've read about in the newspaper or seen on the local news.

13. I will contact role models and seek their advice, guidance, and counsel. People remember when they were my age and are eager to help.

14. I will seek out recommended magazines, articles, books, biographies, videos, and motivational and how-to books, and use them for education and motivation.

15. The light is always green. You cannot go full speed with one foot on the brake.

16. I am always "in school," and I will not waste my summer by failing to read about and speak to people who can inspire me.

17. I will avoid friendship with people who do not share my goals and commitments. Nonsupportive relationships waste time and energy.

18. I will not seek immediate results, as I understand life is a journey and not a destination.

19. I will read a newspaper each day.

20. I will entertain myself in ways that challenge and expand my mind. As someone said, a mind once expanded never returns to its original size.

21. I will pay attention to my diet and overall fitness, as they are the keys to a healthy and productive body and an enthusiastic mind.

22. Drugs are stupid. People who believe in drugs don't believe in themselves.

23. I understand that jobs of the future require more preparation and training than ever, and I am determined to obtain the necessary background.

24. A well-rounded, competent student studies math and science.

25. People are not born "deficient in mathematical ability." Through hard work and dedication, the subject can be mastered.

26. It is essential that I learn to speak and write standard English. This is not "acting white," but acting smart.

27. A strong vocabulary is the key to communication, and I will read books on vocabulary enrichment.

28. I expect sometimes to be teased, even ridiculed. This will not stop me; it will only make me stronger and more determined.

29. I control my body and will not create a child until I am spiritually, psychologically, educationally, and financially capable of assuming this awesome responsibility.

30. Life is difficult. I expect setbacks and will learn from them. Struggle creates strength.

31. Every day is precious, and one without growth is squandered.

32. *There is only one me, and I'm it!*

Call to the Black Leadership

The black leadership must stop focusing on nonsense.

It is nonsense to spend time and energy accusing the networks of racism for failing to have more black comic characters in their prime-time lineup. If people don't want to watch, stop watching. If people stop watching, the studios scramble around trying to figure out why their current stuff ain't selling.

We live in an era where, through the Internet, "our images" can be readily accessed. Niche programming creates networks like BET, UPN, or WB, that "cater to minorities." It is simply silly to suggest that network businesspeople have an agenda beyond making money, securing their jobs, and maintaining their lifestyles. It is not in their best interest to be racist. And, believe me, one thing people in Hollywood are good at is pursuing their self-interest.

In the mid-sixties, the Los Angeles Dodgers played their arch rival, the San Francisco Giants. The Dodgers accused Giants pitcher Juan Marichal, a native of the Dominican Republic, of intentionally intimidating batters. During one of Marichal's at-bats, black Dodger catcher Johnny Roseboro, in throwing the ball back to the mound, intentionally threw the ball extremely close to Marichal's head. Wrong move. Marichal, bat in hand, turned and clubbed Roseboro on the head. Medics took Roseboro to the hospital, and he required stitches.

The incident jeopardized both players' careers.

My uncle and I discussed this, and he said, "Larry, look at these two brothers, almost throwing away their careers for their two white owners. The owners [Horace Stoneham and Walter O'Malley] were probably sittin' in an owners' box, sippin' wine." (The Dodger owner, Walter O'Malley, did encourage the former New York Giants to move to the Bay Area to continue their heated and extremely lucrative rivalry. "Bad blood" between the Dodgers and the Giants means good money.) My uncle was right. Roseboro and Marichal forgot the big picture. The healthier they stay, the more money they make. If they injure themselves or get arrested and convicted of assault, what will O'Malley and Stoneham do? Get new players, dummies!

I urge the black leadership to focus on the big picture. How can our people be safer, healthier, and more productive? Answer: parental choice of schools; moral and legal discouragement of the young, irresponsible, and unwed from having children; the repeal of the war on drugs; the privatization of Social Security; guarantees of adequate police presence and protection; laws allowing citizens to carry concealed weapons; the repeal of business regulations that strangle the formation of inner-city and urban businesses; the repeal of the requirement of licenses for cabdrivers or beauticians; and the repeal of minimum wage laws.

As Aristotle, in *The Nicomachean Ethics*, once put it, "Anyone can become angry—that is easy. But to be angry with the right person, to the right degree, at the right time, for the right purpose, and in the right way—this is not easy."[73]

Who Are You Calling an Uncle Tom?

In 1997, Morley Safer interviewed me on *60 Minutes*. Safer asked how it felt to be called an "Uncle Tom" by fellow blacks, to be accused of betraying them. We had the following exchange:

LARRY ELDER: You're white. If a white person said of you, because of his perception of your affection for blacks, "You're a nigger-lover," you would quite properly call this person a racist. If a black person says to another black person, because of that person's perceived affection for whites, "You are an Uncle Tom," I don't see the difference.

MORLEY SAFER: Racism is racism.

ELDER: [nodding] Racism is racism.

Oh, and how did I respond to the black man referred to in the beginning of the chapter, the one who attacked me personally because of my views? The exchange went this way:

Q.: Larry Elder, is there a connection between your beliefs and the house and the white woman you have waiting for you in the hills?

ELDER: I appreciate that you are so concerned about my personal life. I happen to be single, but if I did have a white woman waiting for me in my house in the hills, I don't suppose you'd be satisfied until I murdered her and then blamed it on the white man.

2

WHITE CONDESCENSION IS AS BAD AS BLACK RACISM

Race remains America's unresolved dilemma.

—SENATOR BILL BRADLEY

What Is White Condescension?

What is white condescension?

Professor Shelby Steele defines white condescension this way: that whites bend over backward to show their good motives and unbiased minds. This provides a way of regaining the moral authority lost due to slavery and Jim Crow.

Economics Professor Walter Williams bases white condescension on emotional and irrational white guilt—that whites feel, if not personally, at least responsible by heritage for the "black plight." Thus, Williams offers universal amnesty to whites "so that white people can quit acting like damn fools."

Good motives aside, white condescension does more damage than good. White condescension says to a black child, "The rules used by other ethnic and immigrant groups don't apply to you. Forget about 'work hard, get an education, possess good values. No, for you, we'll alter the rules by lowering the standards and expecting less.' " Expect less, get less.

Much of what passes for white compassion is nothing more than white condescension. For example, the chancellor of the University of California school system, as well as the presidents of all the system's universities, supports affirmative action. What these academics are really saying is rather insulting. Quite simply, they do not feel black students capable of competing. They do not feel black students capable of performing on standardized tests, a major component of the system's admission criteria. So, rather than urge improved K–12 performance by black students, these compassionate educators support lowering standards to achieve "racial diversity." Yet, if you ask them *personally* how *they* became so successful, most likely they will say through "hard work." But this formula apparently does not apply to people of darker skin. This is not only wrong, but insulting.

I recently received a letter from one of those "I-feel-your-pain" white men, about a jazz festival he had attended. He said that the majority of those in the audience were white, but there were some blacks. He wrote:

> One of the defects of the concert was that security made no effort to make patrons remain seated or go to the side to groove and dance. People who stood up in place blocked the views of those behind. On Saturday afternoon, a group of blacks became seized with the energy and stood up to dance, remaining up after the end of the number. They were entirely

self-centered and in no way mindful of the hundreds of others whose views they were ruining. Not a single Caucasian said a word. It was like a silent understanding that dealing with this particular problem was the responsibility of blacks because whites might conceivably be thought of as proceeding from an improper motive. Better to endure in silence. Blacks ultimately lost patience and began yelling, softly at first and then more loudly—"Down in front!" This became a chant and soon the standees realized that they were the target of the displeasure, and nodded sheepishly in apology, grabbed hands, and sat down in embarrassment. Throughout, whites remained respectfully deferential, and, in May, 1999, in the USA, that was the right thing to do.

"And in May, 1999, in the USA, that was the right thing to do"? Talk about white condescension!

How about, "For crying out loud, sit the hell down! I'm trying to watch a concert over here!"

Now, me, if I'm watching the concert, I want to see the stage. I'm not thinking about Johnnie Cochran, Louis Farrakhan, or the NAACP. How about, "Excuse me, pal, would you mind sittin' the hell down so I can see?" What is this? Some guy stands up in front of you where you're trying to watch a concert, and because of political correctness of not wanting to be perceived as racist, you don't get to see?

Another example of white condescension: Democratic presidential candidate Bill Bradley came to Los Angeles to speak before 150 black ministers. "I was spellbound," said one. "Spellbound"? Another said, "A most powerful and refreshing message." "Powerful and refreshing message"? And yet another attendee said the speech caused her to feel "a connection to him as a human being."

What generated all of this enthusiasm for Senator Bradley, a notoriously plodding and decidedly non-"spellbinding" speaker?

Well, Bradley said that race remains "America's unresolved dilemma." Bingo! Pay dirt! *Ching-ba-da-bing!* Music to a black preacher's ears, this stuff about "America's unresolved dilemma."

Exactly what is this "unresolved dilemma"? That Mark Fuhrman never performed the moon walk on *Soul Train*? That the Ku Klux Klan denied Al Sharpton's petition for candidacy as a member of their board of directors? That the Three Tenors did not invite Puff Daddy?

Bradley's remark perpetuates the nonsense that so many black leaders eagerly embrace: that all problems facing the black community stem from one thing, and one thing only—racism. This mind-set argues that the problem of children having children stems from racism. Black-on-black crime is a product of white racism. And underperforming schools? White racism.

For many black leaders, "feeling our pain" remains more important than identifying the true source of problems and proposing steps to remedy them. The issue of teen pregnancy, for example, far outweighs white racism as the black community's most vexing problem. The 1996 Welfare Reform Act imposed a time limit on welfare, as well as so-called family caps, so that additional babies do not bring additional benefits. The results following the 1996 Welfare Reform Act have simply been dramatic. Welfare rolls declined far more rapidly than experts predicted and far greater than simply as a result of an improved economy. The welfare recipients knew that the "unlimited, unconditional benefits for nothing" jig was up. Polls show that even welfare recipients agreed with welfare reform.

But, what about Senator Bradley? Senator Bradley opposed the 1996 Welfare Reform Bill. So, while Senator Bradley agrees that race remains America's "unresolved dilemma," he was AWOL on welfare reform, when blacks needed him most.

In many inner-city schools, the majority of school children read, write, and compute below grade average. The majority of inner-city parents want choice in schools, so that their kids may escape from an underperforming, government-assigned school. Where is Senator "Race Remains America's Unresolved Dilemma" Bradley on this issue? He supports only limited or trial vouchers, whatever that means.

People like Bradley complain about the "economic gap" between blacks and whites. To close this gap, many scholars urge the privatization of Social Security—allowing workers to invest their monies in stocks or bonds. This would disproportionately benefit blacks. Many blacks enter the work market earlier than whites, and die sooner. Thus, projections show that a black man, who dies at age sixty-five, could, with privatization of Social Security, die with substantially more money than under the current system.[1] A son or daughter could start a business, pay for college, invest in real estate. Where does Senator Bradley stand on this issue, which could so disproportionately benefit black America? He opposes Social Security privatization.

More white condescension: a Time-CNN poll showed that 89 percent of black teens found little or no racism in their own lives.[2] Interestingly, white teens were more likely than blacks to consider racism a major problem! A recent example: a friend and her son walked out of a supermarket and passed a black woman speaking on the phone. "Excuse me, do you have a pen I could borrow?" said the woman.

My friend, a businesswoman, reached into her purse and produced an inexpensive pen with her corporation's logo. Handing the woman the pen, my friend said, "Here, take this." The woman and her son continued toward their car.

"Wait," said the black woman. "Don't forget your pen." "That's all right," said my friend, and she opened the door of her expensive European car. The black woman exploded, "I can afford my own pen. How dare you think I can't afford my own pen. I don't need your pen."

My friend sputtered, "But, but I only meant—"

"I don't care what you meant. You white people think you're

superior. Well, you're not." She threw the pen at my friend and turned around and stomped off.

Now, my friend's son sided with the black woman! "Blacks," he said, "rightfully get offended when they see white superiority."

"White superiority?" said my friend.

But her son insisted that the fragile sensibilities of blacks required whites to tread gently. "To do otherwise," he argued, "is racism." Oh.

Blacks Do Not Need Sympathetic Whites to Protect Blacks' "Self-Esteem"

The racism-is-everywhere-crowd likes to point to studies showing that little black girls, at least initially, prefer to play with little white dolls. Thus, the black psyche remains traumatized by the tyranny of the alleged American standard of beauty: the blonde, blue-eyed woman.

But researchers at the University of Arizona found that, no, young black women are far more satisfied with their bodies than young white women.[3] Obsessed with the Barbie doll image, young white girls fretted about not having long blonde hair, a tall physique, and a tiny waist. "The white girls had a very fixed image of what beauty is," said anthropologist Mimi Nichter. "And because the girls didn't match up—as few of us do—they felt very dissatisfied and frustrated with themselves."

Black women, however, reported being quite satisfied with their bodies. Moreover, young black women relied far less on physical characteristics in forming a positive self-image. "[Young black girls] told us that [the ideal girl possesses] a nice personality, gets along well with other people, and has a good head on her shoulders," according to researcher Sheila Parker, Ph.D.[4]

What percentage of white teens were dissatisfied with their

bodies? Ninety percent! What percentage of black teens were *satisfied* with their bodies? Seventy percent!

Professor Patrick Turley of the UCLA School of Dentistry, who co-authored studies on black and white female models from the 1950s to the present,[5] noted that in the past black models possessed features described as "Caucasian-like." "It has been my feeling over the past twenty years," Turley says, "that this concept of beauty has been changing. If we look at television, motion pictures, supermodels, (or even radio personalities!), we can see that successful people in these fields no longer need to appear 'Caucasian-like.' "

Turley and his co-author sought to determine whether, for example, Caucasian female models "display fuller lips than they did many decades ago." Turley says, "The results of the study are quite interesting. The African-American models [of today] displayed fuller lips than the Caucasian models who displayed fuller lips than the average Caucasian female. Surprisingly, when we compare the faces of African-American models to the average African-American profile we found that they were the same. African-American models displayed profiles that were as full as the average African-American face." Quite simply, the American standard of ideal beauty is changing. Thin features out, thicker features in. Collagen anyone?

Turley continues, "We conclude from these studies that today in American society the African-American female does not have to display Caucasian-like features in order to be considered beautiful. It now appears that the non-Caucasian face with fuller lips is now viewed as more beautiful than the traditional thin-lipped Caucasian."

So, the case against America, home of the racist, grows weaker every day. If blacks are "taught" that white women have superior looks, it ain't working. And, in case you were wondering, the American Association of University Women reports that black *boys* possess greater self-esteem than white boys. So, apparently, black boys, just as black girls, have successfully fought off the attempt to deplete their self-esteem.

Studies show young blacks and young whites watch exactly the same television shows. And don't forget the Time-CNN poll found that 89 percent of black teens report little or no racism in their own lives.

Things ain't so bad. "I think this speaks well for American society," concludes Professor Turley, "in that our attitudes have changed: many characteristics of the African-American face are now viewed as more attractive than the average Caucasian face."

Well, well.

Some black activists tell us that "the media" or "Madison Avenue" somehow undermines the self-image of black boys. "But researchers have repeatedly found," according to columnist John Leo, "that self-esteem of blacks is no lower than that of whites, and often quite higher. A summary of this research, published in *U.S. News & World Report*, points out that this consistent finding goes all the way back to the mid-1960s."[6]

White Guilt and Affirmative Action

Many whites support affirmative action as a sort of reparation for blacks. A longtime Los Angeles liberal talk show host and staunch supporter of affirmative action once said to Internet reporter Matt Drudge, "Do you think Larry Elder, given his voice, would even be on the radio, if he weren't black?" Remember, this remark came from a toe-tag liberal—a true believer in cradle-to-grave big government—who publicly asserts his support for affirmative action! Yet, not very deep down inside, he clearly believes that affirmative action gives blacks an artificial boost without which they could not complete. With friends like these . . .

A Jewish friend accompanied me to an inner-city seminar on

"How to Get into Hollywood." A young black writer stood and offered his opinion on why Hollywood seemed impenetrable to blacks. He said, "I've been trying to get into Hollywood for a long time. It ain't nothin' nobody can do to crack this. I could have went to film school, but, like, I knew what I wanted to do. So I decided to just go out and go for it. But ain't nothin' happenin'. So, don't nobody expect nothin' from these people. . . ." And on he went.

On the drive home, I asked my friend her opinion of the young man. She said, "Well, he meant—"

I cut her off and said, "No, no. I want to know what you thought of the young man."

She repeated, "Well, I think what he was trying to say—"

Again, I cut her off and rephrased the question. "Beth," I said, "suppose a Jewish kid from Brentwood High had stood up in a meeting and expressed himself that way."

She said, "I would have been appalled. His grammar, his diction, his . . ." Suddenly, she caught herself and realized she applied a lower standard to this black teenager than she would have to a Jewish youth. She simply expected less of this black person *because he is black*.

Many whites fail to hold blacks to the same standard to which they hold themselves. Around their own dinner tables, these whites preach that hard work and education lead to success. They preach that whether facing success or failure, always assume personal responsibility for one's own actions. Yet, when it comes to blacks, whites often fail to preach what they practice. They fail to demand responsible behavior from blacks, blaming bad conduct on "environmental factors." How smug. How condescending.

"Black Leaders" and "Black Role Models"

And what about this expression "black leader"? Why—in the 21st century—do blacks need a "leader"? Who is the Western European Caucasian leader? The Eastern European Caucasian leader? The Mexican-American leader? The Jewish-American leader?

How condescending for the media to constantly speak of a "black leader." The media apparently perceives other groups as smart enough, competent enough, and intelligent enough to somehow, some way, lead themselves. Not so for blacks.

One day, a white guy walked into my dad's downtown restaurant. "Did you hear what your leader said on television last night?"

"Who?"

"Your leader, Jesse Jackson."

"My leader?" my dad said. "Who's your leader?"

The white man said, "Why, why, well, nobody."

My father said, "So, I'm intelligent enough to run my own business, but not intelligent enough to make decisions without a leader."

The white guy said, "Well, what I meant was, you know, like . . . uh . . . ."

I recall something said a few years ago by silver-medalist figure skater Debbie Thomas. Reporters frequently asked Thomas, the first black to win a medal in figure skating in the Olympics, what black skater inspired her. To this, an exasperated Thomas finally said, "I don't need to see somebody black do something before I think I can do it!" Hear, hear!

And what of "role models"? An *L.A. Times* article on Al Gore's coarse-tongued campaign manager, Donna Brazile, noted that she put down Colin Powell and J. C. Watts, two of the black community's most prominent "role models."

Why do only blacks seem to have or need "role models," and why do these "role models" have to be black? We all need influences, people to look up to, yes, role models. We all need someone to say, as my dad said to me, "Don't keep your head down and your mouth poked out." Not a bad lesson for anybody. No matter your race.

The Media Treat Blacks Like Children

On April 3, 1996, the plane carrying Commerce Secretary Ron Brown crashed in Croatia. Commentators immediately eulogized Brown's life, focusing on his "triumph" in overcoming prejudice and adversity to become the nation's first black secretary of commerce.

Newspapers featured large photos of President Clinton and Ron Brown embracing and shaking hands. But, think about it. In that large picture of Ron Brown and the president, who was less likely to have "made it"—Brown or Clinton?

Bill Clinton's biological father died in a car crash before Clinton's mother gave birth. His abusive, alcoholic stepfather beat his mother.

Ron Brown, on the other hand, came from a nuclear, intact family. His father worked as the manager of Harlem's famous Hotel Teresa, where that era's black entertainers stayed. Brown met, interacted with, and learned from the leading black luminaries of the day—Billie Holiday, Duke Ellington, Count Basie, Leontyne Price.

Brown attended the predominantly white Middlebury College in Vermont, where he became student body president, a feat, by the way, not equaled by Clinton when he attended undergraduate school at Georgetown University. Brown then demonstrated his management and strategic skills as the campaign manager of Jesse Jackson's 1988 presidential race. Brown so impressed party officials, they voted him chairman of the Democratic National Committee.

Brown achieved at every level, arguably overcoming fewer adversities than the president. Yet, during the Ron Brown coverage, the media described Brown's achievement as almost a freak of nature, rather than the product of good family structure, values, focus, and hard work.

During the 1984 Democratic Convention, the children of Walter Mondale spoke. They were poised and articulate. After they spoke, the commentators said little. Then the children of Jesse Jackson addressed the convention. Announcers fell all over themselves, telling viewers how "terribly, terribly articulate" they found the Jackson children. Well, duh. Jackson's kids went to the same type of tony prep schools as did Mondale's. How were they *supposed* to speak?

But, bent on saying kind things, the announcers applied a second, lower standard to blacks with the same education and credentials as whites. My message to this condescending white announcer: Dude, when blacks do something as well as whites, please don't act as if someone just reinvented the wheel. OK?

Dick Morris, former presidential aide, and I met at a broadcasting convention. I told him that I resented his and the president's use of the term "African-American." "Why are blacks referred to as 'African-Americans'?" I said. "Do we usually refer to former governor Mario Cuomo as 'Italian-American Mario Cuomo'? Do we refer to former presidential adviser Dick Morris as 'Jewish-American Dick Morris'? Do we refer to former secretary of state Henry Kissinger as 'German-American Henry Kissinger'? Do we call Ronald Reagan 'Irish-American Ronald Reagan'?"

He paused and said, "I never thought about that. You know, if I were referred to as a Jewish-American, I would resent it." "Go tell the president," I said.

The American lineage of most blacks pre-dates that of most whites. Yet when newspapers write of whites with English, German, Irish, French, Polish extraction, they do not use hyphens to identify their ethnic heritage. The term "African-American" is both separatist and condescending, especially since blacks pre-date some whites' arrivals in America by as many as three centuries.

The media's pandering toward blacks is almost painful. In 1998, Mark Willes, the publisher of the *Los Angeles Times*, told the *Wall Street Journal* that he wanted quotations from more minorities in news stories. To ensure this, he said that he would base the compensation of managers, in part, on whether stories included quotes from minorities![7] A quota on quotes!

The *Los Angeles Times* once ran a cover story about a government employee caught on tape referring to women as bitches and using ethnic epithets. But only until local television news, where they showed the man's picture, did we learn that he was black! Now tell me. If this employee were white and used racial and sexual epithets, do you think the paper would omit any reference to his race? Yet, in this case, they did. Why? Double standard. Whites get judged one way and blacks in another, less demanding, oh-they-can't-help-themselves, way.

Another illustrative story: *Spider-Man* comics run in five hundred newspapers. In June, 1996, in 499 newspapers, the following panel ran.

Spider-Man is walking in Central Park and overhears a voice saying, "Thought you'd get away, huh? Take that!" Spider-Man springs into action, charges down the hill, and, lo and behold, two black kids are playing with plastic toy guns. Their mother dressed down Spider-Man for his overreaction, and Spider-Man sheepishly apologizes.

In 499 newspapers, the cartoon depicted black children. But not in the *Los Angeles Times,* a traditional, big city liberal newspaper. In the *Los Angeles Times* the Spider-Man comic had been changed! Spider-Man rushes down the hill only to find two *white* kids playing with plastic toy guns.

The *Times* competitor, the local *Daily News*, busted them and ran a story on the switch. The *Los Angeles Times* editorial editor admitted that "this strip perpetuates the stereotypical view of young black kids as carrying guns, threatening people, and that sort of thing."[8] So, now the cartoons, too, also serve as a public relations bureau for the downtrodden.

Marlon Brando appeared on *Larry King Live* and attacked what he considered Hollywood's insensitivity. "Hollywood is run by Jews. It's owned by Jews. But they should have a greater sensitivity about the issue of people who are suffering . . . we have seen the nigger, the greaseball, we've seen the Chink, we've seen the slit-eyed dangerous Jap. We have seen the wily Filipino. We've seen everything, but we never saw the Kike, because they knew perfectly well that there's where you draw the wagons around."

Local news stations repeated Brando's outburst. When the *Larry King Live* Brando excerpt was replayed in Los Angeles, the station left every epithet he uttered intact, except when it came to the word "nigger." Local news *muted* the word. You saw Brando's lips move, but heard no sound. So, Asians heard Brando say "Jap" and "Filipino." Italians heard him say "greaseball." Jews heard "Kike." But the news director found the black psyche far too fragile to hear the word "nigger." The station felt Asians, Jews, and Italians sufficiently strong enough to handle the insult. But, blacks, well . . . The media treat blacks like kids, incapable of handling the truth. Call this "the Brando Rule."

Here's a classic. On March 16, 2000, former Black Panther H. Rap Brown was a fugitive. Authorities sought him in connection with the murder of a deputy sheriff and the wounding of another. He was at large for several days.

The cops caught Brown. On March 21, 2000, the *Chicago Tribune* ran the following headline: "Marshals Arrest Ex-Black Panther Sought In Slaying of Deputy." On the same date, the *New York Times* ran the following headline: " '60s Rights Leader Is Arrested In Death of Sheriff's Deputy." In the *Washington Post*, the following day's headline read: "Al-Amin Calls Slaying Case a 'Government Conspiracy.' " But the *Los Angeles Times* decided to tone down the decibel. Just a bit. Its headline? "A Former Firebrand Lands In Hot Water"! What?! That's sort of like saying Jeffrey Dahmer had an eating disorder, or that Charlie Manson was kind of cranky. How about a headline like this: "Former Black Panther Found, After a Tiff With Police." Or "Ex-Black Panther And Authorities Trade Insults." Or "H. Rap Brown, Former Black Panther, Suddenly Popular." Worse yet, the *L.A. Times*, mind you, reprinted its story from the *Washington Post*. In other words, same story, different headlines.

How bad is condescension in the media? When pollsters themselves uncover less racism than they thought, some quickly discount their own results. For example, in 1997 a Gallup poll[9] showed that 93 percent of whites said they would vote for a black president. In 1958, only 35 percent of whites said they would. And in 1958, only 4 percent of whites approved of black-white marriages. Now almost two-thirds do.

But Frank Newport, Gallup's editor in chief, discounted his own findings! Newport said that whites say what pollsters like to hear, and that "whites' reluctance to express racist attitudes is important in and of itself."[10] So if polled, blacks tell the truth. But whites lie, largely, one supposes, to downplay the existence of racism. Why, for example, accept that "only" 89 percent of black teens found little or no racism in their own lives? Perhaps the accurate "black answer" is even higher, say 95 percent. Yet, Gallup does not show the same kind of skepticism toward *black* answers to questions that it shows for those of whites. Why should we not find that blacks have a reluctance to express optimism about racial issues, and that this reluctance is, to paraphrase Newport, "important in and of itself?"

Apparently, when pollsters poll blacks, blacks give it to them straight. But when polls show a lack of white racist attitudes, pollsters dismiss their own findings.

The Human Rights Commission of Los Angeles recently asked community leaders to speak about race relations in the year 2000.

My panel specifically addressed "Racism and the Media," and I was asked to speak, along with a white editor of the *Los Angeles Times*, and a black activist columnist.

I argued that the media focuses on "racism, racism everywhere" stories, rather than on the true, larger, and far more positive, picture. I mentioned the Time-CNN poll, for example, showed that 89 percent of black teens found little or no racism in their own lives.

The *Los Angeles Times* editor interrupted. "Excuse me, that hasn't been my experience. I've been to a lot of high schools," he said, "and kids *do* talk about racism." Yet only two weeks earlier, the *Los Angeles Times* itself published a story on racial attitudes of white, black, and Hispanic teens. The article said that nearly 82 percent of black teens felt optimistic about the future, compared to only 71 percent of whites![11] So, in essence, this *Los Angeles Times* editor said, *Screw the more reliable data. Forget about those 82 percent optimists. I'm gonna focus on the disgruntled 18 percent.* The *Los Angeles Times* guy ignored his own paper's polling data in favor of his negative anecdotal experiences, which, he decided, presented a truer picture of the world.

Next spoke Dr. Earl Ofari Hutchinson, a black activist who writes a syndicated column. Hutchinson represents the state-of-the-art victicrat, a whining, crying, blame-the-white-man emotional black toe-tag liberal who cannot see the forest for the trees. He frequently attacks me in his column, once referred to me as a "shock jock," while predicting my career's demise. (Sorry, Doc, still here.)

He accused the *Los Angeles Times,* this notoriously left-leaning, I-feel-your-pain newspaper, of racism. First, Hutchinson held up two *Los Angeles Times* photos. "These photographs," he said, "indicate *unconscious* [italics mine] racism." The first photograph showed a black street vendor in Santa Monica. The accompanying article discussed a shopkeeper's anger toward the street vendors for taking away business. Hutchinson stated that he dined in Santa

Monica two or three times a week and that he sees few black vendors. Yet, the *Los Angeles Times* selected this picture. "Why?" asked Dr. Hutchinson. "To malign blacks—unconsciously, now, mind you." Oh.

The second photograph showed a karaoke bar recently opened on Skid Row. The photograph showed mostly black faces. "A mischaracterization," said Dr. Hutchinson, "of Skid Row. Skid Row, after all, features a wide variety of races, yet the photograph unfairly suggests blacks dominate Skid Row." Oh.

The white *Los Angeles Times* editor, who sat next to Hutchinson, never made a comment. After Hutchinson's attack, I turned to the *Los Angeles Times* editor and asked whether he agreed with Dr. Hutchinson's characterization of those photos as evidence of racism.

Turns out, the editor personally helped to select these photos, yet said nothing during Hutchinson's attack! When I demanded a response from the editor, he finally admitted that, no, he was not guilty of racism in selecting those photographs. After further prodding, he called Hutchinson's accusation baseless. Wouldn't he know, since he helped select the photos in the first place?

Yet the editor had said absolutely nothing until *I* demanded that he respond to the charge of racism. But, the same editor nearly took my head off when I pointed to the polling data showing black teens' obliviousness toward racism in their own lives. That, the editor would have none of. But a direct charge of racism, coming from a black activist, well, the less said about that, the better.

This is white condescension.

The editor's attitude, like that of many whites, is one of resignation, of accepting the black victicrat attitude, however silly. Instead of standing his ground, saying, "Excuse me, I don't accept being called a bigot simply because I disagree," he said nothing.

The Media Underreport
"Whites Not Guilty of Racism" News

Bad news sells. Most everybody understands this. During the Reagan economic recovery, the president frequently complained about the media's incessant focus on bad stories. During good times, complained Reagan, the media ignores the big picture, and focuses on some out-of-work guy in "West Cupcake."

And, a journalist can always find some pissed-off victicrat who blames the system, racism, sexism, ageism, looks-ism, anti-Semitism, or any other multitude of "isms." In 1972 Richard Nixon beat George McGovern in a landslide. Still, McGovern received millions of votes. A determined enterprising reporter could file story after story about the "large number" of McGovern voters, forgetting that they represent a small percentage of the whole. This resembles the way the mainstream media covers racism. Not only does bad news sell, but bad news about "racism" really sells.

Many journalists know as much about the environment as they do about Economics 101—next to nothing. To the question, "Is there a cancer epidemic," only one-third of cancer experts agreed. How many journalists feel we face a "cancer epidemic"? According to S. Robert Lichter and Stanley Rothman in their book, *Environmental Cancer: A Political Disease?*,[12] nearly 85 percent of journalists feel "there is a cancer epidemic." So, if a liberal-minded reporter sniffs a pro-environmental story, particularly if there is a "bad guy" developer, expect an anti-business pro-environment story. Expect an absence of pro-business talking heads, but a lot of anti-business experts and academicians included in the story.

President Clinton announced a crusade against "environmental racism," the alleged practice of placing hazardous dumpsites near poor black areas. Clinton ordered the Environmental Protection Agency to issue a report, documenting this "environmental racism." Unfortunately, after this study, the EPA found no credible evidence of environmental racism. Dissatisfied, the administration ordered a second report. Same result. The government published neither report!

The *Detroit News* broke the story[13]:

> The Environmental Protection Agency ignored some of its own ethnic population studies in pushing to link environmentalism and racial discrimination, internal documents show.
>
> The documents, obtained by the *Detroit News*, concluded that whites were more likely than blacks to live around highly polluted sites on the nation's "Superfund" priority cleanup list.
>
> That study never reached the highest levels of the agency as it developed its "environmental justice" policy, and has never been made public.
>
> EPA investigators four years ago began their analysis of the communities around some of the most polluted land in the country, looking for signs of "environmental racism."
>
> They didn't find any, the documents show and interviews confirm. So, EPA staffers said, the agency set aside the results and started over.
>
> The next year, the agency completed an exhaustive survey of the racial demographics around every one of the 1,234 polluted "Superfund" sites in the country. Again, the study failed to find evidence that would bolster the agency's drive to meld civil rights laws into environmental regulations. Again, the agency shelved the report and never released the results.

Did other papers run this not-guilty news?

According to a search of 536 U.S. newspapers, only five papers picked up—or made some reference to—the *Detroit News* story. When, however, the *San Jose Mercury News* accused the CIA of playing a major role in the nation's inner-city crack trade, nearly every paper ran with it. Never mind that the *New York Times, Washington Post*, and *Los Angeles Times* had long debunked the allegation of a major CIA role in the inner-city drug trade. Later, the *San Jose Mercury News* published a near retraction of its story.

The more shrill the "white racism" stories, the better. They're burning black churches! The CIA puts drugs in the black community! Doctors practice racism! Banks redline! NBC, CBS, ABC, and CNN practice broadcast racism! What do these stories have in common? They are all mostly untrue. Yet, popular opinion holds otherwise, a result, in large part, of a widespread whites-are-out-to-get-blacks media bias.

"Racism" in Redlining and Health Care

What about the allegation of redlining, that banks and insurance companies refuse to lend or insure because of discrimination against blacks? Blacks are rejected for mortgage approval about twice as often as whites, leading many to assume that *redlining*—a practice that denies creditworthy black applicants loans for properties in "undesirable" locations—is alive and well.

But according to a September 1999 report by the federal government's Freddie Mac, blacks are two times more likely than whites to have bad credit histories. The *Washington Post* reported that whites making $25,000 a year or less had better credit ratings than blacks making $65,000 to $75,000. Even Hugh Price, head of the Urban League, conceded, "If people have bad credit, they'll be denied loans, end of story."[14]

On February 25, 1999, the *Washington Post* ran an article with the following headline, "Georgetown University Study Finds Disparity in Heart Care; Doctors Less Likely to Refer Blacks, Women, for Cardiac Tests." The article discussed a Georgetown University report, published in the *New England Journal of Medicine*, in which the authors argued, among other things, that doctors referred black and female patients to heart specialists for cardiac catheterization only 60 percent as often as they do for white male patients.

U.S. surgeon general David Satcher said, "This study deals with a very serious problem. It's a matter of life and death whether a patient gets cardiac catheterization and a follow-up with a coronary artery bypass or another therapy. . . . Blacks are 40 percent more likely [than whites] to die from heart disease, and this could be one factor."

According to the *Washington Post*, "The study . . . is the latest in a growing body of medical literature documenting race- and gender-based disparities in healthcare, especially in the treatment of cardiovascular disease."

But, Houston, we have a problem.

On July 29, 1999, in a rare admission of a screwup, a red-faced *New England Journal of Medicine* published a near retraction. Oops, the *Journal* editors admitted that the earlier study had grossly mischaracterized its findings. The doctors messed up the statistical analysis. Turns out that doctors do not refer blacks and women to heart specialists only 60 percent as often as they do for white males. According to Reuters, "Blacks and women were 7 percent less likely to be recommended for cardiac catheterization," the surgeon general said. "Black women were 13 percent less likely." A far cry from "only 60 percent" as often.

Not content to let the doctors-are-racist angle go, the *New England Journal of Medicine* deputy editor Gregory Curfman and editor in chief Jerome Kassirer said, "Although racism and sexism are prevalent in American life, the evidence of racism and sexism in this study was overstated." In other words, just because we didn't find much evidence of racism, we ain't givin' up.

The obsessive determination of white toe-tag liberals to find racism everywhere diverts time, energy, and attention from actual problems. Failing to discuss the problems of crime, illegitimacy, and the lack of personal responsibility simply puts the problems facing the black community off for another day. Failing to talk candidly about the problems facing the black community is a dangerous act of cowardice. White liberals do blacks no favor by this double and lower standard of expectation of black achievement and assumption of responsibility.

Whites Cower in the Face of Black Hostility

A few years ago, a small group of determined Larry Elder–hating blacks launched a boycott of my show. Sponsors received letters with my face, as well as "anti-black" statements I allegedly made. The letter read as follows:

> The following are some of the statements that Larry Elder has made about Black [*sic*] people:
>> Blacks are morally corrupt.
>> It is understandable to be racist against Blacks [*sic*].
>> Blacks are lazy.
>> Blacks are uneducated.
>> Blacks are the cause of crime in America.
>> Blacks feed upon and enjoy victimhood status.
>> The young, the Black [*sic*] and the poor are being pimped by the old, the Black [*sic*] and the rich.
>> It's understandable why some blacks are upset about the burning of Black Churches, [*sic*] but lets [*sic*] put this into perspective . . . Blacks have committed over a BILLION hate crimes against whites in the past 30 years.
>> It's OK for white people to refer to black people as NIGGERS.

Think about this for just one minute. My employer is Disney, whose family-oriented image remains central to the company's success. Any host who said "It's OK for whites to call black people niggers" would find a pink slip in his mailbox before the next commercial break.

Still, sponsor after sponsor defected from the show, costing the station substantial loss in advertising revenues.

During the height of the boycott against me, the management of my radio station invited my detractors to meet. That way, the station felt, we could convince them of our sincerity. We wanted them to know that, no, I wasn't hired as an Uncle Tom but rather as an individual with different, if not politically incorrect, views on a number of issues.

I warned the management not to have the meeting. "These guys are nutcases," I said. "Inviting them in will only embolden them and confirm their clout." As near as we could tell, the "protest" consisted of no more than thirty or forty individuals, using computers and fake addresses to generate an "avalanche" of complaints. Their flyer brazenly describes my letter-writing detractors as "the black community."

So, out went letters to the "protestors." We got the addresses from letters of complaints sent to clients. Only fourteen responded, and about seven showed up, including someone named Keith, sporting dreadlocks and a boombox and carrying an infant child. (Nothing against dreadlocks, mind you, he just didn't look exactly dressed for success.)

Keith proceeded to tell the general manager that my hiring represented a concerted, conscious effort on the general manager's part to undermine the black community. Keith then launched into a stream-of-consciousness, scarily illogical tirade about the white and Jewish conspiracy to oppress the black man, a suppression culminating in the hiring of Larry Elder.

The general manager, a Jewish liberal, who ran the station for nearly thirty years, was almost in tears. "Do you think," he said, "given my record in the community, I would do such a thing to you people?"

Uh-oh. A mistake, using the term "you people."

"You people?" Keith demanded. The general manager said, "Well, I meant, 'you black people.' "

"Black people?" Keith said.

The general manager then offered, "I meant, 'you African-American people.' "

And so it went.

At the end of the meeting, Keith and his group packed up to leave, taking with them generous portions of the catered cold cuts and soft drinks. Keith turned to me and said, "Not only will our efforts continue—we intend to redouble them. And, as for you, Mr. Elder, we want you to resign your job and leave Los Angeles."

"And leave Los Angeles?" I said.

So much for management's effort at outreach, an effort that made about as much sense as an Anti-Defamation League outreach to David Duke. Some people are simply shrill, emotional boneheads and should be regarded as such. But, sympathetic bleeding-heart whites refuse to dismiss even the most reckless and nonsensical voices as irresponsible—beyond redemption—hotheads.

Deafening Silence in the Face of Baseless Attacks Against "Institutional Racism"

When groups like the NAACP make idiotic statements, few non-blacks dare say anything. Recently, the NAACP launched a defense of the shifty, oft-sued black boxing promoter Don King. Kweisi Mfume, president of the NAACP, wrote Attorney General Janet Reno, urging the Justice Department to back off on its investigation of the boxing promoter. Mfume said, "Don King is revered in his profession and in his community for his accomplishments in boxing, business, and, more importantly, for what he has done for worthy causes of all kinds across racial, ethnic, and religious lines." He called the investigation of King a "violation of the internal guidelines of the Justice Department."[15] Hold the phone.

Don King? "Revered in his profession and in his community"? Isn't anybody out there laughing?

First of all, isn't Janet Reno one of the good guys? Isn't she the attorney general in an administration headed by one whom many blacks call "the first black president of the United States"? Doesn't Bill Clinton enjoy a near 95 percent popularity rating within the black community? Didn't Janet Reno, before becoming attorney general, enjoy a positive reputation among blacks in Florida, where she served as the state attorney?

Yet this does not stop the NAACP from essentially charging the Justice Department with racism. And for what? To protect Don King, a man sued for fraud by boxer after boxer, many of whom are just as black as Mr. King?

"Revered in his profession"? In the book, *Muhammad Ali: His Life and Times*, author Thomas Hauser quotes Jeremiah Shabazz, Ali's spiritual adviser from the Nation of Islam: "Because if you want my view, Don is one of the dirtiest rottenest pieces of scum that ever lived. On a couple of occasions, he gave me some bucks to bring Ali to him, and I'm ashamed to say, that's what I did. But Don King is an evil megalomaniac. He's a closet Hitler, a tyrant in the police-state mold. Sometimes he'll make alliances the way dictators work with the armed forces in their country, but in the end he wants everything for himself."[16]

I once interviewed Larry Holmes, who, too, sued Don King. He said, "Don cheats everybody. I mean, if he can get away with it, you know, that's Don King. . . . See what Don King does, what no other promoter does, Don King will say, 'Look . . . the fight they gonna say is worth $30 million. But I ain't gonna give you 30. I'm gonna give you $20 million.' You say, 'No, I want the 30.' He says, 'No, I'm gonna give you 20. And here's 10 of it right up front.' And that's how they get 'em. And then they don't see that other 10 that they were supposed to get. And that's how Don does it. You know he's damn good. He beat the government twice."

And, following Muhammad Ali's beating at the hands of Larry Holmes, Don King owed Ali a million dollars. King sent someone with $50,000 in cash and a release. The aide opened the briefcase, handed Ali the release, as Ali lay in bed recovering from the Holmes beating. Ali took a pen, signed the release, and accepted the $50,000 in cash, agreeing to a shortfall of $950,000. "Revered in his profession"?

The late sportscaster Howard Cosell stood by Ali's side when boxing stripped Ali of his title after he refused induction into the service. Cosell once said, "To this day, I get furious when I think about it. Muhammad Ali was stripped of his title and forbidden to fight by all fifty states, and that piece of scum, Don King, hasn't been barred by one."[17]

Did someone from the Clinton Justice Department hold a press conference and call the NAACP "full of it"? Of course not. By the way, Mr. Mfume is one of the "worthy causes" for which Don King "is revered," since King made contributions to the NAACP.[18] Could this play a role in Mfume's adoration? Just a thought. Who knows, maybe someday somebody will bring it up.

Meanwhile, in Los Angeles, a Hispanic city councilman, Mike Hernandez, got busted doing cocaine on city time and on city property. Some white city councilpersons urged Hernandez to re-sign. A black city councilman called those same whites "West Side Ku Klux Klansmen."[19] That was that. The race card kept Hernan-dez in office, despite his admission of cocaine use.

And Washington, D.C., mayor Marion Barry triumphantly re-turned to office despite his capture on video camera smoking crack and trying to get a woman, not his wife, in bed. On the tape, he later calls the woman a "bitch" for setting him up. But after his jail term ended Barry played the race card back to the top.

Another example: I interviewed Fred Goldman, the honorable father of the slain Ron Goldman. We talked about the civil judg-ment against O. J. Simpson versus the failure of the criminal jury to find him guilty. Why the different outcomes, I asked. Goldman said that his legal team put on a different, better, and more streamlined case than did the prosecution in the criminal case. "But," I suggested, "isn't the biggest difference the racial composition and mind-set of the civil jury versus the criminal jury?" Indeed, in the civil case, the sole black juror, an alternate, said she didn't believe the authenticity of the thirty-plus photographs showing Simpson wearing the "ugly-ass" Bruno Magli shoes. She called the Browns and Goldmans "bullies" for bringing the civil lawsuit and felt the entire case was a setup from the beginning! "Given the comments of this black alternate juror," I asked Goldman, "don't you believe that the predominantly black downtown criminal jury was simply bent on an acquittal, evidence be damned?"

Goldman replied that one ought not assume that the remarks of one person reflect the feelings of others. On one level, his restraint was admirable, but my friend Fred Goldman was wrong. The fact is that during the trial polls showed 75 percent of blacks believed that O. J. Simpson was not only not guilty, but innocent!

Simpson, of course, got away with murder because the Dream Team played the race card before a willing and receptive, predominantly black jury. Period. But political correctness, or political politeness, prevented even Fred Goldman, whose son was murdered, from expressing the obvious. *This silence makes things worse.*

Remember the *Time* magazine cover of O. J. Simpson, when illustrators darkened Simpson's features? Racism, many blacks cried! And *Time* publicly apologized. Yet, *Time* frequently stylizes covers on criminal defendants. A *Time* cover on Unabomber Ted Kaczynski, then still a suspect, referred to him as a "mad genius"! When did a shrink call Kaczynski "mad"? Yet, no outcry. Similarly, stylized covers on Oklahoma City bombing suspect Timothy McVeigh produced no charges of bias.

From time to time, you do find a white person with "noogas" who refuses to be bullied, demeaned, and made to feel guilty. Recently, Reverend Jesse Jackson attacked Silicon Valley, proclaiming it hostile to minorities. He announced a plan to purchase stock in a number of the area's publicly held companies so that he could attend meetings and urge a change in hiring policy.

To Jackson's charge, the CEO of Cypress Semiconductor, T. J. Rodgers said, "If top African-American students choose to be doctors or educators instead of engineers, why blame Silicon Valley?"[20] He invited Reverend Jackson to submit résumés of any qualified black technicians because, Rodgers said, demand is high. Your serve, Reverend Jackson.

President Clinton set up an advisory committee to spend a year touring America, holding town meetings to get opinions. How many gave honest, deeply held opinions? Blunt public candor about race invites charges of bigotry if you're white or charges of Uncle Tom–ism if you're black. Who wins?

The answer: We all lose if we refuse to tell the truth. To refuse to do so is either condescension, spinelessness, or political correctness/politeness run amok.

Will Somebody Please Say Something About Reverend Al Sharpton?

Consider the way the media deals with Reverend Al Sharpton.

This race-hustling, loud-mouthed, ham-fisted state-of-the-art victicrat recently came to California to protest the police shooting of a young black teenager.

But, wait a sec. Isn't this the same Al Sharpton who, during the infamous Tawana Brawley case, falsely accused a former assistant district attorney of raping and sodomizing Ms. Brawley?

Young Tawana Brawley stated that white racists abducted, raped, and sodomized her, scrawling the initials "KKK" on her in human feces. A grand jury later found the entire incident a complete hoax. Most likely, Ms. Brawley, afraid of punishment for staying out too late, fabricated the entire story. This did not stop

Reverend Sharpton from riding the Klan versus Brawley lie to the headlines. Sharpton accused Steven Pagones, an assistant district attorney, of the crime. "We stated openly that Steven Pagones did it. If we're lying, sue us, so we can go into court with you and prove you did it. Sue us—sue us right now."[21]

Pagones did. He sued Sharpton and two others for defamation. A jury unanimously concluded that Sharpton defamed Pagones, assessing hundreds of thousands of dollars against Sharpton and his codefendants. To this day, Sharpton refuses to apologize, never having paid one penny to Pagones. Sharpton's punishment? Hillary Rodham Clinton, during her New York senate race, visited him, seeking his support. Does anybody care that the first lady kisses the ring of a man who falsely accused another of rape? Wouldn't this outrageous accusation and the finding of liability end the career of your average activist? This inexplicable silence emboldens professional black victicrats like Al Sharpton and the local "Al Sharptons." This does a disservice to America and to the black community in particular.

Sharpton, mind you, didn't simply diddle on his income taxes or dump some litter on the interstate. He falsely accused a man of rape, an accusation causing the man to endure death threats and causing his child to be taunted by classmates.

Black Racism, OK, But White Racism . . . ?

This brings us to "Niggardly-gate." A white aide to the newly elected black mayor of Washington, D.C., used the word *niggardly* during a meeting. Soon, the defenders of all that is pure and just and fair attacked him. Why? The word *niggardly* is racist. Somebody better tell Merriam-Webster, who defines "niggardly" as follows: "like or characteristic of a niggard; stingy; miserly."

Then the rumor mill kicked in. The aide began receiving phone calls accusing him of having used the word *nigger* rather than *niggardly*. The accusations grew so loud, some demanded his resignation, accusing him of making an "inappropriate racial comment."

The pressure mounted, and rather than simply tell the accusers, "Get a dictionary," the embattled aide apologized and offered his resignation, stating that the rumor "has severely compromised my effectiveness." Later, the mayor, who steadfastly refused to defend him during the flap, hired him back only after conservative pundits blasted the race card-ers for hysteria.

And don't let a white guy make an "insensitive" racial remark. His bosses will pink-slip him quicker than you can say "Louis Farrakhan." Former CBS Sports analyst Jimmy "the Greek" Snyder saw his job go up in flames. In a restaurant, most likely after Snyder knocked back more than a couple, someone asked why blacks do so well athletically.

Snyder said, "The black is a better athlete to begin with, because he's been bred to be that way, because of his high thighs and big thighs that goes up into his back and they can jump higher and run faster because of the bigger thighs. The white man has to overcome that. But they don't try hard enough to overcome it. I'm tellin' you that the black is a better athlete, because he practices to be a better athlete and he's bred to be the better athlete because this goes back all the way to the Civil War, during the slave trade. The slave owner would breed his big black to his big woman so that he could have big black kids. I mean, that's where it all started."

OK, so the man did not have a Ph.D. in anthropology. Still, no one before this incident ever accused Snyder of racism. Indeed, in his besotted state, he was trying to explain why blacks are superior athletes, and criticizing whites for not trying hard enough to overcome their inferiority. So, put the remark down in the "dumb" column, but do you get fired over this? Apparently so. Snyder got canned.

And, remember former Dodger general manager Al Campanis's meltdown on national television? On *Nightline*, on the anniversary of Jackie Robinson's major league debut, Ted Koppel asked Al Campanis why there were so few black managers, whether prejudice stops them. Campanis said, "No, I don't believe it's prejudice . . . they may not have some of the necessities to be—let's say—a field manager or perhaps a general manager." For his "they lack the necessities" remark, the Dodgers canned him. They canned the same Al Campanis who *volunteered* to room with Jackie Robinson. They canned the guy who taught the infielder how to turn the double play, so as to avoid being spiked by the vicious white racist base runners. But, that was then, and this is now. And Campanis died, hurt and humiliated.

Golfer Fuzzy Zoeller lost two million dollars in endorsements following the 1997 Masters, won by Tiger Woods. By tradition, the winner gets to select the clubhouse food for the next year's event. To this, Zoeller told CNN reporters, "Tell him [Woods] not to serve fried chicken next year . . . or collard greens or whatever the hell they serve."[22]

Never mind that pro golfers know Fuzzy Zoeller to be a jokester, kind of a fairway jester. He promptly apologized, later gave another tearful apology. But, bye-bye, two million dollars.

Tiger Woods initially refused to accept his apology, saying he wanted to talk with him. This is the same Tiger Woods, mind you, who in a *GQ* magazine article only weeks earlier made insensitive anti-gay jokes. A gay publication, the *Advocate*, noted Woods's remarks but dismissed them because of the golfer's youth and naïveté. So, they cut Woods some slack, but not Fuzzy. And the beat goes on.

In Brooklyn, a white teacher, teaching a class of blacks and Hispanics, read a book called *Nappy Hair*,[23] written by black author Carolivia Herron. The book tells of a black girl's emotional journey of self-acceptance. In the story, a young girl discovers that her "nappy hair" was given to her by God and is therefore OK. The children loved it, just as they enjoyed the previous stories about the Haitian child who made a doll from a broom and the Vietnamese girl who was teased because her clothes were like pajamas.[24]

Yet parents (only one of whom had a child in the teacher's class) and community members denounced the teacher, calling the book *Nappy Hair* racist, shouting racial epithets at the teacher and physically threatening her.

When Herron learned of the protests against the teacher, she said she "was shocked and saddened."[25] She says that *Nappy Hair* is about a little girl who discovers pride in her ancestry by loving her hair.[26]

The teacher, who transferred following the initial uproar, later resigned, saying she feared for her safety.

Will some adult step forward and say, "Look, this is stupid. The book was written by a proud black woman. The theme is 'be proud of who and what you are.' Now grow up."

In a recent issue of *Sports Illustrated*,[27] Atlanta Braves relief pitcher John Rocker launched a volley of racially insensitive remarks.

Rocker, who helped the Braves beat the New York Mets in the playoffs, showed little love for the Big Apple: "Imagine having to take the [number] seven train to the ballpark, looking like you're [riding through] Beirut next to some kid with purple hair next to some queer with AIDS right next to some dude who just got out of jail for the fourth time right next to some twenty-year-old mom with four kids."

About New York, Rocker said, "The biggest thing I don't like about New York are the foreigners. I'm not a very big fan of foreigners. You can walk an entire block in Times Square and not hear anybody speaking English. Asians and Koreans and Vietnamese and Indians and Russians and Spanish people and everything up there. How the hell did they get in this country?" And, for good measure, Rocker called a teammate a "fat monkey" and criticized the driving of Japanese women.

Baseball commissioner Bud Selig said, "The attitudes and the opinions expressed have no place in our game or in our society. The remarks are under review and we will take the appropriate action."[28]

Rocker, of course, promptly apologized. Too late. Selig fined Rocker $20,000 and suspended him for several games.

Some people, like Hall of Famer and Atlanta Braves executive Hank Aaron questioned whether Rocker could continue to play baseball!

But wait a minute. Didn't black Green Bay Packer defensive end Reggie White, in an address to the Wisconson state legislature in March, 1999, say about Hispanics, "[They] were gifted in family structure . . . they can put 20, 30 people in one home." Didn't he say that white people were "blessed with the gift of structure and organization." And that black people were "very gifted in what we call worship and celebration. A lot of us like to dance. If you go to black churches you see people jumping up and down." And, about gays, that "homosexuality is a decision." Didn't he say that Asians were "gifted in creativity . . . they can turn a television into a watch," and that Native-Americans avoided slavery because they "knew the territory, and the Indians knew how to sneak up on people."

Did White's comments illicit a condemnation from the NFL commissioner? Or from other football players?

And after an NBA playoff game, Detroit Piston's Isiah Thomas and Dennis Rodman suggested that white player Larry Bird received praise primarily, in Rodman's words, "because he is white."[29] What did NBA commissioner David Stern do? Relying on a subsequent apology, Stern did nothing, and levied no fines. And Stern did nothing when former NBA player Charles Barkley, annoyed at reporters' post-game questions, said, "That's what I hate about white people."[30]

How about a little perspective here? In their book, *Pros and Cons*[31] authors Jeff Benedict and Don Yeager note that 21 percent of players in the NFL have been charged with serious crimes, including attempted murder and sexual assault. Which is worse, John Rocker's big mouth, or the behavior of a player like the St. Louis Rams's Leonard Little, who killed a woman in a drunk driving accident?

And in the NBA, apparently, illegitimacy is an epidemic. ESPN broadcaster Len Elmore said, "For every player with none [child out of wedlock], there's a guy with two or three."[32]

And what about the NBA's Latrell Sprewell who choked his coach at a practice session! Sprewell—over 6'5" tall and weighing nearly two hundred pounds—twice attacked his older, smaller coach, leaving marks on the coach's neck. No police investigation. The NBA union went to bat for Sprewell, and even got his termination lifted. Soon Sprewell inked a more lucrative contract in a bigger city with a better team. But as for Rocker, hangin's too good for him.

A white guy once called my show, pained about white condescension, the reluctance of whites to deny false or exaggerated charges of racism. "You're right," he said. "But what can I say? This is wrong, I am not a bigot. I am tired of being called one, and this diminishes the true charge of racism. I'm sick and tired of it. But what can I say about it?"

"You just said it," I replied.

3

THE MEDIA BIAS—IT'S REAL, IT'S WIDESPREAD, IT'S DESTRUCTIVE

The "liberal media" are a fiction created by political paranoids to discredit all journalism that annoys them.[1]

—*NEW YORK TIMES* FORMER COLUMNIST RUSSELL BAKER

An image of reporters as people different and apart from the mainstream of the country has been created, and it just ain't so.[2]

—CBS'S DAN RATHER

[This country should have a] marvelous middle ground between capitalism and communism.[3]

—WALTER CRONKITE

What is News?

What a newspaper prints and what a television newscast runs is, by definition, subjective. What is news? In the end, news is what news gatherers say it is.

Every day, news directors get faxes from organizations, think tanks, colleges and universities, special interest groups, and research organizations. Many start with, "A new study shows..." Question: which ones to print? The media prints stories that confirm their view of the world. White racism abounds; the environment is under attack; nasty businesspeople need government regulation and restraint; capitalism exploits the defenseless; men oppress women; and the rich get richer at the expense of everybody else. Often, reporters know nothing about the special interest groups putting out the various position papers, and, certainly, reporters do not have the time, inclination, or aptitude to check out the stats or methodology producing the desired, politically correct conclusions.

No, the liberal bias is not a conspiracy. And no central authority sends out a fax. That isn't necessary. Watch a political event that attracts large numbers of the press. What do they do there? They mingle. After the event, they have drinks, interact, and maybe even dine out. Members of the media interact with other members, thus forming a consensus about what's important and what's newsworthy.

In his book, *Boys on the Bus*,[4] Timothy Crouse describes the herd mentality behind the media. Once a thesis gets established— such as there's a growing gap between the rich and the poor—it becomes an unquestioned fact. The mainstream media then prints stories with this assumption, devoid of any real critical analysis. Elaine Povich, former Capitol Hill reporter for the *Chicago Tribune*, said, "One of the things about being a professional is that you attempt to leave your personal feelings aside as you do your work."[5]

So the media, unlike other human beings, can, at will, turn on and off its emotions, prejudices, and ideological biases. No, it's more likely that their world view—it takes a village—frequently becomes part of the story.

What Liberal Bias?

A 1996 study by the Roper Center for the Freedom Forum found that 89 percent of Washington, D.C., journalists voted for Bill Clinton in 1992.[6] Contrast this with the 43 percent of Americans who voted for Clinton. How many D.C. journalists voted for George Bush? Seven percent.

And what ideological label do Washington, D.C., journalists place on themselves? Back in 1962, 28 percent called themselves conservative, but this figure has shrunk every year since then.[7] Now 91 percent describe themselves as moderate to liberal, while only 2 percent call themselves conservatives.[8]

Similar polls document the lopsided, left-leaning nature of newspapers all across the country. Political scientist Stanley Rothman and S. Robert Lichter, the heads of the nonpartisan Center for Media and Public Affairs, conducted a 1980 survey of journalism students. According to that survey, only a third of Columbia University journalism students believed the free enterprise system fair to workers. And a whopping 40 percent believed in government ownership of corporations! Eighty-five percent described themselves as liberals.[9]

That was approximately twenty years ago. Assuming these men and women continued in their field, they now run newspapers as editors and television stations as directors and managers. Scary, ain't it?

A couple of years ago, the *Los Angeles Times* did a piece on Dick Armey, the congressional majority leader. The article described him as a "hardline conservative." Hardly the most conservative member of Congress, Armey nevertheless got labeled "hardline conservative." Fine. How often, then, does the *Los Angeles Times* refer to a politician or public figure as a "hardline liberal"? Surely, someone like former antiwar activist and now California state senator Tom Hayden would deserve such a title. As would Jesse Jackson, or feminist Gloria Steinem, or Hillary Rodham Clinton.

But does the *Los Angeles Times* use the expression "hardline liberal"? A search shows that in the last ten years, the *Los Angeles Times* used the expression "hardline conservative" seventy-one times. How often over the same period did we see the expression "hardline liberal"? Twice. Well, sort of. In one instance, the news-paper used the expression to refer to former Soviet president Mikhail Gorbachev. In the other case, an article used the expression "hardline" in one place, and the word "liberal" in another place, thus producing the computer match. But no American politician or public figure, however leftist, seems to earn the expression "hardline liberal."

Some biases, like that one, hit you in the face, others are far more subtle.

A few years ago, Congress debated the Brady Bill, the measure to provide a five-day waiting period before one could purchase a handgun. Accuracy in the Media, a watchdog organization, surveyed the debate coverage by NBC, CBS, ABC, and CNN.

The study found that journalists routinely called the Brady Bill supporters "gun control advocates," while calling opponents "gun control lobbyists." Get it? Advocate, good. Lobbyist, bad.

Never mind that Sarah Brady runs Handgun Control, Inc., a nonprofit organization just as the NRA is a nonprofit organization. This makes Sarah Brady and the president of the NRA, Charlton Heston, both lobbyists or, if you prefer, both advocates.

During any given news segment, television news uses "talking head" experts to give us a pithy opinion. During this Brady Bill coverage, networks used "pro–Brady Bill" talking heads by a two-to-one margin over the anti–Brady Bill pundits.[10]

A two-year study, released in January 2000, by the Media Research Center,[11] another media watchdog, analyzed 635 stories on gun policy by ABC, CBS, CNN, and NBC. They found that 260 stories could be classified as neutral. Thirty-six opposed gun control. But a whopping 357 advocated more gun control![12]

During the two-year study of the networks, 300 of the 635 stories dealing with gun policy aired during the evening news shows. Of these, 164 advocated gun control, while 20 opposed it. The three network morning shows produced a total of 353 segments on gun policy. Of these, the MRC rated 193 as anti-gun, 15 as pro-gun, and 145 as neutral. The MRC analysts also compared sound bites in the nightly news, and found 296 advocates and 150 opponents of gun control.[13]

The way the media deal with illegal aliens also shows bias. For states such as Texas, Florida, New York, and California, immigration issues boil. In California, hundreds of thousands of Mexicans enter the country illegally. A backlash against the growing number of illegals produced Proposition 187, a ballot initiative to withhold public monies for the education, and most of the health care, of illegals.

As an aside: I opposed Proposition 187 and feel that America's demand for cheap, unskilled labor fuels the market for hardworking illegal aliens from Mexico and other Third World countries. The fact that taxpayers underwrite education and health care for illegals is an indictment against America's welfare state, not against hardworking illegals who enter the country to seek a better life.

But the issue here is whether mainstream media fairly cover both sides in this debate. Many people feel, wrongly in my view, that illegals "take jobs" from Americans. Although I disagree, the position deserves a fair airing. And, in many newspapers, writers subtly, and sometimes not so subtly, champion the cause of immigration, whether legal or illegal.

For example, the *Los Angeles Times* routinely describes Mexican workers who illegally enter the country as "immigrants." Get out Webster's. The dictionary defines "immigrant" as one who comes "into a new country, region, or environment, especially in order to settle there." Many illegals, however, come to America only during the harvest season, then return later to Mexico. They are not, therefore, "immigrants." But the word *immigrant* sounds wholesome, while "illegal," or even worse, "illegal alien"—a more descriptive term—sounds foreboding and unwelcoming.

Journalists reveal bias in other, more subtle ways. Take the controversy over spanking. In 1997, the American Medical Association published a report in their *Archives of Pediatrics and Adolescent Medicine*. The report, echoing a recommendation by the American Academy of Pediatrics, said that its studies showed spanking encourages aggression and violence. How many network and media outlets carried this story? CBS, ABC, NBC, and more than a hundred newspapers.

But, get this. The very same magazine *in the very same issue* published another report *on the same topic, reaching the opposite conclusions*. This study, however, was *more comprehensive* than the earlier one, tracking more children and studying them over a longer period of time. The conclusion? Spanking, done judiciously, does not increase aggression or violence. How many media outlets and newspapers carried the second, pro-spanking study? Not one network and only fifteen of the same newspapers that published the first story bothered to mention the second.[14]

A *U.S. News & World Report* study revealed that twice as many college-educated Americans oppose spanking compared to those who did not finish high school. And most reporters attended college, right?

How Bad Is Media Bias?

Real bad.

ABC anchor Peter Jennings, following the 1994 Republican "takeover" of Congress, said, "Ask parents of any two-year-old and they can tell you about those temper tantrums: the stomping feet, the rolling eyes, the screaming. It's clear the anger controls the child and not the other way around. It's the job of the parent to teach the child to control the anger and channel it in a positive way. . . . Imagine a nation full of controlled two-year-old rage. The voters had a temper tantrum last week." He continued, "Now what? The screaming two-year-old has our attention, but the country, like the family, can't run for long on vituperation."[15] Let's put him down in the "undecided" column.

Other examples complied by the Media Research Center include the following:[16]

- "If we could be one-hundredth as great as you and Hillary Rodham Clinton have been in the White House, we'd take it right now and walk away winners. . . . Thank you very much and tell Mrs. Clinton we respect her and we're pulling for her." Dan Rather, at a May 27, 1993, CBS affiliates meeting, talking via satellite to President Clinton about his new on-air partnership with Connie Chung.
- "Do you think this is a party that is dominated by men and this convention is dominated by men as well. . . . Do you think before tonight they thought very much what happens in America with rape?" Tom Brokaw, to rape victim Jan Licence, after her victims-rights speech on August 13, 1996, at the Republican National Convention.
- "The legacy of the Reagan administration will be with us for years. The deficit under Reagan totaled more than a trillion dollars. Some day we're going to have to pay those bills. As officials look to cut spending and taxes at the same time, we can't afford another round of voodoo economics. . . . I remember that campaign slogan one year, 'It's morning again in America.' Well, it may have been morning for some, but for a lot of people in this country it's become a nightmare." CBS *60 Minutes* correspondent Ed Bradley, in an April 28, 1996, speech to Benedictine University in Illinois; aired May 11, 1996, on C-SPAN.
- "After eight years of what many saw as the Reagan administration's benign neglect of the poor and studied indifference to civil rights, a lot of those who lived through this week in Overtown [rioting in a section of Miami] seemed to think

the best thing about George Bush is that he is not Ronald Reagan. . . . There is an Overtown in every big city in America. Pockets of misery made even meaner and more desperate the past eight years." Reporter Richard Threlkeld, on ABC's *World News Tonight,* January 20, 1989.

• "The bottom line is more tax money is going to be needed. Just how much will be the primary issue on the agenda when congressional leaders meet with the president later today, Wednesday, May the 9th, 1990. And good morning, welcome to *Today.* It's a Wednesday morning, a day when the budget picture, frankly, seems gloomier than ever. It now seems the time has come to pay the fiddler for our costly dance of the Reagan years." Bryant Gumbel, opening NBC's *Today* show on May 9, 1990.

• "Reagan was an exceedingly likable guy, just a heck of a nice fellow, despite his politics. He was funny and loved a good joke, the dirtier, I'm afraid the more ethnic, the better. I don't think he brought very much to the presidency, except charisma and success." Walter Cronkite, on *Cronkite Remembers,* May 23, 1996.

• "And then there was Anita Hill, the poised daughter of so many generations of black women who have been burned carrying torches into the battle for principle. The cause of civil rights and social justice has so often fallen to them to defend. Harriet Tubman and Sojourner Truth were slaves by birth, freedom fighters by temperament. Rosa Parks was a tired seamstress who shoved history forward by refusing to give up her seat on the bus. . . . The latest to claim her place in line is Anita Hill, a private, professional woman unwilling to relinquish her dignity without a fight." Associate editor Nancy Gibbs, *Time,* October 21, 1991.

• "TV viewers saw a well-orchestrated image of a moderated Republican Party, portraying itself as pro-women, pro-minorities, and pro-tolerance. This is in sharp contrast to the delegates on the floor, 60 percent of whom self-identified as conservative Christians." NBC Radio News–Westwood One reporter Bonnie Erbe, hosting *To the Contrary* on PBS, August 16, 1996.

- "In light of the new welfare reform bill, do you think the children need more prayers than ever before?" Bryant Gumble, to Children's Defense Fund leader Marian Wright Edelman, September 23, 1996, *Today* show on NBC.

- "There is something very creepy about the welfare debate. . . . The politicians have gotten together and decided it's a good idea to throw a million or so children into poverty. But they can't say that. The proponents of this so-called reform effort have gone out of their way to avoid being seen for what they are—men and women of extreme privilege who are taking food out of the mouths of infants and children, the poverty-stricken elderly, the disabled." Former NBC News reporter Bob Herbert, July 22, 1996, in a *New York Times* column.

- "The whole week was double-ply, wall-to-wall ugly . . . the Republican Party reached an unimaginable slouchy, and brazen, and constant, level of mendacity last week. . . . [Bush] is in campaign mode now, which means mendacity doesn't matter, aggression is all and wall-to-wall ugly is the order of battle for the duration." Senior editor Joe Klein, on the Republican National Convention, August 31, 1992, *Newsweek.*

- "Just how tightly scripted is this convention? Well, a Russian television reporter said today that this is as tightly controlled as anything the Communist Party ever put on, Tom." NBC reporter David Bloom, in an August 14, 1996, *Nightly News* story about the Republican Convention.

- "You think government should do a lot more than it's doing in terms of making children a priority, doing things for kids. We're clearly living in an age where people are anti-government. How do you get across the message that we all need to see everybody's kids as our own, we need to have more programs, the government needs to be more involved?" Questions to Hillary Rodham Clinton from *Today* show substitute cohost Maria Shriver (who called Clinton's book, *It Takes a Village,* "really terrific"), January 16, 1996.

• "I was a correspondent in the White House in those days, and my work—which consisted of reporting on President Reagan's success in making life harder for citizens who were not born rich, white, and healthy—saddened me. My parents raised me to admire generosity and to feel pity. I had arrived in our nation's capital [in 1981] during a historic ascendancy of greed and hard-heartedness. . . . Reagan couldn't tie his shoes if his life depended on it." *New York Times* editorial page editor (and former Washington bureau chief) Howell Raines, in his book *Fly Fishing Through the Midlife Crisis.*[17]

The Media and Economics 101

Media bias deprives people of information necessary to make informed decisions. A reporter's bias appears not only in what he or she says but also in information not included. For example, most people believe that minimum wage laws promote prosperity and provide a safety net for low-rung workers and protect them against money-grubbing bosses who would pay almost nothing if only they could get away with it. But how many people know that nearly 90 percent of economists believe that minimum wage laws *destroy* entry-level jobs?[18]

One of the few issues on which nearly all economists agree is that minimum wage laws destroy jobs, the very entry-level jobs held by teens, women, and secondary household earners. Study after study documents the adverse effect on these vulnerable workers. But rarely will the typical daily newspaper or local or national TV news show present this data. Remember that Nobel Laureate economist Milton Friedman called minimum wage laws "perhaps the most anti-black law on the statute book." And economist Walter Williams writes that the government in apartheid South Africa used minimum wage laws to shut out low-skilled black workers.

For over thirty years, my dad ran a small café in a working-class area of Los Angeles. From time to time, Congress would raise minimum wages. I watched as my mom and dad sat at the kitchen table, with paper and pencil, trying to figure out how to absorb the increased costs. Defer the hiring of a new dishwasher? Lay off a waitress? Raise prices, the reaction to which would likely depress sales?

A handful of newspapers like the *Investor's Business Daily* and the *Wall Street Journal* showed that even during an era of economic prosperity, minimum wage hikes still decreased opportunities for blacks, teens, and secondary wage earners. Yet the rest of the media routinely ignore the avalanche of economic data documenting the pernicious nature of minimum wages. Even the *New York Times,* in an editorial supporting a recent minimum wage hike, said that studies show that "only" as many as a hundred thousand jobs will be destroyed as a result of the minimum wage hike. "Only" a hundred thousand jobs destroyed? When AT&T laid off thousands of workers, this made national headlines. Yet when Congress proposes a bill that, according to the *New York Times,* may destroy up to a hundred thousand jobs, nothing but yawns.

Even the *New York Times,* back in 1987, wrote an editorial questioning the appropriateness of minimum wage laws. The editorial headline read, "The Right Minimum Wage: $0.00"[19] But that was then, and the *New York Times* soon rediscovered its mission and supported minimum wage hikes even though they earlier acknowledged the damage done. Go figure.

Media members within the same organization can't even agree on how many Americans work for the minimum wage. Considering the following quotes, all made by members of ABC News, and all within a few days of each other.

On April 23, 1996, ABC economics correspondent Tyler Mathisen, on *Good Morning America*, said, "About 3.7 million Americans, wage-earning Americans, are paid the minimum wage or less."[20]

Later that same day, ABC anchor Peter Jennings on *World News Tonight* said, "On Capitol Hill today, the minimum wage and how best to embarrass your opponent. For ten million Americans, it's a very personal issue."[21]

The next day, April 24, again on *Good Morning America*, ABC reporter Bob Zelnick said, "In fact, only about 330,000 employees, most of them part-timers, today work for the minimum."[22]

And a few days later, on April 28, ABC anchor Carole Simpson, on *World News Sunday* said, "An estimated 9.7 million Americans make the minimum wage or close to it."[23]

So, what's the real number? Ten million? Three hundred thousand? That leaves a lot of space in between. More importantly, very few heads of households work for the minimum wage. So, it is a myth that the typical minimum wage toiler is a married guy with three kids, trying to make ends meet.

For sheer unadulterated gall, look no further than the Association of Community Organizations for Reform Now, also known as ACORN. ACORN goes from state to state, raising signatures for ballot initiatives to increase the minimum wage. ACORN eventually came to California, to gather signatures to put a minimum wage hike proposal on the ballot. To accomplish this, the organization needed to hire lots of workers. So ACORN filed a lawsuit, seeking to exempt itself from California's minimum wage and overtime laws!

The *Investors Business Daily* published excerpts from ACORN's brief, where it explained why *they* needed an exemption from paying the very minimum wages their organization was attempting to increase. Said the brief, "The more ACORN must pay each individual outreach worker—either because of minimum wage or overtime requirements—the fewer outreach workers it will be able to hire."[24] Well, duh.

About the only economic experts who still believe in increasing minimum wage are those who work for the Clinton administration. David Card and Alan Krueger, both of Princeton, authored a study "proving" that minimum wage hikes do not hurt employment. Economists Card and Krueger studied fast food restaurant employment in California and New Jersey, after those states raised their minimum wage. They concluded that there was no evidence of job loss.[25]

But, when other researchers tried to duplicate the results, they could not. Turns out that those working for Card and Krueger simply picked up the telephone and asked employers whether they intended to increase, decrease, or keep employment flat. Researchers seeking to duplicate the results of Card and Krueger went one step further. They requested *payroll cards* in order to verify employment.

When researchers requested payroll cards, the non-effect of hiking minimum wage completely disappeared. In fact, both Pennsylvania and New Jersey suffered a decrease in employment following their minimum wage hike.

In 1981, the federal Minimum Wage Study Commission concluded that a 10 percent increase in the minimum wage reduces teen employment by 1 percent to 3 percent. Other studies by top economists confirmed these results. Nobel laureate economist Gary Becker, after reviewing the Card-Krueger study, concluded that "the Card-Krueger studies are flawed and cannot justify going against the accumulated evidence from many past and present studies that find sizable negative effects of higher minimums on employment."[26]

Still, Clinton allies use the Card-Krueger study to promote increases in minimum wage, and the media routinely cites the study's results without mentioning other academicians' opposition.

Again, as mentioned, nearly 90 percent of economic experts polled believe minimum wage undermines employment. Suppose 90 percent of cardiovascular surgeons believed triple bypass operations to be unnecessary. The nightly news *leads* with that story. But, when economists, nearly unanimously, oppose minimum wage, big deal.

Most reporters, like most laypeople, know little and care even less about fundamental economics—the laws of supply and demand; what creates scarcities; the definition of fair market value; the definition of exploitation; the relationship between high taxes and low productivity. Yet, these very reporters will cover Midwestern manufacturing plant workers who proclaim themselves casualties of NAFTA. The "I feel your pain" mind-set of a journalist immediately sympathizes with the workers. Never mind that an evolving, dynamic economy inevitably creates winners and losers. Nor will there be a "sound bite" from an economics professor giving this non-PC point of view.

Media bias manifests itself in what a basketball player might call "shot selection." What issues should reporters explore, and how prominently should the newspaper feature the articles? Newspapers routinely provide stories about the former welfare beneficiary suffering because the return to work meant the denial of certain benefits. How many of these poor-person-who-falls-through-the-cracks stories have we seen? Yet how often have you seen a newspaper story discussing the possible relationship between the welfare state and illegitimacy?

How often do we see articles asking how a pro-women, pro-minority, pro–affirmative action, pro–benevolent government society produces a culture that sees 70 percent of black children, 35 percent of Mexican-American children, and 25 percent of the nation's children as a whole born out of wedlock? Does the welfare state, with its ready food stamps, AFDC, day-care vouchers, WIC program, transportation vouchers, and Head Start create a disincentive to marry? Is it possible that the welfare state damages all of us, inasmuch as the family unit remains the best vehicle to teach the values of moral behavior, hard work, and sacrifice? With no father around, is it possible that the woman "marries" the government, thus providing the children with no in-house male role model? Few members of the mainstream media raise these economic and social questions, let alone publish articles about it.

The Media Feel Blacks' Pain

Let's examine how the media handle the politically sensitive affirmative action debate.

In California, voters debated Proposition 209, the initiative to ban race-based hiring, contracting, and admissions to colleges and universities. Well, the measure passed. And, for the first time in a long time, college administrators could not (or weren't supposed to) use race as a factor for admissions. Well, what happened? The total number of blacks and other minorities admitted to the University of California system failed to decline, as doomsayers predicted. Indeed, the numbers actually rose a bit. A minority student who, under affirmative action, would have gone to UC Berkeley, now got into the University of California at Riverside or University of California at Irvine. And, because the kid's background and aptitude are now better matched with the college's admissions standards, the minority student's chances for graduation improved. How? Students who entered school under "special criteria"—a fancy term for special credit for race—dropped out at a much higher rate than did students who entered based on grades and test scores. Affirmative action, therefore, induced a mismatch of student and college, as if a Triple-A ballplayer suddenly found himself batting cleanup in the major leagues.

Again, minority enrollment at the University of California schools did not go down after the elimination of affirmative action. So how did our fair, objective media cover this? Headlines could have read, "Despite Predictions, Minority Enrollment Up" or "Post-Proposition 209 Picture Brighter Than Predicted" or "Minority Enrollment Down at UC Berkeley, But Up Overall." But no, a typical headline, such as the one in the *Daily News,* read "UC Minority Enrollment Down Sharply."[27] The writer focused on "elite" departments that showed declines and ignored overall admissions improvement!

The article covered the "decline" in minorities who enrolled in the law and business schools of the University of California system. But carefully read the article. The real story is there, the reader just has to ignore the headline and look for the information. And suddenly the situation ain't so bad. The number of minority students enrolling in medical school showed little change. And at the more than six hundred graduate academic programs in the UC system, black enrollment actually *increased* by 2 percent.[28]

Remember the "they're burning black churches" headlines? *USA Today* led the charge: "Arson at Black Churches Echoes Bigotry of Past."[29] "Arson Strikes Black Churches at Record Pace."[30] "Church Burnings Called a Provocation for Race War."[31]

But, uh-oh, once the hysteria died down, some uncomfortable facts emerged. Not only was arson against black churches down dramatically since 1980, but mosques, synagogues, and white houses of worship saw more arson than did black churches.

In the South, prior to the burning-black-churches frenzy fire marshals reported *no* arsons against black churches as a result of racial animus. President Clinton took to the radio airwaves, and somberly lectured the nation on the need to deal with this problem. He even recalled growing up in Arkansas, where, according to the president, racists burned black churches. The *Arkansas Gazette,* however, checked into Clinton's story to determine whether, during his childhood, arsonists did, in fact, burn black churches. But the paper found none, zilch, zero, nada instances of a black church burned as a result of a racist arsonist. Clinton, uh, stretched the truth. But a fact to a toe-tag liberal is like kryptonite to Superman. No matter. Few papers reported the president's distortion.

Of the burned black churches, arsonists burned most for non-racist reasons. Many black rural churches are constructed of wood and sit alone in rural areas, making these structures an arsonist's dream. Nearly one-third of those arrested for burning black churches were black!

Furthermore, the media hysteria about black churches created copycat criminals. Only after the "reporting" of a "rash" of black church burnings did fire marshals begin to see an uptick in burned black churches. The media stories educated would-be arsonists about the desirability of this juicy target of rural wooden stand-alone churches. Finally, *USA Today* acknowledged its error and ran a story retracting much of its previous hysterical coverage.

And then there is the shrinking Fort Bragg story. A few years ago, military officials discovered racial epithets painted on the doors of the barracks of black soldiers. But, uh-oh. Weeks later, authorities begin zeroing in on a suspect—a black officer. The *Los Angeles Times* carried the initial, lengthy story on page A-9. But a week later, when the military, citing strong evidence, investigated a black officer and suspected him of painting the racial epithets, the story suddenly diminished in importance. And where did they place the short article fingering the black suspect? Page A-17.

So, when the paper thought the suspect white, this warranted great attention. But when the suspect turned out to be black, the story's interest declined. Why? Isn't the idea of a black guy writing racial epithets on another black guy's door inherently newsworthy? Guess not, because as far as the media go, the wrong guy wore the black hat.

In January 1997, angry parents confronted a white South Carolina kindergarten teacher who wrote on a black student's face, "Where are my glasses?" because the child forgot to bring her prescription glasses. Well, THE FIT HIT THE SHAN. National news! In a world where the Johnnie L. Cochran Doctrine tells us "Race plays a part of everything in America," this means one thing. The South Carolina teacher is . . . RACIST!

Next scene. The Southeast Region executive director of the NAACP accuses the school and the teacher of violating the child's civil rights. The teacher receives a twenty-day suspension without pay. She undergoes sensitivity training, and issues a public apology. And, for good measure, when she returns to work, some twenty-five protesters greet her, several holding signs with such slogans as "White teacher, black child. No way."

Around Memorial Day of that same year, *USA Today* published a tiny article about the alleged misconduct of a first grade Georgia teacher. The teacher wrote "Book" on the face, arms, and legs of a student who forgot to return an overdue library book. There was no national outcry.

Two stories, similar facts, one an insignificant story of fleeting local interest, the other major news. *Pourquoi?* Well, the Georgia incident involved a white teacher and a white student. The South Carolina incident, on the other hand, involved a white teacher and a *black* student. And we all know what comes next.

Not that it matters, but newspapers offered no other information about the South Carolina teacher's "racist" past. You know, stuff like whether she had done this before, whether other parents had complained about her "racism." Turns out the teacher also writes on white children. Again, not that it matters.

The Georgia and South Carolina cases are almost identical. Same part of the country, roughly the same grade level. Both occurred in small towns. In fact, the white-on-white writing was worse. There, the Georgia teacher reportedly wrote on the kid's face, arms, and legs. Yet, somehow, the South Carolina teacher's "Where are my glasses?" gets magically transformed into "Segregation now, segregation tomorrow, segregation forever."

Same old media hustle. If the case smacks of interracial conflict—even if it's a stretch—go for it!

The media, thanks to the likes of Jesse Jackson, use the term "African-American." But the media fail to call Supreme Court Justice Antonin Scalia an "Italian-American," or former presidential candidate Michael Dukakis a "Greek-American," or Bill Clinton an "Irish-American." Blacks lived in America as long, if not longer, than most any other group with the exception of Native-Americans. Yet, newspapers regularly use the hyphenated ethnic-American term for blacks without doing so for Italians, Poles, Germans, British, French, and so on.

Blacks fought in every American war from the Revolutionary War to the war in Kosovo. This makes blacks as American as anybody, no hyphen needed. Yet the editorial code of many big-city newspapers mandates the use of the separatist term.

When the Media Like You, They See No Evil, Hear No Evil, Write No Evil

In 1999, John F. Kennedy, Jr.'s plane crashed into the Atlantic en route to Martha's Vineyard. Certainly, America mourned, along with the Kennedy and Bessette families. But, good Lord, who anointed JFK, Jr., "America's Prince"? And who decided that the Kennedy administration be called "Camelot"? When did the Kennedys become "America's Royal Family"?

Perhaps somebody didn't get the memo, but when Founding Father Alexander Hamilton pushed for a monarchy, his colleagues told him to shut up.

When John F. Kennedy, Jr.'s plane, also carrying his wife and sister-in-law, went down, a choked-up Dan Rather talked of the "Kennedy Curse" and spoke movingly of the days of Camelot. Barbara Walters, too, weighed in about how unpretentious, good, wonderful, luminescent, honorable, decent, self-sacrificing, tender, successful JFK, Jr., was. Well, yeah. The son of a rich and famous family, Kennedy chose from an array of options most could only dream of. Though a mediocre law student, he landed a job with the prestigious Manhattan district attorney's office, where a lot of applicants vie for just a few seats.

Kennedy proceeded to flunk the bar twice, a dishonor that, in private practice, gets you fired.

With great fanfare, he started a magazine. *George* lost so much money that, around the time of JFK, Jr.'s death, many openly speculated about the magazine's survival. When you cut through it, JFK, Jr.'s best asset comes down to this: He wasn't a jerk. Despite looks, wealth, and privilege, JFK, Jr., remained remarkably down-to-earth. Fair enough, but "America's Prince"? Give me a break.

After JFK, Jr.'s death, the media told us about the rip-roaring success of *George* magazine and about his finely honed editorial skills. (One of *George* magazine's stock questions is, "What's your favorite vegetable?")

Remember, a fact to an emotional toe-tag liberal is like kryptonite to Superman.

Flat out, the media loves John F. Kennedy, Robert F. Kennedy, Ted Kennedy, and the Kennedy family. Why? Here's where things get confusing. First, John Kennedy was not Richard Nixon, a man loathed by the left even before Watergate gave them real reason to. JFK eloquently spoke about civil rights, and his brother, Bobby, about injustice. And, certainly, compared to other leaders of that era, the Kennedys were social progressives.

But the Kennedy family's "progressiveness" on civil rights also needs further analysis. The NAACP criticized Kennedy for dragging his feet on comprehensive civil rights legislation. Kennedy, fearing alienating the South, wanted to delay any legislation until after the 1964 reelection.

Lyndon Johnson did the heavy lifting on civil rights. But the press rarely fawns over Johnson's accomplishments: passing the 1964 Civil Rights Act, the 1965 Voting Rights Act, and the 1968 Equal Housing Act. As discussed, President Kennedy appeared to oppose race-based preferences.

In fact, Richard Nixon became the first president to authorize an affirmative action program with numerical goals and quotas. Newspapers had a field day publishing excerpts from Nixon's

Watergate tapes, excerpts featuring demeaning epithets against Italians and Jews. Yet, *New York Times* writer Seymour Hersh in *The Dark Side of Camelot*[32] writes that John F. Kennedy derisively referred to countries in Central Africa as "boogie republics." His brother Robert Kennedy, attorney general, allowed FBI head J. Edgar Hoover to wiretap Martin Luther King.

Yet, suddenly, at the death of JFK, Jr., the same liberal pundits rewrote, before our very eyes, the Kennedy record to suit their romantic notions.

The Media Dislike Hitler, Stalin, and Reagan—Not Necessarily in that Order

The media dub the 1980s the "Decade of Greed." Yet the 1990s saw more mergers and acquisitions, and by some measures a widened gap between the rich and the poor. Why, then, do the media call only the eighties the "Decade of Greed"? Answer: Ronald Reagan. Reagan served from 1980 to 1988, during a period of explosive job creation and income growth. Despite lowering the top marginal tax rate from 70 percent to 28 percent, Ronald Reagan watched tax revenues soar, while the economy created 20 million new jobs. Charitable contributions increased from both individuals and corporations.

The media's contempt for Ronald Reagan borders on the pathological. Just after the "stock market crash" of October 1987, *Time* magazine almost gloated over how the crash exposed the flaws of "Reaganomics."

The magazine offered this "objective" analysis of what happened: "What crashed was more than just the market. It was the Reagan Illusion . . . he stayed a term too long . . . [his] dream of painless prosperity has been punctured."[33] (Note the prosperity continues.)

And the *New York Times* ran an editorial criticizing Reagan for staying calm during the "crisis" of the "crash." Referring to Reagan's statement on the night of the "crash," that the "underlying economy remains sound," the *Times* opined: "With the fire alarm wailing on Wall Street and the country anxious for leadership, it gets an astonishing rerun of Herbert Hoover."[34]

The press despises Ronald Reagan's so-called trickle-down policies. Reagan hated high taxes. He believed, and historical records back him up, that high taxes destroy productivity, making a country far less prosperous. An economics major in college, Reagan further argued that lowering taxes would increase money coming into federal coffers because it kick starts people into working harder, smarter, and with less need to conceal income.

But guess who else felt that way? JFK. That's right, JFK. In the December 24, 1962, issue of *U.S. News & World Report*, "Kennedy's Latest Word on Tax Cuts, Plans for Business," in urging a tax cut, Kennedy said that "it is a paradoxical truth that tax rates are too high today and tax revenues are too low—and the soundest way to raise revenues in the long run is to cut rates now.

"The experience of a number of European countries has borne this out. This country's own experience with tax reductions in 1954 has borne this out, and the reason is that only full employment can balance the budget—and tax reduction can pave the way to full employment. The purpose of cutting taxes now is not to incur a budgetary deficit, but to achieve the more prosperous expanding economy which will bring a budgetary surplus."

But when Reagan says it, the media sniffs "trickle-down."

Even public high school textbooks diss Reagan. Charts on the Reagan years in one popular text, *The American Pageant* by Thomas Bailey and David Kennedy, show the federal deficit numbers in historical dollars. But, by not showing the numbers as a share of the Gross National Product, their charts make the Reagan years' deficits look outrageous. As a share of the GNP, Reagan's deficits are really much smaller than FDR's. Ditto for a chart on the national debt. As a share of the GNP, it was lower under Reagan than it was for Kennedy, Eisenhower, and FDR. According to a professor at the University of Dayton, "The appearance to mislead seems intentional."[35]

And according to leading reviewers, the popular textbook *History of US* by Joy Hakim is also biased. It ignores how Reagan tax cuts doubled government revenue and raised per-capita income. It also makes no mention of how real term charitable giving expanded 56 percent between 1980 and 1989.[36]

Want more proof? The book *Bartlett's Quotations*[37] compiles profundities, witticisms, and thought nuggets from famous Americans. For FDR, the book has thirty-five entries. For Jack Kennedy, twenty-eight. For Jimmy Carter, six.

But, for Ronald Reagan, who served a full eight years, *Bartlett's* contains exactly three quotations. Indeed, Reagan biographer, Dinesh D'Souza writes that *Bartlett's* editor, Justin Kaplan, didn't even attempt to conceal his hatred for Reagan: "I'm not going to disguise the fact that I despise Ronald Reagan."[38]

Well, say Reagan's critics, the national debt soared under his watch. Oh, please. Since when did toe-tag liberals care about expenses and deficits? Furthermore, Reagan dealt with a Congress controlled, in part, by the Democrats during much of his term. Read the Constitution. *Congress* authorizes spending. And Congress consistently refused cuts.

During the 2000 election year presidential race, media bias was in full bloom. John McCain, a Republican from Arizona, became the media's darling. McCain, whose budget plan resembled President Clinton's, seemed less threatening than other Republicans to the mostly liberal-leaning media. The press took delight in McCain, often calling him a "maverick." They overlooked the fact that McCain called *himself* a "Reagan Republican." The media attributed McCain's self-description to the perceived need to trade favor with right-wing Republicans.

If John McCain were truly a "Reagan Republican" would the media have gushed about him? Mike Wallace, in a *60 Minutes* piece on McCain, twice used the word "maverick": "John McCain is, first of all, a 'maverick,' a conservative, a Vietnam POW who survived five bitter years in prison in Hanoi, and he wants to be president of the United States. It is the 'maverick' part that makes McCain a long shot for the GOP nomination he seeks."

McCain's economic program, with its limited tax cuts and modest downsizing, resembled Clinton's budget package. McCain, like many liberal Democrats, attacks the tobacco industry, an industry that is a legal industry both subsidized and taxed by the federal government.

McCain also urges campaign finance reform, and members of the media wrote lengthy articles about the alleged, pernicious influence of "soft" money in campaigns.

Critics recently criticized McCain for using the term "gook" to describe his Vietnamese captors. But McCain used the term several times in front of reporters *months* before anybody decided to report it. Would a similar remark by, say, Ronald Reagan or Newt Gingrich enjoy this McCain-type media protection?

A McCain cover story in the liberal magazine *The New Republic* flatly declared, "This man is not a Republican."[39] Not that the magazine was complaining, mind you.

No, the media embrace of McCain turns primarily on one thing: McCain is most decidedly *not* a Reagan conservative.

Syndicated columnist Donald Lambro interviewed Lyn Nofziger, Reagan's former political director: "I don't think [McCain's] a Reagan conservative. I don't think he knows where he is. I think he's evolving and he's evolving leftward."[40] No wonder the media liked McCain—for a Republican, that is.

In South Carolina George W. Bush soundly beat McCain. McCain's campaign manager, Mike Murphy, said he intended to regroup. "They [Bush's people] used their base, the Christian right. So we had every right to use ours, which is the media."[41] Any questions?

The typical journalist's hatred toward Ronald Reagan seeps

through in many other ways. Consider the way the media handled Lorraine Wagner. Who is Lorraine Wagner? As a thirteen-year-old girl, she wrote to the then thirty-one-year-old actor, Ronald Reagan, one of her favorites. To her surprise, Reagan responded, and they maintained a correspondence for some fifty years.

During that time, Reagan, of course, experienced the ups and downs of fifty years, including divorce and remarriage, election and reelection as governor of California, and, of course, election and reelection to the presidency. About his first wife, actress Jane Wyman, Reagan wrote, "I know she loves me, even though she thinks she doesn't."

In 1999 Lorraine Wagner sold those 276 letters quite legally to a collector, who promptly put them up for auction at an opening bid of $400,000! An Associated Press story on the selling of the letters led with the following headline, "Letters Shed New Light on Reagan's Life." Nowhere in the Associated Press article on this sale do we learn whether Ms. Wagner sought or received permission from the Reagan family.

My office contacted Reagan, and Nancy Reagan authorized the following statement: "We've never believed that letters should be sold without the permission of the person who wrote the letters."

No, Ms. Wagner did not get permission. (On my radio show, she admitted she was wrong for not having asked the Reagans.) Isn't this relevant to the story? Wouldn't you think columnists would scream bloody murder? Invasion of privacy! Violation of trust! But, since it's Reagan, what the hey. . . .

Zippergate

During the height of the "obstruction of justice and perjury" Clinton scandal, I appeared on the *Rivera Live* show on CNBC.

Geraldo Rivera pointed out that polls find the American people indifferent regarding the alleged misdeeds of the president. Yes, I said, the polls certainly show that. That's because you in the media consistently refer to the scandal as "Zippergate," "Sexgate," or "Monica-gate," rather than "Perjury-gate" or "Obstruction-of-Justice-gate." I told him that as long as members of the media flippantly label these very serious allegations, the public will not take this seriously. "Zippergate," "Sexgate," "Monica-gate," indeed.

The words of West Virginia democratic senator Robert Byrd say it all. Pre-impeachment, the media consistently described the declarative Senator Byrd as "the conscience of the Senate," "the elder statesman of the Senate," "the keeper of the Senate tradition." Following the Senate vote that refused to convict the president, Senator Byrd all but conceded the president's crimes, even though Byrd himself refused to vote to convict: "I have no doubt that he has given false testimony under oath and that he has misled the American people. . . . What he did was deplorable. Inexcusable. A bad example.[42]

"And that he has—there are indications that he did, indeed, obstruct justice. The question is, does this rise to the level of high crimes and misdemeanors? I say yes."[43]

Yes, the "fair-minded" Byrd, and a member of the president's own party, held the president morally, if not legally, guilty. "Zippergate," "Sexgate," "Monica-gate"?

Political Correctness

The left-of-center political magazine, the *New Republic*, wrote about the *Washington Post*'s policy of "diversity." So bent on being minority friendly, the newspaper that almost single-handedly brought down Richard Nixon, now pulls punches. For example, former D.C. mayor Marion Barry, after getting busted and doing time for drugs, decided to regain his office. Black reporter Milton Coleman, assistant managing director for metropolitan news, supervised the coverage of Marion Barry.

Now, Mr. Coleman had already achieved some degree of fame when he published the infamous "Hymie" and "Hymie-Town" remarks by Jesse Jackson. For that effort, the Nation of Islam leader, Louis Farrakhan claimed Coleman worthy of death, publicly stating, "We're going to make an example of Milton Coleman. . . . I'm going to try to get every church in Washington, D.C., to put him out . . . whenever he hits the door tell him he's not wanted. If he brings his wife, she can come in if she leaves him. But if she won't leave him, then you go to hell with your husband. If he is a traitor and you love to sleep in the bed with a traitor of your people then the same punishment that's due that no-good filthy traitor you'll get it yourself as his wife. One day soon we will punish you with death."[44] Perhaps chastened by that experience, Coleman seems intent on making sure the world understands that he is no one's "Uncle Tom."

During the Barry campaign, rumors surfaced that the candidate was buying votes. The *New Republic* reports that Coleman killed the story, as well as other negative pieces on Barry. "One day, I had lunch with the mayor," said Coleman. "The guy I had lunch with was a much more sophisticated, astute politician than the guy we had been portraying, and that part of my mission would be to change that."[45] Hey, is this a newspaper or a public relations bureau?

Even his staff were bothered by Coleman's bias. "People felt that stuff was being held, watered down, refocused," said one of his reporters. "And one of the things that Milton said . . . was, 'Look, you know, I have to answer to these people. These people are my neighbors and friends. And you guys are a bunch of white folks, you don't know what I'm talking about, but I live in black Washington.' It just shocked people."[46]

And remember, the CEO of the *Los Angeles Times*, Mark H. Willes, shortly after he became the paper's publisher, went one better than Coleman. Most stories, Willes noted, use "experts" and "sound bites" from white males. To encourage reporters to use minority and female "experts," Willes tied his editors' salaries to the frequency of female and minority quotes in their reporters' stories!

He further stated that the *Times* must offer stories that are "more emotional, more personal, less analytical" to attract women readers.[47] Pointing to Los Angeles's 40 percent Hispanic population, Willes even considered establishing a "Latino desk." But even the Latino *Times* reporters resisted, claiming that this would "ghettoize" their careers.

An obvious display of media bias surfaced during the Million Man March, led by the anti-Semitic, anti-Catholic, homophobic Nation of Islam leader Louis Farrakhan. Previously, on a trip to Los Angeles, Farrakhan denounced inner-city Korean American shopkeepers, calling them "bloodsuckers" for making money in but taking money out of the black community. He ridiculed rape victim Desiree Washington's accusations against Mike Tyson, saying, "She said, 'No, Mike, no,' I mean how many damn sisters have you said no and you mean yes all the time? . . . I'm talkin' to women now—we gonna' *talk* now. . . . The days of the B.S. is all over. You not dealin' with a man that don't know you, and the damn deceitful games that you play."

Yet, when Farrakhan announced the Million Man March to Washington, the media showed a surprising lack of hostility. Imagine David Duke announcing a Million White Man March.

Some editorials denounced the march, but surprisingly few, given Farrakhan's track record, including saying "Judaism is a gutter religion." Farrakhan later denied that he had said that. Confronted with an audiotape by a CNN interviewer, he contended that he had said Judaism was a "dirty religion," not a "gutter religion." Is that any improvement?

The Promise Keepers marched on Washington two years after the Million Man March. The Promise Keepers, an organization of male Christians, urges its members to live up to their religious and moral responsibilities to their wives and families. Their goal, not unlike Farrakhan's, is to implore men to uphold their moral and spiritual responsibilities.

In 1995, the *Los Angeles Times* wrote softly on the Million Man March: "In a moving display of pride and mutual support, hundreds of thousands of black men stood shoulder to shoulder. . . . Basking in the racial solidarity of attending the largest gathering of African-Americans in the nation's history, participants embraced each other. . . ."[48]

But a couple years later, when the Promise Keepers gathered for their rally, the stories were not quite so glowing. The *San Francisco Chronicle* wrote that two years earlier, the Million Man March had assembled to "repent their sins and recommit themselves to their families," and conceded that the Promise Keepers gathered to do "essentially the same thing." But the article went on to report that the gathering of "mostly white men" was controversial and that NOW President Patricia Ireland attacked the Promise Keepers as a dangerous "stealth male supremacist group."[49] A *Los Angeles Times* article on the rally quoted a black man, complaining about the dearth of blacks at the Promise Keepers rally.[50]

Now, why does the *Los Angeles Times* care about the lack of the Promise Keepers' diversity, but make no reference to the total absence of whites, Hispanics, and Asians during Farrakhan's march? Farrakhan excluded non-black men. Yet, the media apparently deemed the Promise Keepers' exclusion as something negative, while Farrakhan's exclusion went uncommented upon.

The Media Expect White Dads to Be Present and Responsible—Not So with Black Dads

On April 20, 1999, in Littleton, Colorado, two teenagers, Eric Harris and Dylan Klebold, planted pipe bombs at Columbine High and opened fire on students and teachers, killing twelve students, one teacher, and themselves.

We soon learned the professions of the parents of Harris and Klebold, and that one parent worked inside the home. Pundits soon began asking obvious questions. Who are these parents? How could they have bred such animals? Where were they when the teenagers plotted this massacre?

A few months later, in Decatur, Illinois, authorities suspended, for up to two years, seven black high school students involved in a brawl at a football game. Well, in came Jesse Jackson to demand immediate reenrollment. "Racism," said Jackson, explains this severe punishment for what Jackson called a "simple fistfight." Unfortunately for Jackson, a videotape soon surfaced, showing the "simple fistfight" to more closely resemble an all-out brawl. Later, it was reported that the seven students involved had a combined absence rate of over 300 days in their high school careers.

In the case of Columbine High, the media immediately raised questions about the quality of Harris's and Klebold's parenting. Yet no one seemed to ask the same question of the parents of the so-called Decatur Seven. The mothers of several of the kids appeared during press conferences and stood at Jackson's side. But photos of the Reverend Jackson, the students, and their mothers revealed one glaring absence—fathers. Surely, these seven kids had dads. Where are they? We don't know, because *nobody asked!* Again, one standard of civility is expected for parents of white, suburban kids and another, lower, standard is expected of parents of black kids.

What Liberal Bias?

According to Media Research Center, Dan Rather spoke to radio talk show host Mike Rosen, of station KOA, in Denver, Colorado, on November 28, 1995. Rather said, "I'm all news, all the time.

Full power, tall tower. I want to break in when news breaks out. That's my agenda. Now respectfully, when you start talking about a liberal agenda and all the, quote, liberal bias in the media, I quite frankly, and say this respectfully but candidly to you, I don't know what you're talking about. . . ."

And the Media Research Center quotes Jack Nelson, *Los Angeles Times* senior White House correspondent on CNBC's *Politics '96*, March 9, 1996: "When you're talking about pure journalists, I mean reporters, when you're talking about reporters, not columnists, I don't think there's any liberal bias. I don't think there really ever has been."

During a trial, lawyers use "premptory challenges." These challenges allow a lawyer to get rid of a juror for any reason, no matter how subjective or unfair. Why does the system allow this? Because people come to the table with biases, preferences, predilections, leanings. It is simple human nature. Why should reporters be exempt?

Reporters, like all humans, have blind spots, emotional trigger points, and a world view based on a set of values, teachings, and experiences. When the overwhelming majority of those responsible for spotting, gathering, reporting, and disseminating news are self-described liberals, small surprise that their biases seep into their news stories.

The Media Deny Their Liberal Bias: Are They Lying or Just Dense?

Actually, neither. The following story about my mom illustrates the problem.

When I was a child, Doris, a teenager, came to live with us. The daughter of a Tennessee friend of my mom's, Doris moved to Los Angeles to attend college and live with us for several years. Our family became attached to and protective of Doris. She became like a sister to my brothers and me. Doris dated George. George was extremely handsome. I mean Harry Belafonte–Sidney Poitier in their prime type of handsome. He was tall and muscular, with a beautiful face and sparkling white teeth.

My mother hated George. Don't ask me how or why, but my mom intuitively felt he was up to something. She never spoke favorably about him and would question his motives for things he said to and did for Doris.

One day my mom and I were talking about George, and I called George "handsome." My mother looked at me and said, "You think George is handsome?" She was dead serious.

"Come on, Mom," I said, "of course he's handsome. He looks like an actor." My mom said, "I don't see it. I don't find him handsome at all." Finally I said, "Mom, you dislike George, don't you?" She did not respond. "Because you dislike him so much," I continued, "you are not even capable of seeing how he looks to other people. And Mom, I gotta tell you, the man is handsome." "Really?" Mom said, "I just don't see it." And she truly did not.

So it is with the media. The media so dislike—fill in the blank—Newt Gingrich, welfare cutbacks, Republicans in general, the whole notion of trickle-down economics. So convinced of their righteousness, that they fight the good fight, most reporters blind themselves to their own bias. This makes them well intentioned, but unfair, one-sided, and guilty of failing to provide the public sufficient information to make up their own minds.

By the way, Mom was right about George. Turns out, he was married to another woman at the time he dated Doris. Doris found out, and the relationship ended. But he truly *was* handsome.

4

THE GLASS CEILING—FULL OF HOLES

Have dinner ready. Plan ahead, even the night before, to have a delicious meal, on time. This is a way of letting him know that you have been thinking about him and are concerned about his needs. Most men are hungry when they come home and the prospect of a good meal are [sic] part of the warm welcome needed.

Prepare yourself. Take 15 minutes to rest so that you'll be refreshed when he arrives. Touch up your makeup, put a ribbon in your hair and be fresh-looking. He has just been with a lot of work-weary people. Be a little gay and a little more interesting. His boring day may need a lift.

Clear away the clutter. Make one last trip through the main part of the home just before your husband arrives, gather up school-books, toys, paper, etc. Then run a dust cloth over the tables. Your husband will feel he has reached a haven of rest and order, and it will give you a lift, too.

Prepare the children. Take a few minutes to wash the children's hands and faces (if they are small), comb their hair, and if necessary change their clothes. They are little treasures and he would like to see them playing. Minimize all noise. At the time of his arrival, eliminate all noise of the washer, dryer, dishwasher, or vacuum. Try to encourage the children to be quiet. Be happy to see him. Greet him with a warm smile and be glad he is home.

Some don'ts: Don't greet him with problems or complaints. Don't complain if he is late for dinner. Count this as minor compared with what he might have gone through that day. Make him comfortable. Have him lean back in a comfortable chair or suggest he lie down in the bedroom. Have a cool or warm drink ready for him. Arrange his pillow and offer to take off his shoes. Speak in a low, soft, soothing and pleasant voice. Allow him to relax and unwind.

Listen to him. You may have a dozen things to tell him, but the moment of his arrival is not the time. Let him talk first. Make the evening his. Never complain if he does not take you out to dinner or to other places of entertainment. Instead, try to understand his world of strain and pressure, his need to be home and relax.

The Goal: Try to make your home a place of peace and order where your husband can renew himself in body and spirit.

—HOW TO BE A GOOD WIFE, A HOME ECONOMICS
HIGH SCHOOL TEXTBOOK, 1954

The Pigs Are Coming

That was then, this is now.

Today's American women now fire on all cylinders. Still, many "feminists" and others see male coconspirators systematically holding women down.

In pushing for "gender equity legislation," President Clinton said, "Today women earn about 75 cents for every dollar a man earns," and that the gap persists because of "the demeaning practice of wage discrimination in our workplaces."[1]

The American Bar association claims women remain under siege. Although women make up 44 percent of incoming law students, only 16 percent of tenured law professors are women.[2] The American Bar Association (ABA) blames this on sexism.

President George Bush's Federal Glass Ceiling Commission Report found, guess what, a glass ceiling! The Glass Ceiling Commission noted few women running Fortune 500 corporations and therefore suggested that corporate sexism thwarts female upward mobility.

The Pacific Research Institute for Public Policy issued a report that found legitimate reasons to explain why women earn less than men. Horrors! Feminist economist Myra Stober of Stanford University blasted the report's coauthor, Katherine Post. "She should come and sit in my office and listen to the stories of the women in the corporations I work with, all of whom are in their late 40s and 50s and are available for those jobs and qualified and are not being chosen."[3]

Feminists like Andrea Dworkin argue that chauvinism stems from a deep-seated hatred of women, a hatred that remains *even in marriage*. "One of the differences between marriage and prostitution is that in marriage you only have to make a deal with one man." She also said, "Marriage . . . is a legal license to rape," and "The hurting of women is . . . basic to the sexual pleasure of men." And how about this one: "All men benefit from rape, because all men benefit from the fact that women are not free in this society."[4]

University of Michigan law school professor Catharine MacKinnon suggests that the male interest in pornography provides a foundation for hatred toward women. "Sooner or later," writes MacKinnon, "in one way or another, the consumers want to live out the pornography further in three dimensions. Sooner or later, in one way or another, they do. It makes them want to; when they believe they can, when they feel they can get away with it, they do. Depending upon their chosen sphere of operation, they may use whatever power they have to keep the world a pornographic place."[5]

Exhibit A: Corporate Chauvinism

NationsBank, headquartered in North Carolina, recently merged with California's Bank of America. As with any merger, consolidation of positions followed, with many dual spots completely eliminated. Newspapers soon wrote articles noting that not a single female bank executive from Bank of America survived the merger. Implication: sexism, chauvinism.

Some articles pointed out that male executives at Bank of America also got cut, but at least *some* survived. Not so with women. What else could explain this other than sexism, the unwillingness of the good ol' Southern banking boys to accept female California executives.

Assume, for a moment, the accusation to be true, that Nations-Bank does not like female executives. And because of this chauvinism they refused to recognize and appreciate the talent of female Bank of America executives.

First, expect the highly competitive banking industry to gobble up these "talented female executives." Second, a move of blatant chauvinism risks offending the substantial and growing female customer base. Nearly one in four Americans now works for a woman, and women start businesses at a faster rate than do men. These businesses also have a lower failure rate than male-founded enterprises. And nearly 25 percent of married women outearn their spouses.

So, chauvinism, like racism, is stupid and inconsistent with the best interests of the organization. But, again, let's assume Nations-Bank guilty as charged.

Enterprising female executives can turn assets into liabilities by starting a new bank. Let's call it the United Female Friendly Bank. Because, after all, female consumers of the old bank do not wish to continue doing business with an enterprise that refuses to hire and promote their own. Expect female depositors then to flock to the female-friendly, nonsexist bank.

Good people, in a highly competitive market for talent, ultimately land on their feet. The best defense against unfair workplace treatment remains performance. If the current boss does not appreciate performance, the new boss will.

Sympathetic reporters love stories like these, where, on the surface, it appears a woman got the shaft. Never mind that, in this case, men lost their jobs, too. Or that, NationsBank, as the "winner" in this merger, probably feels its executives superior. After all, NationsBank is the acquiring company and, thus, calls the shots. Sorry. Welcome to Life 101.

Besides, just how bad *are* male bosses? After all, an international poll of women showed that most women, in nearly every country surveyed, prefer male bosses. Of the twenty-two countries polled—including the United States, Great Britain, Chile, China, Colombia, Estonia, France, Germany, Hungary, Iceland, Japan, Lithuania, Mexico, Spain, Taiwan, and others, whose combined population represents more than half the world—only women in India preferred female bosses. In Honduras and El Salvador, women were evenly split in their preference of male versus female bosses.[6] Do women around the world lack self-esteem? Are they self-loathers who prefer oversight by their male oppressors? Or is it that, maybe, just maybe, male bosses ain't all that bad.

Do Women Make Less Money for the Same Work?

Many, like President Clinton, bemoan the "gender pay gap." The assumption, of course, is that chauvinism, the repression of women, causes this gap.

Do women earn less money than men? Yes. Too bad, however, that those who jump on the sex discrimination bandwagon refuse to examine the facts.

Girls get better grades in high school than the boys. Women earn more college degrees than men, and females outnumber the males in graduate schools.[7] Sounds like the girls are beating the guys so far. But here's where the differences begin. Women tend to major in lower-paying "humanities" fields rather than in higher-paying disciplines such as engineering, science, and technology.

Clinton's 75-cents-on-the-dollar figure for women is accurate, when you compare *all* women to *all* men. Kinda like comparing apples to trucks.

Just for grins, let's assume that women *do* earn only 75 cents to every dollar a man earns, for the *same job*. What should a smart, dastardly, money-grubbing bottom-line-oriented boss do—fire all of his men and hire women at three-quarters on the dollar! Think about it. If, in fact, a pool of women exist who can perform the same work for less, any manager who hires men should be fired. To do otherwise hurts the bottom line. But activists want it both ways. On the one hand, they accuse male bosses of greed, thus the need for these "protective laws" in the first place. On the other hand, they, in essence, accuse male bosses of stupidity by paying inflated labor costs just for the joy of hiring fellow men. It doesn't make sense.

Economist June O'Neill, former head of the respected Congressional Budget Office, specializes in labor matters. O'Neill, in analyzing the alleged "gender pay gap," compared apples to apples. She studied the salaries of women in the same industries as men, with the same academic background, who have been on the job the same length of time, and discovered virtually no difference in pay.[8]

In fact, the wage gap between women aged twenty-four to thirty-three who have never had children is virtually nonexistent compared to men of the same age.[9] And a 1993 U.S. Census Bureau study shows that women who work at full-time jobs and have never married earn $1,005 for every $1,000 of their male counterparts.[10] Pacific Research Institute fellows Katherine Post and Michael Lynch say that as far back as the 1970s, never-married women in their thirties who worked continuously outearned never-married men: "There is vast evidence that women who choose to remain single, invest in education, and work long hours, have in the past and continue to fare about as well as men in the labor market."[11]

Feminists refuse to acknowledge a simple fact. A lot of women think the corporate rat race sucks. Polls show that both men and women, when given a choice, would prefer a stay-at-home mom to nurture and raise the children. Many surveys of women with MBAs find that ten years after receiving their degrees, 20 percent don't work at all—most of those having opted out of the workplace in favor of family life.[12] A Korn Ferry study shows that only one-third as many women (14%) as men (46%) actually *want* to be a CEO someday.[13] Many female professionals, and many men, for that matter, simply refuse to put in the time, effort, energy, and sacrifice required to become number one. Why should this be considered a bad thing?

Feminist lawyer Gloria Allred and I recently argued over the basic differences between men and women. "Aren't women inherently and instinctively more nurturing than men?" I said. She responded by asserting that women deserve equal pay for equal work. "Fair enough," I said. "Now care to answer my question?"

In fact, women get "punished" in corporate America for taking time out to rear children. Given the competitive nature of the corporate ladder, anyone, male or female, who takes several months to several years "time out" gets hurt, or left behind his or her peers. In corporate America, to have a real shot at the top title of a Fortune 500 company, an upwardly mobile executive must work well over forty hours a week, and make an average of four or five geographical moves during a twenty- to thirty-year career, sacrificing family life for career.

We live in a high-tech information age, minimizing the advantage of muscle and brawn and increasing the emphasis on camaraderie, esprit de corps, teamwork, and creativity. This means that a woman with the training, background, smarts, and drive no longer faces a disadvantage because of her generally smaller physical stature.

I once met a female steel executive and asked her whether she had encountered much chauvinism on her way up. "Yes," she replied, "but I considered that their problem, and I let my performance speak for itself."

Businesswoman Darla Moore recently appeared on the cover of *Fortune* magazine. A successful executive in her own right, she married Richard Rainwater, who helped the Texas millionaire Bass brothers grow their remarkable fortune. Ms. Moore left a successful career to manage her husband's portfolio, increasing it many times over.

The *Fortune* magazine cover story on her called her "The Toughest Babe in Business."[14] Female readers wrote angry letters bemoaning the cover's use of the term "babe," and urging that this kind of thing sets women back.

Darla Moore dismissed the criticism as the kind of hypersensitivity that gets in a woman's way. She wrote a letter in response to the critical comments, and said, "I have this to say to the women who find the use of the word 'babe' inappropriate or even horrifying: I seriously doubt, as long as you retain this attitude, that you will ever appear on the cover of *Fortune*—or that you will ever accomplish enough in business to merit this distinction.

". . . I'm certainly not suggesting that women should look the other way when confronted with true sexual harassment or genuinely offensive behavior. I also strongly believe that trying to be sexy in the workplace is a formula for failure if there ever was one. But being someone with sex appeal is a terrific formula for success. It means you're comfortable with who you are. And it means you can learn to appreciate who other people are. True sensitivity means not getting all wound up in a bundle every time you think you hear an insult. Anyone who wants to play in the big leagues of business has to learn to focus on what's important—and not be thrown off by smaller things. You also have to accept, as a woman, that men are never going to treat you like another guy, because— guess what—you aren't another guy.

". . . You know what I think is one of the world's biggest wastes of time for a woman? Networking with other females. Where is that going to get you if men are the ones with all the power? Every single one of my mentors has been male. At no time have I even encountered a woman who would have been a smart choice to help pull me up the ladder, to give me the tools and the power needed to make a difference."[15]

What should women do to improve their prospects? The same thing men should do. Push for lower taxes, less regulation, and a downsized government. These measures increase competition and, therefore, options for those who are or feel they have been mistreated. The more vibrant an economy, the more businesses competing, the greater the consequences for any company mistreating or failing to competitively compensate proficient employees.

Economist Wendy Lee Gramm says that a strong economy means expanding opportunity and more demand for less-experienced workers, such as women. "Competition [for workers]," she writes, "also makes discrimination, glass ceilings and other inefficient work practices economically undesirable." Therefore, she says, "Women's advocates should support free and competitive international markets, lower capital-gains taxes, lower income taxes and fewer burdensome government regulations."[16]

But President Clinton considers himself a friend and ally of women and accurately credits his victory to having received more of the female vote. Clinton's prescription for helping women? Expand the Family and Medical Leave Act. Push legislation mandating equal pay for equal work. Encourage lawsuits from women who feel victimized by sexual harassment. Wrong formula.

Economist Gramm says, "Many government programs work against women by weakening the economy or creating employment barriers that are harmful. Requiring certain benefits like maternity leave raises the cost of employing women and may cause marginal companies to close their doors and hire no one at all. The higher costs may make some companies reluctant to hire women."[17]

The Family and Medical Leave Act increases the cost of doing business. It makes hiring those likely to use the Family and Medical Leave Act—women—more expensive. It imposes burdens on businesspeople. The law requires an employer to provide leave for family emergencies or other "important" personal matters. The employer must—during the leave—keep the job open and continue to pay health benefits. Many activists think this a good thing, that the businesses recognize the "dual responsibilities" of women and force employers to demonstrate flexibility and sensitivity. But a business exists to make money, not as a device for social engineering. And, given the choice between an equally competent man versus an equally competent woman, shouldn't a rational boss take into consideration the additional burdens imposed by law should he hire the woman?

This law raises the price of hiring a woman. What, a prospective employer might say, happens if she gets pregnant? Oh, the employer thinks, she has two kids. What happens when the inevitable crises come up? How can I afford to keep a job open, and pay benefits despite her absence? Of course, the "feminists" and other toe-tag liberals don't give a damn about a company's bottom line. Companies, in their minds, possess an unlimited bag of money to accommodate the it-takes-a-village mentality.

"Feminists" simply do not trust enlightened employers to institute policies that make sense for employer, employee, and the bottom line. Some "feminist" activists refuse to believe that companies, out of their own self-interest, will say, as many have already done, "Hey, if we want to attract top-notch females, many of whom have children, we need to do something."

And, what of the other employees who must pick up the slack for the woman out on family leave? What about single workers, perhaps less likely to use family leave? The Family and Medical

Leave Act assaults the relationship between a willing employer and a willing employee, mandating, controlling, directing, and demanding that employers "do the right thing,"—provided, of course, government gets to pick "the right thing."

Similarly, laws proposing equal pay for equal work make employers nervous. A salary is something negotiated between employer and employee. The employer can fire and the employee can quit. This provides power on both sides. But, no, says the government. Mean-spirited employers (mostly male) would surely take advantage of weak women who, of course, are devoid of options. What is "equal work"? Is it where both men and women perform the same job? But what if one has more experience than the other? Should this matter? What if the female worker, anxious to get her foot in the door, willing and knowingly accepts lower pay than a male incumbent for the same work. Should the government step in and say, "Wait a second, what are you guys doing to her?"

The commission found that in 1994, only two women were CEOs of Fortune 1000 companies.[18] Therefore, sexism. But the strides women are making in corporate America are nothing short of breathtaking. The commission also discusses the numbers of women at second-tier corporate positions, the top twenty through forty slots in a given corporation. There women composed nearly 50 percent. And, from the mid-1980s to 1992, the percentage of females in top executive positions of Fortune 1000 industrials and Fortune 500 service companies increased from less than 2 percent to 9 percent, a blinding increase of more than 400 percent in one decade.[19] A poll of CEOs of small and midsized corporations showed that nearly half expect the next CEO to be a woman.[20]

In short, expect many more women to assume top spots in major corporations.

"Pale Males" and the Glass Ceiling

Former secretary of transportation Elizabeth Dole speaks of a "glass ceiling." Vice President Al Gore speaks of a "digital divide." Here's a new one: the "silicon ceiling." President Clinton appointed a woman named Dr. Anita Borg to something called the Federal Commission on the Advancement of Women, Minorities and Disabled in Science, Engineering and Technology. Said Borg, "We really have to think about supporting efforts to recruit people at a whole lot of different places." Borg bemoans the dominance of "pale males," white men who dominate the computer industry.[21]

She works to shatter the "silicon ceiling" that excludes women and minorities.

But Borg herself holds a degree in computer science at NYU. Of doctorates in computer science and computer engineering, what percentage go to women? Eighteen percent. In fact, the percentage of women receiving computer science degrees fell from 37 percent in 1984, to today's 27 percent.[22]

A recent article described Borg as a "technogeek." If a "technogeek" requires a computer background to enter computer fields, and, if women don't get these degrees, then perhaps the smoking gun ain't sexism. Maybe women just don't like the computer fields. That may or may not change, but don't point the finger at sexist managers. Nearly one-third of Microsoft's work force consists of women. The government accuses Bill Gates of mercenary predatory practices. Is Gates also lowering standards to create a "female-friendly" work force? No, more likely, Gates being Gates, wants the best. And, in the end, that is the "solution" for women.

Sexual Harassment in the Workplace Doesn't
Hold Women Back

Civil rights complaints in the private and public sector more than doubled from 1990 to 1998, to a total of 42,354. As a percentage of all civil rights complaints, employment cases compose 65 percent of the overall increase.[23]

Job-bias lawsuits totaled 21,540 in 1998.[24] These cases included allegations of discrimination in hiring, promoting, termination, or pay based on race, color, religion, sex, national origin, age, and disability.

More than 70 percent of all of these cases result in dismissals. Of those that go to trial, either by judge or jury, only a third end up awarding the plaintiff any damages.[25] Twenty-one thousand five hundred forty (21,540) cases out of an "employment universe" of what? More than 130 million people? True, cases did double over an eight-year period of time. But does this mean we have more sexual harassment and discrimination in the workplace, or does this mean new laws embolden employees to take their complaints to the Equal Employment Opportunity Commission (EEOC)?

According to surveys, approximately 40 percent of women report harassment at work.[26] Does sexual harassment hold women back? Certainly, a lot of male employees and superiors and managers make inappropriate remarks and do inappropriate things to women. Yes, many men are pigs.

But, again, the best defense against inappropriate male conduct directed toward women is competence. Competence makes you valuable to your organization. If a woman feels aggrieved, she should take her concerns to management. Her bargaining power is the perception of her value to the organization. If the organization fails to appreciate her value, she should walk. Quickly. Ideally, to the nearest competitor.

A corporation with a reputation for tolerating sexual harassment will soon find it difficult to attract women. And most corporations have manuals and internal policies discouraging inappropriate sexist behavior. One can, therefore, sue a company for tolerating sexist behavior and failing to abide by its own rules and regulations.

Smart women simply overlook some boorish behavior by men. Off-color jokes and stupid remarks may be irritating, but a smart woman deals with this. She makes it clear to the speaker that she finds the remark unfunny and inappropriate. But hypersensitivity creates an atmosphere where everybody walks on eggshells, no one knows what to say to each other, and camaraderie and productivity suffer.

Men and Women *Are* Different

Many police departments operate under judicial consent decrees, a finding that the department engaged in historical discrimination. A consent decree mandates increased hiring of minorities and females. As a result, many police departments actively recruit female officers. In Los Angeles, the City Council passed a resolution that the police department become 42 percent female. One small problem: where to get the female cops! Not enough applied to even get remotely close to 42 percent of the force. So the department eliminated the height requirement, made the written test easier, and, many say, dumbed down the physical aspect of training at the academy.

Jill Stewart, former writer for the *Los Angeles Times*, covers the Los Angeles Police Department's effort at "outreach" to women. Stewart says, "This shows all the logical thinking of a three-year-old. Even the military, which has courted female recruits for far longer, has only ever achieved a 15 to 20 percent saturation of females. This kind of aggressive recruiting of groups that aren't interested is the worst kind of politically correct bullshit."

Few departments come close to 40 percent female officer population. Why? Maybe, just maybe, a whole lot of women simply do not want to become officers. Maybe, just maybe, the required aggression turns women off. So, too, does the military-oriented command-and-control atmosphere of a police department. And many criminals don't respect female officers, finding them too small and nonthreatening. Some departments find female officers *more likely* to use deadly force than a man. Why? Perhaps because the bad guys challenge them more readily than they do male officers.

In any event, females simply do not seem to find police work appealing. Fine. Similarly, many women do not want to be coal miners, garbage collectors, or ditch diggers, all fields where women are "underrepresented." Tell the activists who bean count and falsely conclude that sexism shuts out women to wise up.

Sexual Harassment Hypocrisy

Anita Hill accused conservative Supreme Court nominee Clarence Thomas of sexual harassment. Representative Barbara Boxer (D-California) took to the floor and demanded hearings, "One thing I know is that there just aren't enough women on Capitol Hill to represent the women in our democracy and there should be more. If there were, then the seriousness and scope of these issues would be better understood."[27] The National Organization for Women condemned Thomas's nomination and mobilized to defeat it.

But recall Hill's accusations—that Clarence Thomas asked her out and made unseemly comments, such as, "There's a pubic hair on my Coke [can]." She never alleged touching, or that Thomas attempted to force himself on her, or that Thomas propositioned her. Furthermore, she followed Thomas from job to job, soliciting a recommendation from him, long after the alleged acts took place.

When Hill pursued a job as a law professor, Thomas wrote her a sterling recommendation. She allegedly told a couple of friends about the harassment at or around the time of its occurrence, but she never identified the harasser by name. Thus, a classic "he-said, she-said" over, comparatively speaking, minor allegations.

And then there's the Paula Jones double standard. Jones, an Arkansas government staffer, accused Bill Clinton of sexually harassing her while he was the governor of that state. She said, "I was approached by one of Bill Clinton's bodyguards . . . and I was given a number and I asked him what it was; I held out my hand, and he said, 'It's a number to a hotel room.' The governor would like to meet with me. Well, I was surprised, and I kinda talked it over with my coworker, and we didn't have any reason to believe that we couldn't trust him, so I agreed to go up to the room and meet Mr. Bill Clinton.

"I got to the room and Governor Clinton, he opened the door to meet me. It was a room that did not have any beds in it, had couches and stuff like that, a meeting-type room, and he asked me about my job and how I liked it, and who my boss was. And I told him, and he mentioned that he liked the way my curves were on my body, and he liked the way that my hair went down to the middle of my back. Then, he kind of leaned over and he put his hands up my leg, which, it happened so fast, and tried to kiss me on the neck. It happened so fast, he leaned over and kissed me on the neck, as he was putting his hand up my leg, and I backed up and said, 'I don't want to do this. I think I need to be goin'.' "

A little more serious than a pubic hair on a Coke can, don'tcha think? Jones alleged far more serious conduct than the accusations against Clarence Thomas. And Jones told friends at or around the time of the alleged harassment, and she—unlike Anita Hill—specifically mentioned the accused by name.

At the time, Jones remained publicly silent, not wanting to get into a dogfight with such a powerful figure. But, when a magazine article during the 1992 presidential campaign suggested that a

"Paula" had had an intimate relationship with Governor Clinton, Jones asked Clinton to deny this and apologize for his earlier actions. Clinton refused. Paula Jones sought help from the National Organization for Women. They did nothing. Because Jones got assistance from a conservative legal foundation, activist women dismissed her allegations. After all, she consorted with the enemy. Never mind the merits of her case or that her case seemed far stronger than the case against Clarence Thomas.

Paula Jones comes from the lower class, and, unlike Hill, did not come across as well groomed, sophisticated, or articulate—a clear case of class bias. But the biggest difference remains the "target." Thomas is conservative and, thus, an enemy as perceived by the left. Clinton's endorsement of "pro-women legislation" made him a sympathetic target, deserving of defense. The left-wing establishment on the whole simply abandoned Jones, despite her more substantial, more serious allegations. They chose politics over principle, calling into question their very commitment to protecting women.

Even if you believe the president's conduct did not deserve impeachment or conviction in the Senate, Jones's charges remain serious. And, as a defendant in a sexual harassment lawsuit, President Clinton attempted to deny her her day in court. Independent counsel Ken Starr's investigation alleged that the president and his aides obstructed justice and committed perjury. Thus, to defeat a female citizen's sexual harassment civil liability lawsuit, the president lied under oath and before a grand jury. OK by me, say liberal female activists.

For years, feminists complained when, in rape cases, courts allowed defense attorneys to examine the sexual history of the accuser. Feminists called this "equivalent to being raped twice." Yet, when Clinton operatives systematically attacked Paula Jones's character, and when the president's attorney suggested examining Jones's life, feminists sat on their hands. Women said nothing when the president's chief zealot, James Carville, famously said about Jones, "Drag a hundred dollars through a trailer park and there's no telling what you'll find."[28]

Later, the president shook his finger and looked America in the eye and said, "I did not have sexual relations with that woman, Ms. Lewinsky." Oops. The famous blue dress with semen stains appeared, and the president had to admit an inappropriate relationship with young intern Monica Lewinsky. But, said his defenders, everybody lies about sex. (Funny, that defense did not seem to apply to Clarence Thomas.)

Another blatant example of the sexism double standard: Clinton campaign volunteer Kathleen Willey said, on *60 Minutes*, that the president grouped her, touching her breast and placing her hand on his genitalia. Feminist Gloria Steinem, in a *New York Times* op-ed piece, denied that the president committed sexual harassment. After all, said Steinem, the president stopped when Willey said, "Stop." But I thought "no" meant "no"! So, feminists apparently allow guys to get one crack at an unwanted touching, and, if the touch-ee says no, then the touch-er commits no offense. Let's call this the "Grope-a-Dope," one free feel.

Steinem's defense of the president was even too much for fellow feminist activist Gloria Allred to stomach. Allred finally said, "Enough's enough," and publicly demanded the resignation of the president. She also called Steinem wrong about the alleged touching of Kathleen Willey, calling the allegation, if true, an example of sexual assault.

After her demand that the president resign, Allred says that she got punished. A CNN booker, claims Allred, retracted her invitation to appear on a talk show where Allred had appeared many times. CNN quickly denied this, but Allred stands by her story, that CNN declared her persona non grata. (A footnote: When the new CNN news division head took over during the height of Perjurygate, he issued a memo. He told reporters to refrain from using the word *scandal* in connection with Clinton. This makes Allred's allegation more plausible.)

Yet, feminists love Clinton. Even when, on the Monica Lewinsky–Linda Tripp tapes, Lewinsky said she asked the president why he didn't settle the Paula Jones suit, and she said he responded, "I can't. There would be hundreds."

The feminist stand in support of Clinton damages women in several ways. First, it gives a green light for men to lie under oath because, after all, "everybody lies about sex." Clinton defenders found his lie permissible because the "question should not have been asked in the first place." (Never mind that the question came about in the context of a civil sexual harassment suit, the lawsuit being a tool encouraged by feminists to "level the playing field" against men.) Second, the president's lawyers provided a roadmap to defend against sexual assaults. Trash the victim, put her on trial.

Things sure get confusing. During the height of the O. J. Simpson case, feminist Tammy Bruce headed the Los Angeles chapter of the National Organization for Women. On ABC's *Nightline*, Bruce labeled the O. J. Simpson case a matter of domestic violence and said that her message gives people "a needed break from all that talk of racism."[29] This upset the national headquarters of NOW, which feared a backlash from supporters. The organization urged Bruce to refrain from making any such statements. Bruce, though, did not back down and said, "I will not be silenced. I will not abandon domestic violence victims for internal NOW politics. I would say Patricia Ireland [NOW national president] owes an apology to the families of domestic violence victims who will die while NOW focuses on petty name-calling."[30] NOW replaced Bruce.

The "In Box" Is Empty

The National Organization for Women recently blasted CBS, NBC, ABC, and CNN for "one-dimensional" portrayals of women before the camera and for insufficient opportunities behind it.

"One-dimensional portrayals of women?" Even if true, this continues the silly notion that television raises children. This ignores the overwhelming influence of the quality of parenting and of community role models, friends, relatives, and teachers, on giving children a sense of values, hope, and upward mobility.

Furthermore, television shows more women in a greater variety of roles—including power positions—than ever before. Two of the six networks' head programmers are now female. Many women occupy decision-making positions in television and in movie studios, green-lighting the kinds of projects that their male predecessors used to approve.

We still see a lot of action movies, horror films, and situation comedies involving single people struggling, married people struggling, separated people struggling, and divorced people struggling. In short, female executives green-light projects for the same reasons that male executives do: to get ratings and make money.

If the extremely violent television movie *The Last Don* makes money, would a female executive refuse to green-light *The Last Don II*? Not if she wants to keep her job.

The Elizabeth Dole Candidacy

Republican Elizabeth Dole declared her candidacy for the 2000 presidential nomination. Her husband, the failed Republican nominee of 1996, urged her entry into the race. Her résumé showed a number of executive positions in and out of government, including secretary of labor and CEO of the Red Cross. She is attractive and articulate. Yet her candidacy went supernova. Why? After being asked repeatedly about agendas or goals for America, she came across like an empty suit. Apparently, the sole reason for her candidacy, the only thing distinguishing her from other candidates was her gender. "Vote for me," she said, in essence, "because I'm a woman."

Few, including women, bought this. This suggests that women, despite the prattling of the feminist left, feel pretty darn good about their "plight." After all, men have a stake in this fight, too. Men marry women, have daughters, mothers, friends, and sisters. And, since nearly a quarter of female spouses now outearn their husbands, men stand to gain by insuring equal opportunity for women.

With the exception of the radical "feminists," women do not perceive men as the enemy. Certainly some women feel men need "remedial education." But most women do not think of men as "out to get them." Someone should tell the emotional left.

But many "feminists" continue to push the myth of the "Glass Ceiling," with the compliance of a news media either too biased or too lazy to look beneath the numbers. This influences many women to incorrectly view the marketplace as one where the great male chauvinist pig lurks around every corner holding a nightstick, waiting to strike them down.

The formula for success for women? The same as for men— drive, energy, education, enthusiasm, and positive attitude, an attitude made more difficult by the incessant wrongheaded harping about the "glass ceiling."

Let's give it a break. If there's a war between the sexes, some-one once said, it's the only one where you get to sleep with the enemy.

5

AMERICA'S GREATEST PROBLEM: NOT CRIME, RACISM, OR BAD SCHOOLS— IT'S ILLEGITIMACY

At thirteen, my older sister was pregnant and unmarried. I followed in her footsteps, becoming pregnant at seventeen, continuing a series of bad choices. My older brother had already begun his walk down his own crooked road, getting arrested by the time he was sixteen on half a dozen occasions for petty crimes. We were linked by fatherlessness. . . . Nothing can stop the killings until the core issues are addressed: the rapid disintegration of the two-parent family . . . [1]

—JONETTA ROSE BARRAS, WRITING IN THE *WASHINGTON TIMES*

The Importance of Dads

A chaplain in a federal prison decided to improve morale. With Mother's Day approaching, he made a deal with one of the major greeting card companies. Supply us, he asked the company, with five hundred Mother's Day cards, one for each man. Sensing good PR, the card company went along.

The inmates enthusiastically sent each mom a card. Morale improved so dramatically that the chaplain decided to repeat the success on Father's Day. Again, the greeting card company agreed to supply five hundred Father's Day cards. The chaplain offered the cards to the inmates.

But not one inmate sent a card to his father. Not one.

In his book *My Father's Face*,[2] author James Robison wrote about the chaplain's experience. The majority of men in prison come from a home with an absentee father, or one in which he doesn't even know his father, or one in which the father was present but abusive. What does this tell us? This demonstrates the importance of fathers, especially for male children.

This chapter discusses the damage done to society and the family by the welfare state, an institution that says to young pregnant women, "marry the government." To the father, the welfare state says, "Get lost. You're not needed, we will enable you to abandon your moral, spiritual, and financial responsibilities. We're in charge here."

Since the 1950s, crime has tripled. Many factors explain this, and no single factor, by itself, caused the explosion. But the absence of involved fathers, depriving children, especially males, of an in-house role model, is the leading suspect. Lots of variables explain the crime rate. Criminals say that crime goes up when the possibility of getting caught, convicted, and incarcerated goes down. And crime is a young man's game. As the youthful population of America grows, so does the crime rate. The nuclear family remains the best vehicle to inculcate values, goals, and morals into the young. But the modern welfare state leads to the breakdown, or nonformation, of nuclear, intact families.

In Africa, observers report a unique and disturbing problem. Baby elephants are attacking rhinoceroses and other animals as never before. Why? Poachers kill off mature elephants for their ivory tusks. And sometimes game wardens, for population control, decide to relocate older breeding elephants. This leaves young elephants to grow up without the socializing and "civilizing" effect of a father figure. Normally, elephant young grow up gentle, obedient, and respectful of their elders. But these young rogue elephants—described by the game wardens as destructive, angry punks—run amok, not unlike what happens with male humans who grow up without paternal guidance and leadership.

This brings us back to the welfare state. Although blacks make up a substantial percentage of welfare recipients, most welfare recipients are not black. But the issue is not the race of welfare recipients but whether the welfare state encourages dependency, and thus makes the situation worse.

In 1960, out-of-wedlock births accounted for 2 percent of white births and 22 percent of black births. By 1994 the rates had soared to 25 and 70 percent, respectively, although more recent trends show improvement.[3] What happened?

Since the mid-sixties, spending for social programs—WIC, Head Start, food stamps, AFDC—exploded. Women learned they could "marry the government," making a fifth wheel out of the biological fathers of their children. The fathers knew that—worst case—the government would step in and provide a so-called "social safety net" for the mother of his child, as well as for that child.

Lyndon Johnson's well-intentioned War on Poverty created the greatest uptick of illegitimacy in America's history. This huge number of children without involved fathers underlies nearly every major problem in America—bad schools, crime, unemployment.

In 1967, Lyndon Johnson established the Kerner Commission to examine the reasons for the rioting of the 1960s. The commission saw an America moving in two directions, one black and one white. It concluded that poverty and racism conspired to hurt the black community.

In reality, the biggest factor negatively affecting black America was the welfare state, created by well-intentioned, good-minded people seeking to eradicate poverty. But neither racism nor lack of money plays the biggest role in the dysfunctional development of a child. Caring, loving parents remain the greatest factor in creating a self-reliant, upwardly mobile, confident adult. A society ignores these lessons at great cost.

For example, in 1987, a wealthy, idealistic philanthropist in Philadelphia, "adopted" 112 inner-city sixth-grade kids, most of whom were products of broken homes. The philanthropist, George Weiss, guaranteed a fully-funded education up through college if only the kids would refrain from drugs, unwed motherhood or fatherhood, and crime. He even provided tutors, workshops, after-school programs, summer programs, and counselors to be available when trouble arose, whether personal or otherwise.

Fast forward. Thirteen years later, how many of these kids successfully made it to college and beyond?

Forty-five never made it through high school. Of these, thirty-five dropped out, one died while in school, four died after dropping out, four are working on a GED, and one graduated trade school.[4]

Of the high school graduates, thirteen are four-year-college graduates; eleven are enrolled in four-year colleges; five are enrolled in two-year colleges; twelve have dropped out of two- and four-year colleges; seven graduated trade school; eight are enrolled in trade school; six dropped out of trade school; and five graduates got no further education.[5]

Of the sixty-seven boys, nineteen have grown into adult felons.[6] Among the forty-five girls, they had sixty-three children, and more than half had their babies before the age of eighteen.[7]

If you took more than a hundred kids from similar backgrounds, but no guaranteed education, the results would have been approximately the same. What do we make of this? The answer is simple: It ain't about money. It's about values. It's about discipline and application. It's about character, working hard when you don't want to. *And these values are instilled in the home.*

In fact, the poorer the child, the more likely a school or college will grant a scholarship, loan, or other financial-aid package.

But a lot of people fail to understand this simple, powerful message. Dads matter.

Recently, the richest man in America, Bill Gates, gave more than a billion dollars for scholarships. He specifically targeted inner-city kids because he felt they are "underrepresented" in technical fields like computer science and engineering. William Gray III, chief executive of the United Negro College Fund, cheered when Bill Gates gave him the $50 million annual fund to target for inner-city children. Gray said gleefully, "The biggest barrier to minority educational attainment is not family values. It's not grades. It's money."[8] No, Mr. Gray, it is not. Just ask George Weiss.

The government, and well-intentioned toe-tag liberals, arrogantly think assistance programs replace quality parenting. Raising a child means a minute-by-minute, hour-by-hour, day-by-day, week-by-week, month-by-month, year-by-year proposition. It is labor-intensive. Quality parenting communicates appropriate behavior by word and by deed. When a child hears his father's alarm go off, then hears the old man grunting when he gets up and heads off to a job, the kid learns. He learns that sometimes people have to do things they don't want to do in order to achieve a goal. He learns that smiling all the time and always loving a job are unrealistic, but that mature people do things they have to do rather than only those things they enjoy doing.

A male child with an absent father learns other things, too. He sees his mom struggling to raise a family without any help from his father. He may perceive women as weak and grow to resent his dad, who appeared to "get away with" shouldering any responsibilities. In his eyes, women become patsies. He sees the woman's role as that of caretaker, of someone who cleans up somebody else's mess. He sees a man as a slickster, as someone for whom the general rules of civility and responsibility do not apply. Just like the baby elephants in Africa.

Children Having Children

In 1965, Daniel Patrick Moynihan, later a Democratic senator from New York, wrote a groundbreaking book, *The Negro Family: A Case for National Action.* "A community that allows a large number of young men to grow up in broken homes, dominated by women, never acquiring any stable relationship to male authority, never acquiring any rational expectations about the future—that community asks for and gets chaos," he wrote. In such a society "crime, violence, unrest, unrestrained lashing out at the whole social structure—these are not only to be expected, they are virtually inevitable."[9]

Critics attacked Moynihan for his "racist," "Eurocentric" view of the world, an unnecessary exaltation of the traditional nuclear family. Just because a single two-parent household is Moynihan's ideal, critics said, this doesn't mean we can apply that to other, culturally different, people.

As mentioned, since the publication of his book, today's rate of 70 percent of black children born outside of wedlock is nearly three times the level Moynihan decried in his report. America's white and Hispanic illegitimacy rate grows even faster. The out-of-wedlock birthrate for whites was 2 percent in 1960. By 1993, Hispanic illegitimacy stood at 33 percent, and the white rate had increased *twelve* times, to 24 percent.[10]

I read Moynihan's book in my freshman sociology class. The kids went bonkers, accusing Moynihan of everything from elitism to white supremacy. Some students questioned the very need for and importance of fathers in the first place!

But given slavery, haven't black families always been unstable? Certainly slavery militated against the traditional two-parent household. Black slaves could not enter into civil marriages recognized by the state. And a father could not "provide for" his family in ways that free men could.

But even during slavery, slave owners generally attempted to *keep* families together because it improved morale and, therefore, productivity. Owners, of course, bought and sold slaves, thus destroying families. But so strong was the slaves' desire for family unification that, after emancipation, slaves walked up and down riverbanks in search of their loved ones.

After emancipation, and through much of the twentieth century, blacks overcame racism, segregation, and Jim Crow to preserve their families. Herbert Gutman, in *The Black Family in Slavery and Freedom*,[11] found that in the early 1900s, blacks' marriages endured at about the same rate as those of whites of similar socioeconomic levels. He also notes that in both the North and the South, "the typical Afro-American family was lower-class in status and headed by two parents," and that even in Harlem, he found few female-headed families.

But for today's explosive black illegitimacy rate, slavery bears little responsibility. In *The End of Racism*, Dinesh D'Souza says, "The worst decay in the two-parent black family unit seems to have occurred not during slavery or as a result of slavery, but much later and for different reasons. Nor is there any evidence that as a consequence of slavery, blacks condoned illegitimacy as acceptable within the community. For the decline and fragility of the contemporary black family, the institution of slavery bears only a minor responsibility."[12]

Why don't organizations like the NAACP lead the charge against illegitimacy rather than concentrating on peripheral issues such as whether the Confederate flag should fly over the South Carolina state house, or how Webster's defines the word *nigger* in the dictionary? In the case of NAACP president Kweisi Mfume, perhaps the *Almanac of American Politics*[13] provides a clue. Before becoming president of the NAACP, Mfume served as a congressman from Baltimore. His entry in the almanac reads, in part, as follows:

The seventh district congressman is Kweisi Mfume, former councilman and radio talk show host, whose name echoes the rebellious Black Power movement of the 1960s, whose personal history is caught up in the social pathology that is at the root of the problems of the black underclass—and who himself has moved on from and above these aspects of the past. Mfume's original name was Frizzell Gray; he was 16 when his mother died, at which point he dropped out of school, held low-paying jobs, and fathered *five children out of wedlock* [italics mine]. Then he took control of his life and moved it in another direction. . . .

Mfume claims to have a good relationship with all of his children, and we have no reason to believe this isn't so. If Mfume would speak, often and bluntly, about his early irresponsibility, he could perhaps become an example of how one can seize control and reshape a life of irresponsibility. But his agenda remains stomping out racism rather than calling for personal responsibility.

Why does welfare damage families? After all, don't some families "need" government welfare?

The Heritage Foundation compared families on welfare versus families eligible for welfare but that, for one reason or another, refused to take it. The results were startling. Heritage reported:[14] "Young women raised in families dependent on welfare are two to three times more likely to drop out and fail to graduate from high school than are young women of similar race and socioeconomic background not raised on welfare.[15] Similarly, single mothers raised as children in families receiving welfare remain on AFDC longer as adult parents than do single mothers not raised in welfare families, even when all other social and economic variables are held constant."[16]

The Heritage Report further showed that children born outside of wedlock were more likely to engage in early sexual activity, and themselves have children out of wedlock. The report further stated, "Compared to children living with both biological parents in similar socioeconomic circumstances, children of never-married mothers exhibit 68 percent more antisocial behavior, 24 percent more headstrong behavior, 33 percent more hyperactive behavior, 78 percent more peer conflict, and 53 percent more dependency. Overall, children of never-married mothers have behavioral problems that score nearly three times higher than [those of] children raised in comparable intact families."[17]

Other studies have found that the best predictor of violent crime in a community is not race or economic status but the proportion of households without fathers. The fact is that, by a three-to-one margin, most juvenile and adult offenders come from homes without fathers.[18]

The results are simply common sense. Without the ideal of two good role models in the house, interacting with each other, going places with dad, watching dad and mom go off to work, a child grows up without a solid moral, spiritual, and financial foundation.

Even poor people agree. In 1985, the *Los Angeles Times* conducted a poll, asking poor people whether poor young women "often" or "seldom" have children in order to get on welfare. More poor people (64 percent) than non-poor (44 percent) agreed that welfare recipients "often" have children to get additional benefits.[19]

The Public Agenda Foundation, in 1996, also surveyed those on welfare. They were read the statement, "Welfare encourages teenagers to have kids out of wedlock," and asked to respond if the problem was "very serious," "somewhat serious," "not too serious," or "not serious at all." Once again, 64% of the respondents—who were themselves on welfare—said the problem was "very serious"![20]

Cleveland Works, is a government-supported organization that assists in getting welfare recipients off welfare and into the job market. Several years ago, I gave a speech before one hundred of their mainly female "clients." I said, "I know you love your children, but, looking back, how many of you would have chosen to become mothers when you did? If you knew then what you know now," I asked them, "how many of you would have had a child when you did?" Not a single woman raised her hand.

In *The Tragedy of American Compassion*,[21] Marvin Olasky traces the growth of welfare. During a mere three-year period in the 1960s, welfare rolls increased nearly 110 percent. President Johnson established "neighborhood centers," whose workers went door-to-door apprising people of their welfare "rights and benefits." We now see that they weren't "helping the needy," they were recruiting welfare dependents.

Until the so-called War on Poverty, the poverty rate declined steadily. At the turn of the century, nearly 70 percent of Americans were poor, but, by the time of the War on Poverty, the rate stood at approximately 13 percent. Then, after generations of declining poverty, the poverty rate more or less flattened out, and has remained so ever since. What happened? Welfare created dependency and decreased the incentive of the welfare recipient.

During the depression, overall adult unemployment stood at 25 percent, and the black rate at 50 percent. Yet, people balked at the prospect of going on welfare. The needy first sought help from relatives, then friends, then churches or other organizations. Most took any menial job offered, and a second or third job, if available. People took extraordinary measures to avoid accepting government assistance.

Of the pride and independence of Americans during the depression, Olasky wrote that there was "a remarkable unwillingness to go on the dole,"[22] because of the shame attached to it.

The people who grow up without knowing their fathers experience problems with intimacy. They show more difficulty in getting and staying married and in maintaining employment. The absence of a father affects the psyche. It is simply hard to love and trust when you don't see it growing up.

Reverend Jesse Jackson and Louis Farrakhan both come from

troubled family backgrounds. Jesse Jackson's mom conceived him with the married man next door. Jackson's father grew quite prominent in the South Carolina town where Jackson grew up, but the man never publicly claimed or embraced Jesse as his own. According to the book *Thunder in America*,[23] young Jesse Jackson endured taunts from other children, "Jesse ain't got no daddy."

Louis Farrakhan's mother had separated from her husband and taken up with a boyfriend, Louis Walcott. Despite her relationship with the boyfriend, Farrakhan's mother became pregnant by her estranged husband. According to a Farrakhan biography, *Prophet of Rage*,[24] this infuriated the boyfriend, and Farrakhan's mother attempted three times to abort Farrakhan with a coat hanger. But when his mother gave birth to him, she named him "Louis Eugene Walcott" and even listed her boyfriend as the father on the birth certificate.

Did the troubled backgrounds of Jackson and Farrakhan contribute to their determined, but often unsound, victicrat view of life? Did their troubled backgrounds produce an "us-against-them, take-no-prisoners" mentality? Who can say? But a bunker mentality frequently results from the necessary, protective shell-like defensiveness of a child aching for acceptance and love.

For Single Moms

Circumstances do not determine destiny. And most single moms turn out decent, law-abiding children, often without the assistance of the child's father. But pressures of time, energy, and money make it more difficult for a single mom to inculcate the values necessary to create a healthy, well-adjusted adult.

Many argue that values trump family structure in importance. Morgan O. Reynolds, director of the Criminal Justice Center at the National Center for Policy Analysis, reports that "Harvard economist Richard B. Freeman finds that church attendance is a better predictor of who escapes poverty, drug addiction, and crime than family income, family structure, and other variables.

"Other criminologists find that even under poor social and economic conditions, churchgoing serves as an insulator against crime and delinquency. These and other findings give evidence of the importance of character formation—teaching the difference between right and wrong and the value of morality."[25]

And a "Murphy Brown" child is another matter. A growing number of emotionally mature, responsible, and financially secure women wish to have children without marrying the father or choose to adopt on their own. Is this in the best interest of the child? The key is this: a safe, secure, warm, loving, hopeful atmosphere in which a child can put down loving roots and grow wings.

Who Pays: The Responsible Pay For the Irresponsible

In 1996, Congress passed the first major change in welfare in over a generation. The Welfare Reform Act of 1996 imposed "family caps" on welfare recipients, denying, in some cases, additional benefits if a woman on welfare had additional children. It also allowed states to craft "workfare" programs, imposing tougher conditions, including job training and seeking work, in order to get a welfare check. Different states imposed different programs, but overall the results bear out the theory that welfare begets dependency. Marian Wright Edelman, president of the Children's Defense Fund, called the bill "the biggest betrayal of children and the poor since the CDF began."

Writes Cato economist Stephen Moore, "The latest government statistics reveal that welfare caseloads have dropped an astonishing 46 percent since 1993. . . . The explanation for this progress is that welfare reforms in Washington and in the states have had a profound impact in reversing the perverse incentives of the Great Society welfare state."[26]

Wisconsin's Governor Tommy Thompson argues that no one should get a check without working. The number of households on welfare in Wisconsin fell from one hundred thousand in 1987, to under ten thousand today.[27]

Teenage pregnancy rates have plummeted following aggressive welfare reform. Three out of one hundred girls age fifteen to seventeen had babies in 1997, down 17 percent since 1991. Birth rates for black teenage girls over the seven-year period was down 24 percent, to seven births per one hundred girls. There were fewer teen pregnancies than would have been predicted without welfare reform, but without a corresponding increase in abortion! Different interest groups try to credit the reduction to abstinence education, or improved use of contraceptives.[28] But welfare reform means there's now a price to pay for non-productive, short-term thinking. Kids aren't stupid.

The poor were right when they told us that welfare is a trap. Its reversal has done just what welfare critics said it would: create incentives for self-sufficiency and personal responsibility.

How fair is the government's war on poverty to those who pay for it, especially those who waited to have kids until they achieved a level of emotional maturity and financial stability? They pay for the irresponsibility and self-indulgence of others. Is that fair?

Gloria Allred, the aforementioned feminist lawyer and radio talk show host, is a card-carrying member of the "it-takes-a-village" mentality. One day while on-air, she received a phone call from a distraught young woman.

The woman, almost in tears, asked Allred, what about me? I've not had children. I decided not to. I wanted to wait until I had the money to afford children, until I finished college. But now I've started working, and money is taken out of my wages to support women who have not made the choices I have made. What about *me*, Gloria? What do you have to say about people like me, people who have lived their lives responsibly, who waited until they could feed and take care of their children in the proper way? What about people like me, who made these kinds of personal sacrifices and are now paying for others who refused to make them?

I waited for the state-of-the-art emotional toe-tag liberal Democrat to give this woman a sincere, heartfelt, and persuasive response. Allred's answer? The federal government needs to increase its efforts at collecting child support.

What?

Memo to the feminists: Nearly all *divorced* women receive some child support. It is estimated that less than 10 percent of welfare moms successfully collect a dime from the biological father of their children (although most of the child support collected goes to the government, to partially offset the welfare paid to the moms). Women go on welfare in large part because the men who father their children do not support them. Many of the men lack skills, and, more importantly, lack the initiative to become providers. The real solution is a government that refuses to subsidize irresponsible behavior. Our government says to men and women: "Have children, however incapable you are of nurturing them, and you can expect taxpayers to pick up the slack." This provides an incentive for irresponsible male inseminators.

For kids and young adults, sex is a combination of danger and off-limits pleasure. Why restrain or engage in safe sex when government welfare shields the male and female from the true consequences of their actions? This provides a disincentive on the part of the young to refrain from premature motherhood and fatherhood.

Allred's caller felt betrayed by the crushing weight of government taxation. She resented the government transfer of her tax monies to another person who irresponsibly brought into the world a child she could not feed, clothe, or educate. The welfare state's response? "Sorry, but you're responsible for the irresponsible."

Needless to say, the caller did not sound persuaded. For bringing into the world a child that you cannot feed, clothe, and educate is the moral equivalent of a drive-by shooting.

Comedian Chris Rock jokes about biological fathers who brag, "I take care of my kids." Rock pauses, then screams, "You're *supposed to!!*"

Hear, hear.

6

THERE IS NO HEALTH-CARE "CRISIS"

In this richest of all countries there is a growing sense of personal vulnerability and personal insecurity because of the way our health care system has failed us. We cannot go on the way we have been going. . . . We do not have a system of health care in America, we have a patchwork, broken-down system.[1]

We can't go on like this, with a cost system that leaves 37 million people totally uninsured and thousands of others on the brink of catastrophe.[2]

This is not some abstract policy debate. This should be about one of the most important things in our lives—our health. And we're going to make sure the finest doctors will be here for you.[3]

I have met people in their 60s, 70s, and 80s who pay from $4,000 to $18,000 a year for prescription drugs on a fixed income. We don't want older Americans choosing between food and prescriptions.[4]

—First Lady Hillary Rodham Clinton

What Crisis?

Democrats, and to a lesser extent, Republicans, tell us we face a "health-care crisis." Thirty million Americans go without health-care insurance. Make that 35 million. Forty million. Now President

Clinton puts the figure at 45 million! A crisis of mammoth proportions! Somebody do something quick to make health care more "affordable." Health-care reformers also tell us that Americans spend a greater percentage of Gross Domestic Product on health care than, say, Canada and other countries. But, tell us, what is the "appropriate" amount to spend on health care? After all, what's more important than health? What's missing from their argument is that the amount a country spends on health care in no way tells us whether we spend the money efficiently or intelligently.

We all know what comes next—more government control, intervention, and regulation. Why, despite the best of government intentions, does the cost of health care continue to go up? What gives?

The answer is simple: the government does not trust the private sector to produce "affordable" health care, "accessible" to all. As a doctor once told me, with a straight face, "The normal laws of supply and demand do not apply to health care." It is precisely that kind of thinking that made health care more, rather than less, expensive, and less, rather than more, accessible. How arrogant.

"Pretty smug, Doc," I said. "So the laws of supply and demand apply to eggs, sweaters, and pocket calculators, but not to your august profession."

Furthermore, health care is complicated. There is interplay between insurance companies, doctors, hospitals, nurses, paraprofessionals, pharmaceutical companies, medical equipment suppliers, and patients. Yet, we somehow trust a government-supervised and -protected post office that operates less efficiently than do private carriers. We trust the government despite the government's control over public education, a monopoly resulting in three-quarters of inner-city children unable to read, write, and compute at grade level. Why, then, do we feel the government capable of running our complex health-care system more efficiently and cheaply than the private sector?

In the early years of the Clinton administration, First Lady Hillary Rodham Clinton tried a complete government takeover of our health-care system, patterned more or less after the Canadian system of socialized medicine that she much admired. The President gave a speech, waving a plastic card and declaring that someday all Americans will have to do is present this card to get "affordable" health care. Presto! Whammo! Voila!

During the "Clinton-care" push, the President placed First Lady Hillary Rodham Clinton in charge. I had a dream that, upon reflection, she would see the folly of her course and write the President a secret memo:

HILLARY'S RX

TO: President Bill Clinton
FROM: Ms. Hillary Rodham Clinton
RE: Health-Care Task Force
NOTE: Confidential Memo/For Your Eyes Only!

Bill:

Bad news. Forget about a health-care plan this year.

Learned a great deal over the last several weeks about our so-called health-care crisis in America. I will share my thoughts, but be warned that you may not like them.

OK, 35 million Americans don't have health-care insurance. But guess what. This does not mean they are without *health care.* Through government-supported health-care facilities, poor people do get treatment. They often line up in crowded emergency rooms, but they get treated, and the overall quality of the care is good.

On the other hand, 215 million Americans *do* have health-care insurance. Hope this doesn't get out, but some task forcers question the wisdom of scrapping a system that performs fine for 85% to "save" the other 15%.

Another thing: I just rechecked our pre-election polling data. Only 20% or 25% of Americans cited health care as a primary concern; most cared more about the economy. But now polls show a majority of Americans concerned about health care.

Could it be that CBS, ABC, NBC, CNN, and C-SPAN's "health-care crisis" bombardment stirred up dissatisfaction with a system most people liked? Odd that the same poll found that people were quite satisfied with their own doctor. (Nobody likes Congress, but people like their congressperson. Our schools stink, but parents love their own kids' schools. People!)

Something else. Remember that analogy between the Canadian and the American health-care systems? Yes, Canada does spend less than 8 percent of GDP on health care vs. our 14.5 percent. But we spend much more on our elderly population than the Canadians do. This kicks up the costs because 30 percent of health-care dollars for an individual are spent in the final year of life.

We have 6 million regular drug abusers, 30,000 homicides yearly, 200,000 diagnosed cases of AIDS, crack babies, and alcohol abuse costing more lost work time and money than any other drug. Twenty percent of adults still smoke, and among young women, cigarette smoking is *increasing.*

With hundreds of thousands of Jane Fonda workout tapes sold and Jenny Craig outlets popping up all over the place, Americans still overeat. Our consumption of fat, cholesterol, and sugar remains high. Most Americans get no or inadequate exercise. These are behavior-conscious acts that have precious little to do with greedy doctors, gouging drug companies, or an "indifferent government."

Another thing. Why, in a society of nearly 260 million Americans, are there only 500,000 doctors? We have twice that many lawyers. Well, it seems that the American Medical Association, with the support of overzealous state lawmakers, have artificially and intentionally limited the number of doctors produced by medical schools. For every med school applicant who gets in, many qualified applicants get turned down.

Even crazier, a lot of medical students who are accepted are from foreign countries. Med schools like them because, unlike American students, they pay full tuition—no grants or loans. Better yet, when they graduate, they go home—at least they're supposed to—posing no competition to the Yanks. Imagine what would happen if we dumped another 500,000 docs on the population? Next thing, they'd advertise, drive down prices, and end up driving cabs, just like some lawyers have had to do!

We also clip the wings of nurses and physician assistants, who, if laws allowed, could fix broken bones, prescribe drugs, conduct annual check-ups—all at a much lower cost.

We talked about price controls, but it is hard to find an economist who agrees with us. The only one I can think of is Laura Tyson, and she works for *us*. How can price controls work? Tell people they can only earn so much, and they ration their services, lower quality, or both. Limit what drug companies can charge, and they will spend less on research and development rather than cut their profit margin. This could kill one of the few American industries that still leads in the international marketplace.

Besides, the government already plays a huge role in health care. Did you know that through Medicare, Medicaid, and other programs, the government already pays nearly 40 percent of all health-care costs? Some even say that this heavy government involvement in health care has *caused* much of the rise in health-care costs. What about the dreaded malpractice-fearing "defensive medicine"? It adds maybe 1 percent or 2 percent to the bill. Ditto for "skyrocketing drug prices"—3 percent at most.

See, when people don't pay for things, demand soars. Last month somebody said, "When you're robbing Peter to pay Paul, you can always count on the support of Paul." At the time I didn't think it was funny. Yesterday I received a memo from a task force member. Turns out that last year health-care costs rose only about 4 percent—just slightly higher than the inflation rate. Trends suggest that our health-care costs are going *down*, not up.

In fact, many big companies and smaller companies have already joined to pressure doctors, hospitals, and drug companies to reduce prices, lest they take their business elsewhere.

So there you have it. An aging, health-care consuming population with bad health habits, an artificially depressed supply of doctors, and 40 percent of health-care dollars paid by taxpayers.

Given this, what's the best possible health-care plan? I'm afraid, Bill, we've pretty much got it.

One more thing—shred this memo.

—HRC

History

Three historical mistakes put us where we are now.

First, in the early 1900s, the American Medical Association urged Congress to license medical schools and to shut down all non-licensed medical schools, including those teaching the use of herbs and other "unorthodox" methods of treatment.

Early in the century, Congress complied and passed stringent licensing procedures, which resulted in the closing of numerous medical schools and a reduction in the supply of medical personnel. The American Medical Association, biased in favor of so-called allopathic doctors—"drug healers," who treat disease by remedies that produce effects different from or opposite to those produced by the disease—forced any and all other practitioners out of the game.

The result: selected doctors' incomes went up, while regulations blocked access to health care for many others seeking different types of treatment. This kept doctors' incomes high, while doing nothing to improve the overall health quality of the country.

Economist Milton Friedman calls the American Medical Association "perhaps the strongest trade union in the United States."[5] He says, "For decades it kept down the number of physicians, kept up the costs of medical care, and prevented competition with 'duly apprenticed and sworn' physicians by people from outside the profession."[6] It takes practically an act of God for a kid to become a doctor.

The medical profession also controls the supply of doctors. On a per capita basis, we have no more doctors now than we did seventy-five years ago! As the median age for Americans goes up, we can expect an aging population that voraciously consumes medical care. The laws of supply and demand would suggest more, rather than fewer, doctors. Yet the minting of new doctors trails the need for services.

The second historical mistake occurred during World War II, when Congress imposed wage freezes. Businesspeople who wished to attract employees had little recourse but to offer non-cash benefits. The government, recognizing businesspeople's "plight," allowed employers to deduct their premiums as a cost of doing business, while it did not treat the medical services received by the employee as taxable income. It seemed like a good deal for both. But it put, for the first time, a third-party payer between doctor and patient, distorting the traditional fee-for-service system used so successfully up until now. It also created the incentive to get your medical care through your employer rather than pay for it directly.

It's like this. I once had an apartment with utilities included. In my old apartment, during hot summer months, or cold winter months, I turned the thermostat off when I left the apartment and put on the heat or air when I returned. Once I moved into the "utilities included" apartment, I left my heat and air on all day, thus insuring a perfect climate when I entered the room.

Now, I knew that somehow I would pay, but that the cost would be distributed over all tenants in the building. So, the conscientious tenant who cuts off his or her air would, in effect, subsidize my carefree use of utilities. Eventually, we all pay, but the effect becomes gradual and diffused over a number of people. Similarly, with employer-provided insurance, and "hidden premiums," employees have less incentive to refrain from seeing doctors for minor reasons, and less incentive to watch and manage one's own health.

Third, the Medicare Act of 1965.

The Medicare Act of 1965 became the final neutron bomb

dropped on the medical profession. In the two decades before the enactment of the Medicare Act of 1965, a typical day in a hospital increased threefold. In the two decades *following* the passage of the Act, a typical day increased eightfold—far higher than inflation over the same period.[7] Besides, where does it say in the Constitution that the non-elderly must pay for the health care of the elderly? We don't pay for their car insurance, do we? Or homeowner's insurance?

But the government said that because certain people lack health care or accessibility or broader coverage, other taxpayers must supply it. As in so many government programs and activities, this one, too, lacked constitutional authority. The Constitution does not empower the federal government to spend the taxpayers' money on health care.

And, as usual, when Congress proposes a program, the ultimate price tag exceeds projections. A lot. For example, Libertarian Harry Browne writes in *Why Government Doesn't Work*, "The elderly now pay from their own pockets over twice as much for health care (after adjusting for inflation) than they did before Medicare began. And most older people now find it harder to get adequate medical service. Naturally, the government points to the higher costs and shortages as proof that the elderly would be lost without Medicare—and that government should be even more deeply involved.

"When Medicare was set up in 1965, the politicians projected its cost in 1990 to be $3 billion—which is equivalent to $12 billion when adjusted for inflation to 1990 dollars. The actual cost in 1990 was $98 billion—eight times as much."[8] The program has been on automatic pilot from the outset.

From time to time, Congress attempts to rein in the cost by imposing a fixed reimbursement schedule. This simply creates an incentive on the part of doctors and hospitals to schedule a lot of unnecessary tests, or to Ping-Pong the patient from specialist to specialist in order to evade the artificial limits. This also forces doctors and hospitals to charge more from private carriers to off-set the low reimbursement rates provided by Medicare.

So, everybody gets hurt: the elderly, because the medical profession becomes less efficient, less innovative, and less cost-effective, and the non-elderly, because practitioners charge them more to offset the lower reimbursement rates provided by the government. Government intervention, however well intended, became the catalyst for the formation of the dreaded HMOs, the health maintenance organizations. Practitioners and businesspeople set up these institutions to standardize health care and to provide lower costs. Many people quite properly complain about "business people" making medical decisions. But government rules and regulations so distorted the fee-for-service system that HMOs became necessary to standardize care and costs.

Regulation Hurts

For thirty years, my Uncle Thurman worked as a machinist at a Chevy plant in Cleveland. A gifted mechanic, my uncle fixed cars in his garage for his friends and neighbors. Whenever the machine at the plant broke down, the company called in a tech from headquarters. The tech would sit at my uncle's machine, manual in hand, and attempt to determine the problem. The tech never even asked my uncle his opinion, even though my uncle could have fixed the problem, if rules allowed it, and certainly could have identified it for the young white-shirted tie-wearing tech.

I once asked my uncle whether any tech ever broke the rules and said, "Excuse me, what do you think is wrong with this sucker?" My uncle said that the techs inevitably assumed the machinists to be formally untrained and, therefore, ignorant about the operation of a machine that they might have run for more years than the tech had been alive.

What does this have to do with health care? Well, my uncle's wife, Maggie, worked for years as a licensed practical nurse at a suburban hospital in Cleveland. For thirty years, my aunt worked in the maternity ward, assisting intern after intern on proper care and feeding of babies and, more importantly, on the appropriate drugs and what side effects the young doctors must guard against.

From time to time, interns would turn to my aunt and say, "Excuse me, nurse, what pills should I use for this?" or "What is the proper amount of cc's for this particular drug?" or "What would you advise?" Smart interns sought my aunt's advice because she knew more about drugs, dosage, and side effects than all but the most experienced doctors.

Suppose my aunt, based on her years of experience, decided to open up a pharmacy to dispense drugs. She could not, because she did not attend medical school, or otherwise possess the appropriate "credentials." The law forbids a "civilian" to open up, say, a clinic to fix broken bones. (Many non-doctors learned to fix bones on the battlefield. When such a person returns home, he or she cannot open up a "Harry's—We Fix Broken Bones" store.)

In some places, regulations prevent nurses and other paraprofessionals from fixing broken bones or performing physical exams. Doctors, through regulation, control many activities capable of being performed equally as well, and at far less cost, by other less expensively trained personnel.

While some states allow midwives to deliver babies, others make babies delivered by midwives a crime.

Think about it. Why does the government require all doctors to attend a licensed institution, to have the same years of training, no matter the area in which the doctor intends to specialize? Certainly, a brain surgeon requires years and years of sophisticated training. But, if someone wishes to set broken bones, for example, why require him or her to undergo the same expensive, lengthy medical training that more demanding specialities require?

But don't we need licensing to insure health care quality? After all, if anybody could open up a clinic, what protects the public?

The answer: consumer awareness and competition. Besides, some studies show medical malpractice may cost as many as 100,000 lives per year, with nearly that many dying from misusing prescription drugs. A board-certified New York OB/GYN carved his initials on the stomach of a patient. We've got bad docs now. Licensing does not prevent negligence.

Dr. Edgar A. Suter, the National Chair for Doctors for Integrity in Policy Research, says, "The 1990 Harvard Medical Practice Study, a non-psychiatric inpatient sample from New York state, suggests that doctors' negligence kills annually three to five times as many Americans as guns, 100,000 to 150,000 per year. With sad irony it has become vogue for medical politicians to claim that guns, rather than medical negligence, have become a 'public health emergency.' "[9]

How do most people get their doctors? Answer: word of mouth. Why recommend a doctor to someone? Answer: confidence in that person's ability.

Civil liability laws allow recourse for negligent care. Would you go to a doctor who did not carry negligence insurance? Most of us would not, so we would ask about insurance during the initial visit. Some people, however, would forgo a practitioner with insurance if it meant lower prices. Government, however, should let citizens make that call.

We didn't always have a heavily regulated health-care system. At the turn of the century, the United States enjoyed the world's lowest infant mortality rate, a standard by which many judge the quality of a country's health care. By the 1990s, the United States ranked nineteenth among nineteen developed nations on infant mortality.[10]

There are, no doubt, many explanations for this. But an open, free market health-care system unleashed by oppressive government regulation would make health care more affordable and more accessible.

Is There a Doctor Shortage?

Walk into your doctor's office. Notice anything missing? What about price lists? Where else do we go, whether shopping for groceries, clothing, or auto work, without knowing the price of the service? But a typical doctor's office contains no price list.

It is pointed out that doctors do this because a third party, whether insurance carrier or government, pays.

Still, you would think that some doctors would compete on prices and would post them, if only to show how competitive their prices are versus their competition. But, no. One reason is that America has an acute doctor shortage. That's right—too few docs. Not that the government sees it that way, mind you. In fact, the assistant secretary of health at Health and Human Services, Dr. Philip R. Lee says the opposite. He said the number of foreign-trained doctors doing residency in the United States has shown "a very dramatic increase in the last five years." Lee said America contains too many doctors, and seeks ways to restrict the number of residency positions available for new med school grads.[11]

Dr. Edward J. Stemmler, executive vice president of the Association of American Medical Colleges, agrees, saying "There is no compelling reason for medical schools to increase their size." In a report to Congress, a commission of health-care experts agreed with him, "The number of physicians exceeds, or will soon exceed, that required to meet national health-care needs."[12]

But a series of articles on the "doctor shortage" appeared in *Fortune* magazine. *Fortune* wrote, "The chance of joining the jobless is about as likely as contracting scurvy. 'For physicians, a job search is like dining at a gourmet buffet,' says Roy Huntsman, a management consultant to 200 doctors in central Florida. 'The choices, and the incomes, are fantastic.'

"A study by Merritt Hawkins & Associates, a Texas recruiting firm, found that 87% of America's 5,000 hospitals are urgently seeking doctors, and that 86% of all physicians in their last year of residency received 50 or more job inquiries, many of which led to offers. Says the firm's chief executive, Joe Hawkins: 'The reality is that there's no such thing as an unemployed doctor in America. But the myth of too many doctors dies hard.'

"The dearth of doctors is mainly a legacy of two glaring public policy errors: freezing medical school places and shutting out foreign doctors. . . . Urged on by state medical societies, state governments stopped building new medical schools. Worse still, almost all America's 126 medical colleges cut back enrollment. Ohio encouraged the cuts by providing the same level of funding for fewer students. Between 1982 and 1991, the number of medical school graduates *declined* 3% to around 16,000 a year."[13] States like Wyoming and others put together bonus and incentive plans in order to attract doctors.

The United States has not authorized a new for-profit medical school since early in the twentieth century. Recently, a man who operates a for-profit medical school in the Caribbean island of Dominica attempted to build one in Wyoming. He had scouted the country, noting that Wyoming's doctor shortage created ideal conditions for a for-profit medical school. He might as well have attempted to build an exotic dancing bar next to a church in downtown Casper. First, the local doctors screamed "murder." They warned of the lack of quality doctors produced by this man. Never mind that 92% of students graduating from his offshore medical school passed their U.S. basic level tests on their first try, a *slightly higher* rate than the U.S. and Canadian averages. And, never mind that the state of Wyoming faces a severe shortage of physicians, with only one doctor for every 642 people, compared to the national average of one doctor for every 441.[14]

Wyoming doctors and the national accrediting agency for medical schools successfully fought the proposed college. Doctors, quite properly, feared intruders on their competition-light field and put up roadblock after roadblock. Yet, doctors sanctimoniously tell us that they are protecting their role, calling themselves "guardians of America's health." No, all too often, doctors serve as guardians of their own income and will shut out competition, however damaging to the overall health of the country.

Meanwhile, doctors cry about government's micromanagement of their industry and complain about declining salaries. Still, the profession certainly remains attractive enough for medical schools to receive twice the applications for available admission slots. A recent Associated Press article said, "Despite doctors' fears that managed health care threatens their livelihood, their annual earnings have risen to an average of $200,000, the American Medical Association said. . . ." That was a rise in earnings of about 50 percent in ten years.[15] What does that tell you?

Remember the doctor who claimed that economics do not apply to medical care? Well, the doctor was right in this sense. The normal laws of supply and demand *don't* work in health care, precisely because government has intruded, regulated, mandated, dictated, distorting incentives all along the way. The doctor pointed out that a new kind of testing equipment, for example, leads to demand for it, thus inflating health-care costs.

"But why," I said, "does a patient automatically demand and get the newest, most cutting-edge testing device?" "Because," he said, "they want it." In other words, the health-care recipient will demand expensive procedures most likely because somebody else pays.

If you're looking at new stereo equipment, the latest stuff contains all sorts of fancy lights, bells, whistles, gizmos, and doodads. And, given the new features, the price exceeds that of "standard" equipment. Most of us, with finite resources, make choices and compromises, settling for less than the most expensive, since we can meet our needs by buying something a little less spiffy. Not so with health care, precisely because the recipient does not have finite resources, but rather the resources of the taxpayers.

So, no, the normal laws of supply and demand will not apply

here. This, in turn, invites still more regulation, always justified on the basis that "the normal laws of supply and demand don't work in health care." And the band plays on.

The Canadians Do It—Why Can't We?

The Clinton-care plan patterned itself after the Canadian system. After all, polls show that Canadians like their health care and its "universal access." Supporters of socialized medicine offer the Canadian health-care system as exhibit A for the "right way" to administer health care. Well, Great Britain also has a state-run health-care system, but when Margaret Thatcher needed surgery, she used private medical care.

But the tide appears to be turning. *Investors Business Daily* published an editorial, "It has taken 30 years for Canada's socialized health-care system, known as Medicare, to destroy what was arguably the second best health-care system in the world, next to the U.S."[16]

The *New York Times* reported that almost all of Toronto's obscenely overcrowded hospitals refused ambulances in January 2000. Polls show a growing number of Canadians willing to pay "user fees" to supplement their health care.[17]

Canadian patients cross the border to go to places like the Cleveland Clinic, where paying customers get state-of-the-art, cutting-edge medical technology. People in Canada wait in lines for hip replacements. According to an orthopedic surgeon in Ontario, the wait for an office appointment is four to eight months, and another twelve to twenty-two months for the surgery. So many Canadians head south of the border, and for ten thousand dollars they get a new plastic hip. The wait for cancer radiation treatments can be three to six months. This potentially fatal delay has prompted the Canadian government to contract with American hospitals to treat Canadian patients. Some contracts even include airfare, meals, and hotels, with Canada's state-run health-care system picking up the tab.[18]

One official, Alberta premier Ralph Klein, even suggests allowing American for-profit private clinics to come to his province, and letting the government pay them to perform surgeries that are unavailable, or only available after a long wait, in Canada.[19]

Sally Pipes, president and CEO of the Pacific Research Institute, wrote in *Investors Business Daily* that she saw billboards on Canadian roads announcing MAGNETIC RESONANCE IMAGING IS COMING, SUMMER 1999.[20]

MRIs came to America, too—fifteen years ago!

We often hear about the "inexpensive" nature of the Canadian health-care system. Well, how much does it cost? No one truly knows. Because of the complicated way resources are allocated and distributed, how do you tell?

The United States, critics say, spends nearly twice as much, by percentage of its gross domestic product on health care, as Canada. Would Americans accept Canada's health-care system? Again, what is the "appropriate" amount of the nation's GDP to spend on health care? What better item to spend one's hard-earned money on than maintaining one's health. And, as mentioned, after paying taxes to cover the vaunted "universal health care," many Canadians still come here and open their pocketbooks again, thus paying twice for medical care.

Canada's reported percentage of GDP spent on health care is likely understated because of the complex system in which some provinces underwrite a part of the overall price tag. Since that Canadian figure disguises all sorts of hidden costs, the actual percentage of health care–related GDP in Canada may exceed our own!

Predictably, the media do not report many stories on the increasingly creaky Canadian socialized medical system. Since so many in the media think health care a "right," they ignore spiraling costs and inefficiencies. But we ignore Canada's lesson at our peril.

The year 2000 presidential candidates, Republicans and Democrats alike, fall all over themselves to guarantee "access" to "affordable" care. Both urge still more regulation.

Also unreported is the experience of the state of Tennessee, a state that sought to provide "universal access." In 1994, Tennessee adopted Tenncare. Twenty-five percent of Tennessee residents belong. The state provided funds for uninsured Tennesseans. The plan is now virtually bankrupt, and a panicky Tennessee legislature now debates ways to shore up the system. Up next, a possible state income tax. Nice work, Tennessee.

But, again, the first argument against national health care remains the Constitution. It does not provide for it.

> **We, the People** of the United States, in Order to form a more perfect Union, establish Justice, insure domestic Tranquility, provide for the common defence, promote the general Welfare, and secure the Blessings of Liberty to ourselves and our Posterity, do ordain and establish this Constitution for the United States of America.

People often misinterpret the Constitution's Preamble that allows government to "promote the general Welfare." Some mistakenly interpret this as a carte blanche for government spending for, you name it, transportation, education, electrification, farming, utilities, water distribution, and so on. Unlike defense, which must be "provided," the Preamble says government may "promote" welfare, but only in ways *enumerated by and allowed for* in the Constitution. No carte blanche.

Even if the Constitution allowed a federal takeover of health care, socialized medicine destroys incentive, creates disincentives to productivity, and results in inefficiencies.

During the Clinton health-care "crisis," 560 economists wrote an open letter to the president, urging him to stop the madness. "Price controls don't control the true cost of goods. People pay in other ways," said an economist who helped gather the signatures. Those signing included Nobel laureate Milton Friedman, William Niskanen, formerly with Reagan's Council of Economic Advisors, and William C. Dunkelberg, a member of the National Federation of Independent Business. One signator even came from the liberal Brookings Institution.[21] This letter slowed down the president's march toward Clinton-care about as much as a speed bump slows down a drag racer.

Why? What's different about seeing a doctor versus seeing an auto mechanic? In both cases, you wish something fixed—a body in one case, a car in the other. In both cases, you rely on expert diagnosis and treatment to fix the problem. Yet, the government interferes far, far less in the auto mechanics industry.

On *60 Minutes*, a congressman put a bunch of Vermont senior citizens on a bus to Canada. There, the seniors found the cost for prescription drugs much lower than in the United States. The congressman demanded, and President Clinton went along with, a call for hearings to investigate why Americans pay more for drugs than do Canadians.

First, the Canadian government picks up much of the cost for drugs. Many of the Canadian drug manufacturers are subsidiaries of American companies. Are the subsidiaries making less money than their counterparts in the States? Of course not. They get paid. But the Canadian citizen does not directly bear the full brunt. They pay, however, through taxes, making the price *look* cheaper to the consumer.

Second, because the Canadian government discourages fair market value pricing, the Canadian pharmaceutical industry remains gaunt and weak compared to America's vital pharmaceutical business. The Canadian government simply removes the incentive to make a buck and, therefore, suppresses creativity and innovation. Is this a good trade-off for "cheaper" prescription drugs?

The price of an airline ticket, adjusted for inflation, declined after deregulation. The price continues to fall. Oil prices, too, decline, despite the 1973 "energy crisis," prompted by the Arab oil embargo. Even at nearly two dollars a gallon, gas prices, adjusted for inflation, remain at 1973 levels. But not so with medical care. Although there is some evidence that prices for many medical procedures are going down, the costs remain higher than would be the case under a completely private system. Even during the last recession, the average doctor's income increased, while incomes of other professions stagnated or decreased.

When Will Doctors Rebel?

Doctors are unhappy. I recently received a letter from a doctor disenchanted with the business of medicine. Here is an excerpt:

Dear Larry:

I have said repeatedly that until the patient becomes involved with their care in a fiduciary manner, the demand for care will continue to overwhelm the supply creating a backlog in patient care. Costs have been distorted by the insurance companies and the government. Medicare has truly distorted the picture. And still, the government continues to add to the confusion and redistribution of funds by suggesting that medications should be paid for.

Just a few interesting things to address in the future: 1) The administrative costs of health care run between 70% and 80% of the health-care dollar. 2) The patient's responsibility for the health-care dollar has decreased from 55% of the dollar in 1975 to 19% of the dollar in 1997. 3) The fact that government and large insurance agencies make health-care decisions completely distorts the concept of capitalism. Deciding a personal healthcare issue based on the "greater good" is socialist and is dangerous. The only way the patient will recapture their decision-making power is to assume financial responsibility. . . .

I have often said, "we are just too good." We continue to treat the poor like the rich; those who can't pay are treated no differently than those with great insurance. Economically speaking, we have driven the value of our services to ZERO when we do it for free over and over again. We are tired of the public's perception that we are rich. I can assure you. IT AIN'T SO.

When I present my colleagues with these depressing issues they shrug their shoulders and tell me that they are just too damn tired to try to change things. They feel defeated and depressed. Ironically, not too many years ago, this country is where the best and the brightest could be found. Now, admissions are down in medical schools. The government is paying medical schools to decrease their admissions. The tide has turned. The brightest aren't going to travel this road. When you and I are old enough to need special care, there will be a "C" student willing to work a 9–5 schedule deliberating life and death issues at our bedside. I shudder.

—Marcy L. Zwelling-Aamot, MD, FACEP

The government now picks up nearly 50 percent of our health-care dollar. The appeal for a health-care "safety net" is certainly understandable and emotionally satisfying. It is, however, without constitutional authority and, in the long run, will make Americans worse off and less healthy.

7

AMERICA'S WELFARE STATE:
THE TYRANNY OF THE STATIST QUO

The lesson of history, confirmed by the evidence immediately before me, shows conclusively that continued dependence upon relief induces a spiritual and moral disintegration fundamentally destructive to the national fiber. To dole out relief in this way is to administer a narcotic, a subtle destroyer of the human spirit. It is inimical to the dictates of sound policy. It is in violation of the traditions of America. Work must be found for able bodied but destitute workers. The federal government must and shall quit this business of relief. . . . We must preserve not only the bodies of the unemployed from destitution but also their self-respect, their self-reliance and courage and determination.

—President Franklin Delano Roosevelt, in his annual
message to Congress, January 4, 1935; in the
Congressional Record, 74th Congress

The number of people receiving public assistance more than doubled from 1960 to 1977. The money spent on public housing rose nearly fivefold in a decade and the amount spent on food stamps rose more than tenfold. Government-provided benefits in kind increased about eightfold from 1965 to 1969 and more than twentyfold by 1974. Whether measured in money terms, in real terms, or as a percentage of the nation's gross national product, welfare spending skyrocketed.

—Thomas Sowell[1]

We could give it all back to you and hope you spend it right. But . . . if you don't spend it right, here's what's going to happen.[2]

—PRESIDENT BILL CLINTON, EXPLAINING WHY THE FEDERAL GOVERNMENT KEEPS THE BUDGET "SURPLUS"

The powers not delegated to the United States by the Constitution, nor prohibited by it to the States, are reserved to the States respectively, or to the people.

—AMENDMENT X, THE BILL OF RIGHTS

The Justification of the Welfare State

The statist government view shared, for the most part, by both Democrats and Republicans, assumes a large government role in nearly every facet of our lives. Whether education, health care, transportation, charity, the statist view says, "Let government do it." Not only does the Constitution forbid the federal government from assuming these responsibilities, most state-run functions can and should be performed by the private sector. Professor William H. Peterson of the Heritage Foundation described what he called the "statist quo": "Like the sea monster Leviathan it's named for, government breeds rotten offspring: moral hazards, sweet-sounding 'social safety nets.' Leviathan thus makes bad situations worse, morphs Uncle Sam into Santa Claus, and drags down American character."[3]

Taking money from some and giving to other "worthy" recipients rests on this premise: that the welfare state is moral; it is right; it is just. Yet, those who argue a moral basis for the welfare state face an obstacle: the Constitution.

The Constitution is more than just a political document. It is more than just a philosophical document. It is a moral document. Founding Father John Adams said, "Our Constitution was made only for a moral and religious people. It is wholly inadequate to the government of any other."

The other well-known Founding Fathers—George Washington, Thomas Jefferson, James Madison, Alexander Hamilton, Patrick Henry—were all deeply religious men.

The Constitution, claim supporters of the welfare state, allows the government to establish a so-called social safety net. Why, then, did these religious, moral Founding Fathers fail to provide for a means to *pay* for this welfare state?

The Preamble to the Constitution says that the government shall "promote the general welfare." The Constitution then goes on to outline the specific and enumerated powers of the state. In other words, it goes on to say the government may promote the general welfare in specific ways and for specific reasons, *and no other.*

The Founding Fathers did not provide for a mechanism to pay for the modern welfare state. The Constitution said that tariffs and duties shall pay for the limited responsibilities and obligations of the federal government.

There was no income tax, under which our current government collects nearly $1.5 trillion. Today's welfare state funds not only constitutionally required obligations like defense, but non-constitutionally-sanctioned social programs such as Medicare, Medicaid, and Social Security. (Both Social Security and Medicare are funded by payroll tax, but a payroll tax is simply a sneakier and less offensive way of saying, "give the government part of your income.")

If the Founding Fathers believed in an activist government, one that pays for half of today's health-care dollars—surely they would have provided a means to fund these programs. But they did not. What does that tell us?

Is Government Welfare Necessary?

In 1871 a fire nearly destroyed the entire city of Chicago, yet, the city rebuilt itself *with virtually no government assistance.*

The mayor of Chicago put a nonprofit agency, the Chicago Relief and Aid Society, in charge of accepting and distributing the charitable contributions that poured in from all around the country. The police maintained order and attempted to keep looting to a minimum. But this was about the extent of the government's role.

Just two weeks after the fire, O. C. Gibbs of the Chicago Relief and Aid Society issued a circular to all Society personnel. The contents of that memo are worth quoting at length:

> Every carpenter or mason can now earn from three to four dollars per day, every laborer two dollars, every half-grown boy one dollar, every woman capable of doing household work from two to three dollars per week and her board . . . Clerks, and persons unaccustomed to outdoor labor, if they cannot find such employment as they have been accustomed to, must take such as is offered or leave the city. Any man, single woman, or boy, able to work and unemployed at this time, is so from choice and not from necessity . . .
>
> Give no aid to any families who are capable of earning their own support, if fully employed. . . .
>
> No aid should be rendered to persons possessed of property, either personal or real, from which they might, by reasonable exertions, procure the means to supply their wants, nor to those who have friends able to help them.[4]

The Society received some criticism for its arguably bureaucratic way of administering aid, but most observers called its work outstanding. The organization's meticulous record keeping and careful investigation of applicants helped to detect fraud, making sure beneficiaries truly needed assistance, unlike the "get-in-line, here's-a-check" mentality of today.

If the city of Chicago, now the nation's third-largest city, could rebuild itself without government assistance, why assume government is required for individuals to rebuild themselves?

Economist Thomas Sowell estimates that nearly seventy cents on the welfare dollar never gets to the intended beneficiary, having been gobbled up in administrative costs, like rent and salaries. Contrast this with the performance of nonprofits like the Salvation Army, where over eighty cents of the dollar gets to the intended beneficiary. Even if one believed in a government-provided social safety net, surely proponents must be concerned about the seventy cents on the dollar that is eaten up by the government costs in transfering the money from taxpayer to federal treasury to beneficiary.

Furthermore, unlike the government, charitable organizations like the Salvation Army require a commitment *from* the recipient in exchange for food, shelter, and clothing. A recipient must at least listen to a sermon on responsibility and spirituality and must agree to attempt to achieve some level of self-sufficiency. The Constitution's separation of church and state prevent government programs from even suggesting spiritual redemption and faith-based responsible behavior in exchange for benefits. "Get in line, here's a check."

One welfare worker told me that many welfare workers encourage dependency. This ensures their jobs.

In 1995, the Cato Institute (a nonpartisan public policy research foundation) published a study calculating the cash and non-cash value of welfare benefits in all fifty states, for a mother with two children. To compare these untaxed welfare benefits with a taxable payroll check from a forty-hour-a-week-job, they factored in FICA payroll taxes, state and federal income taxes, and federal earned income tax credit. The resulting wage equivalent of welfare ranged from a high of $36,400 for Hawaii, to a low of $11,500 in

Mississippi—exceeding even that of a minimum-wage job. The wage equivalent of forty states exceeds eight dollars an hour, and that of seventeen states is more than ten dollars an hour.

In twenty-nine states, welfare pays more than that state's average starting salary for a secretary. Nine states pay more than the first-year salary for a teacher. And the top six states pay more than the entry-level salary for a computer programmer.

The study concluded that, "For the hard-core welfare recipient, the value of the full range of welfare benefits substantially exceeds the amount the recipient could earn in an entry-level job. As a result, recipients are likely to choose welfare over work, thus increasing long-term dependence."[5]

But without government, will people help?

The Myth of the Stingy

President Jimmy Carter once called America the "stingiest nation on earth."

Some indictment. Especially for a nation that, for humanitarian reasons, sent men and women to die in Haiti, Bosnia, and Kosovo. America did the heavy lifting against Saddam Hussein during the Persian Gulf War, supplying the bulk of manpower, matériel, and management.

This nation fought and won the Cold War, standing up to the Soviet Union and Communist China by sending troops to North Korea and Vietnam. Americans give more foreign aid than any other country and frequently "forgive" the debt owed by Third World countries. Americans helped to rebuild Europe and Japan after the devastation of the war.

Josette Shiner, president of Empower America, points out that more than 80 percent of Americans belong to a volunteer association, and 75 percent of U.S. households report some kind of charitable contribution. Shiner writes, "Americans look even better compared to other leading nations. According to recent surveys, 73 percent of Americans made a charitable contribution in the previous twelve months, as compared to 44 percent of Germans and 43 percent of French citizens, for example.

"The average sum of donations over twelve months was $851 for Americans, $120 for Germans and $96 for the French. In addition, 49% of Americans volunteered over the previous twelve months, as compared to 13% of Germans and 19% of the French."[6]

America is the most generous nation in history. But many claim that America's "generosity" stems from the forced extraction of their tax monies by the government. If government didn't *require* "giving," would Americans voluntarily give?

Father Robert Sirico heads an organization in East Lansing, Michigan, called the Acton Institute. He argues that government intrusion in welfare diminishes the incentive to give, and suggests that people would "do the right thing" if government lowered taxes and expected people to help others.

Father Robert notes that 40 percent of taxes go toward social programs of one form or another. To allay the fears of those who think Americans stingy, he suggests the following plan. Allow taxpayers to direct 40 percent of their income tax to specific programs the individual taxpayer likes. On one's 1040, for example, the taxpayer could list various charitable organizations to which the money should go. This insures the same *amount* of money going to welfare. Father Robert, however, expects that, in the not-too-distant future, far less than 40 percent will be necessary. In 1994, the total federal, state, and local welfare outlay for a family of four averaged $35,756. But that total never reaches the intended beneficiary, since the federal government "loses" about 70 percent of the money in bureaucratic costs.[7] Father Robert envisions an amount far less than 40 percent currently necessary, because the private sector will help more efficiently and cost effectively than seen under government programs.

Care to reconsider, Mr. Carter? Americans are arguably the most compassionate, caring, and giving people in the world. We are especially giving when we are not being taxed to death. During the so-called Reagan "Decade of Greed," charitable contributions from corporations went up, as did contributions from individuals. Even though Reagan's lowering of the top marginal tax rate reduced the deduction value of donations, still Americans gave.

I envision horrified expressions on some reading this book. My God, the man advocates social Darwinism—"to the victor belong the spoils"; "kill or be killed"; "I got mine, you get yours." But what distinguishes humans from animals? Conscience. Empathy. Love. A fair, decent society does not let the innocent starve, the poor suffer, or the sick die. So the question is not whether to help, but how.

How Welfare *Should* Work

Sister Connie Driscoll and her partner, Sister Theresa O'Sullivan, run a shelter in Chicago for homeless welfare mothers and their children. The home is called St. Martin de Porres House of Hope. Eighty-five percent of the entering mothers are addicted to drugs. Only 5 percent of its alumni return to shelters, and almost all kick their drinking and drug habits.

According to a recent *Forbes* article,[8] Sister Connie initially thought people became welfare recipients through no fault of their own. "For the first couple of months after we started, I had the same rose-colored glasses as everybody else, thinking these poor people have been abused and victimized. After a while, you have to take the glasses off."

Her anti-government stance gets little support from the Catholic clergy. Why? With that attitude, they would lose funding, and Catholic relief services receive 74 percent of their budget from taxpayer dollars.

How does Sister Connie reinforce the message holding people responsible for their own fate? "We give every woman a job in the house the day she arrives, whether that's cooking, security duty, or helping Sister Theresa teach the children. That's only the beginning. The teaching here is constant. We're telling people who have had no budgeting experience, 'You can't buy your babies $90 shoes.' They're saying it's hip and cool. This is nuts, though. They have to give me 80 percent of their welfare checks and 50 percent of their food stamps. I put the money and stamps into a safe deposit box and return it when they're ready to leave so they have some savings for the first month's rent on an apartment.

"We teach them to pay rent, utilities, and food bills first, then prioritize what else they need. The word on the street is that ours is a tough house, probably the toughest in the city. Everyone's up at 6 in the morning, and in bed with lights out at 10:30 P.M. Children are in bed by 8:00 P.M. (9:00 P.M. in the summer). No men can visit. Other than a 3-½ hour pass to go for job interviews, the women always have somewhere to be: career or computer training, G.E.D. classes, Alcoholics and Narcotics Anonymous meetings, or at a job here in the House.

"The average stint is 7-½ months, and every day we talk about responsible sexual behavior, the dangers of illegitimate childbirth, and how to hold a job."

But are there enough jobs out there? "The work is there," says Sister Connie, "I see plenty of McDonald's 'help wanted' signs for $7.00 an hour along with a $100 signing bonus. The problem is not lack of jobs; it is bureaucracy and lack of accountability. The problem is not lack of jobs, but the inability of people to work and be responsible with a paycheck."

The effort, she says, must come from the community level. If government goes, people step in. Citizens stopped helping only when government took over. Few will tolerate starving neighborhood kids. But citizen motivation becomes difficult when people see government wasting money on ineffective programs or dependency-creating "safety nets."

And they think that the government is "taking care of it," however inefficiently. They have paid their taxes, so, asked to help some more, many think "I gave at the office."

At St. Martin's, alumni often come back to speak with residents. "These women are delirious to be off the dole and working and independent. People equate welfare with compassion, but compassion's got nothin' to do with it. A handout is the least compassionate thing you could do. Compassion means suffering with, doing with, being with. Teaching is 99 percent of what we do."

I had the privilege of interviewing Sister Connie on my radio program:

LARRY: Sister Connie, you know the line that the government's gotta be there because, if the government isn't there, people aren't gonna step up to the plate and do the right thing. When you hear that, how do you respond?

SISTER: I think that's absolutely false. I think the problem is that the government was there and people stepped out. Once the government gets out, then people will step back in again.

L. You've opened your home for welfare mothers and their children—the *Forbes* magazine article says that 85 percent of the mothers are addicted to drugs or alcohol. Your results are just mind-boggling. They're just extraordinary. What percentage of women who come to your home end up staying?

S. Most of them stay.

L. I would have thought that after you laid down the law, that a substantial number would say, "O.K., Sister Connie, I'm going somewhere else."

S. That happens very rarely. This is a very warm house. It's tough, but it's very, very warm. People who come in here know what they're coming into because the word on the street is that we're a very tough house, but we're a very loving house. If you want to get your act together, that's where you want to be. We turn away 50–60 people a day who want to get in here. Every-body knows who we are, so it isn't that they walk away once they know what happens here. They're here because they truly know they can get their lives together.

L. So you turn away 50–60 people because you don't have space?

S. That's correct.

L. 120 beds?

S. That's correct.

L. So the people who come to you are, I would think, really serious about getting their act together.

S. Not necessarily. Some are sent to us by the court system, and they're told that unless you get your acts together, we're gonna take your children away or you'll never get your children back if they're already in custody. So there is some resistance when they first come in, but after a day or two of being there, all of a sudden it dawns on them that this is where they ought to be.

L. The article says that you take 80 percent of their welfare check, and 50 percent of their food stamps and put it in a safe deposit box and give it to them when they're ready to go for first month's rent, utilities, and the like.

S. That's correct.

L. So in a sense, indirectly, in a way, you *are* getting government assistance, in the sense that government assistance is used by you to give them a start in a life outside of your Home.

S. Well, it's not used by us. It's their money. And we never touch it. What we're saying is, if you're going to get government money, you are going to save it for the purpose it was in-tended, and you are not just going to go out and spend it while we are feeding you and housing you for free.

L. Would you like to see a world where there is no government money and our taxes are lowered, and therefore people could give money to organizations like yours?

S. Oh, absolutely. I think that's what's happened over the past thirty years, when they're spending $5.5 trillion on programs that have absolutely failed! Certainly. Once we get rid of the welfare system, then the private sector can take over and people can then become responsible for their lives. Up to this point, they've been able to get their welfare checks, spend it as they wish, and end up homeless, anyway. Can you imagine having that many people come into one house in a large city and less than 1 percent are not getting welfare? Well, if they're evicted from their apartments, where did their money go? We all know where it went. That's what we want to end.

L. Tell me about the support, or lack of support from other members of the Catholic clergy.

S. Well, actually, we get a tremendous amount from other members of the Catholic clergy. That was sort of mixed up in the article. We don't ask the Church for any money because we feel the Church ought to be spending the money on education and other programs. But the Catholic community at large supports us. Of course, Catholic charities doesn't want me to talk about ending government money coming in, because they're heavily supported by government money. And we feel that the communities and the local churches, and not just Catholic churches but all churches, ought to step forward and do this work.

L. And you feel that their fear is unfounded and that if taxes were dramatically lowered, people would step up and donate money and the funding would continue?

S. It certainly would; there's no doubt about it. When you can operate a house as large as ours without any government money or any institutional Church support, you know people are stepping up to the plate. They're doing the job.

L. Give us, Sister, a typical day for one of the women in your house.

S. A typical day would be: rising at 6:00 A.M., getting themselves cleaned up, getting their children cleaned up, getting their areas ready, getting dressed, going into breakfast and getting their children off to school, either the public school or pre-school. Then they start their programs. They have chores to do. They have education, computer training, stress counseling, regular parenting and child guidance. Then, if they need to do something, they're allowed to go out on a 3-½ hours pass if they don't have a program going on at that time. In the afternoons, when their children come home from school, they are tutored by volunteers who come in and do tutoring. Then they get ready for dinner, have dinner, then go into AA and NA meetings. Then they're with their children before they go to bed at night.

L. In your opinion, why are these people homeless in the first place?

S. I think it's a matter of lack of accountability and personal responsibility, and the fact that government money can be had so easily, that they're able to lay back and get their money, and not do anything for it. I can't imagine putting out money without any accountability for how that money is spent. And that's the problem.

Sister Connie Driscoll
St. Martin de Porres House of Hope
6423 S. Woodlawn
Chicago, IL 60637

In *The New Politics of Poverty: The Nonworking Poor in America*,[9] author Lawrence Mead notes that fewer than one in seven welfare recipients claim not to be able to *find* a job! But today's welfare recipient, says Mead, considers low-end jobs chump change, too menial to consider.[10] Contrast this with the attitude of the poor during the Great Depression. Today's ready availability of welfare, even under welfare reform, sends a powerful message to the needy: the state rewards sloth.

I wince every time my father tells this story about me:

When I was entering junior high school, I saw an ad in the back of a comic book, "Sell Christmas cards, make money, win prizes." I desperately wanted the prize, a shiny, black Schwinn bike. So, with permission from my parents, I sent away for a huge box of cards to peddle to friends and neighbors. This way I earned points to purchase a bicycle.

Well, after a few weeks of hustling on foot, my dad felt sorry for me. He decided to advance me the additional money to get the bike. Afterward, I could reimburse him by selling the cards, an effort made easier since I could now bike to my customers.

Let me make a very long story short, and ask you this. Wanna buy a box of cards? That's right. The Christmas cards sat piled up in my dad's closet from the very moment I got the bike. The advance simply destroyed my incentive to sell the cards, since I had accomplished my goal—to get the bicycle.

One of the hardest things in life is to appreciate the value of something you got for nothing.

The Benevolent Uncle Sam

But didn't Big Government solve the depression and, through the Marshall Plan, help rebuild Europe? Doesn't foreign aid help Third World countries?

Only one thing clouds the view that the New Deal stopped the Depression, that the Marshall Plan rescued Europe, and that foreign aid benefits Third World countries: the facts.

Many credit Franklin Delano Roosevelt's activist government with solving the Great Depression. This false belief helps fuel support for Big Government. What most Americans know about the Depression is that things were bad, really bad. Furthermore, most Americans have a vague feeling that somehow, someway, government activism "pulled us out" of the depression. But most economists say government efforts failed to lift America out of the depression, and that much of the government's activism actually made things worse.

During the Depression, which lasted from 1929 until the Second World War, adult unemployment stood at 25 percent, and black adult unemployment stood at 50 percent. But bad government policy helped transform a recession into a depression.

First, the Federal Reserve Board tightened, rather than loosened, money supply. This was a poor decision that was completely avoidable.

Second, Congress passed the Smoot-Hawley Act, legislation that increased tariffs for goods imported into America. Other countries promptly retaliated, and walls of protectionism went up all over the world, exacerbating an already bad situation.

Third, President Herbert Hoover jawboned companies and their CEOs to keep wages high rather than to lower costs by reducing salaries or eliminating positions. And, finally, FDR passed all sorts of government-aid programs, including farm subsidies, the National Recovery Act, and Social Security, the last of which was subsequently expanded to include far more than the help for widows and orphans envisioned by FDR.

In reality, World War II "rescued" the world from the Depression. The war's aftermath resulted in the dismantling of trade barriers erected at the beginning of the Depression, the very trade barriers that deepened the economic plight. So, it is simply false to assume that, but for government, the Great Depression would have ruined capitalism.

In *Out of Work*, a book about unemployment in twentieth-century America, economists Richard Vedder and Lowell Gallaway say, "The common interpretation is that this Depression, this misery, this inequality, reflected rigidities and imperfections in the markets for goods and resources. Yet the evidence we have presented is more consistent with a far different story. The market, particularly the critical market for labor, was prevented from operating in a normal fashion by the interventions of government.

These intrusions turned a severe shock that started a recession into a major depression. Government failure, not market failure, was the problem . . ."[11]

And William H. Peterson of the Heritage Foundation says, "The Great Depression sprang from three fatal mistakes—the fed's jacking up of money-supply growth in the 1920s, which fueled the stock market boom; the Smoot-Hawley Tariff of 1930, hiking import duties to their highest level in U.S. history and inviting deadly foreign retaliation against U.S. exports; and the Revenue Act of 1932, hiking the top income tax rate from twenty-four percent to sixty-three percent."[12]

So, no, the Depression does not represent some colossal "failure" of the market, or "failure" of capitalism. No, government made a bad situation worse.

But didn't the post–World War II Marshall Plan play a critical role in rebuilding Europe? Doug Bandow, author of *Perpetuating Poverty: The World Bank, the IMF and the Developing World*,[13] says, false. Great Britain received the most Marshall Plan aid, he shows, yet recovered slowly. France, Germany, and Italy began to recover even before the Marshall Plan. Meanwhile, Japan received less aid, yet dramatically outperformed the European Marshall Plan recipients. Economist Tyler Cowen calls the Marshall Plan's "success" "a modern myth."[14]

Jeff Tucker, who edits the *Free Market*, is equally as blunt: "A year after the Marshall Plan began sucking private capital out of the economy, the U.S. fell into a recession, precisely the opposite of what its proponents predicted. Meanwhile, the aid did not help Europe. What reconstructed Europe was the post-Marshall freeing up of controlled prices, keeping inflation in check, and curbing union power—that is, the free market. As even [Paul Hoffman, the man Roosevelt put in charge of distributing the Marshall Plan] admitted in his memoir, the aid did not in fact help the economies of Europe. The primary benefit was 'psychological.' Expensive therapy, indeed."

Tucker continues, "The actual legacy of the Marshall Plan was a vast expansion of government at home, the beginnings of the Cold War rhetoric that would sustain the welfare-warfare state for forty years, a permanent global troop presence, and an entire business class on the take from Washington. It also created a belief on the part of the ruling elite in D.C. that it could trick the public into backing anything, including the idea that government and its connected interest groups should run the world at taxpayer expense. Moreover, the Marshall Plan did damage. Over the next five years, 'Marshall money' would corrupt nearly every Christian Democratic Party in Europe, turning them into carbon copies of the U.S. Democratic Party. Those political parties in turn worked to create monstrous welfare states and regulatory controls that continue to hinder European economic growth today."[15]

But surely, foreign aid assisted many Third World countries in getting on their feet? Again, false. As with domestic welfare plans, foreign aid turns out to create dependency while stunting growth.

Author Bandow, for instance, says, "Since World War II, the United States alone has provided $1 trillion (in current dollars) in foreign aid to countries around the world. The result? According to the United Nations, 70 countries, aid recipients all, are poorer today than in 1980. An incredible 43 are worse off than in 1970."[16]

What went wrong? The pillars of economic prosperity are basic: democracy, rule of law, property rights, and free enterprise. Corrupt totalitarian regimes, single-party states, and military dictatorships run and thus ruin many Third World countries. "Free money" somehow seems to disappear in the hands of these corrupt leaders, with the remainder misspent on big public works programs and other ego-driven look-what-I've-done-for-you-lately projects. The dictator says to the people, "Look at the money I've secured for you." And this creates a disincentive on the part of that country's citizens to struggle for personal and economic freedom, the true path to economic self-sufficiency.

Does Government Welfare Work?

In 1910, before England's massive welfare state, there were 26,877 registered mutual-aid societies, and some estimate there were at least as many unregistered ones. These charitable organizations provided people with medical care, aid to orphans and widows, burials, and other benefits. When, however, England decided to federalize welfare, the number of mutual-aid societies plummeted. Taxpayers undoubtedly felt that, since the government took over aid to the needy, individual assistance was no longer required. And, since individuals saw taxes going up to support a welfare state, they felt less inclined to give more on top of that which the government already extracted.

Unfortunately, history provides us with "guinea pig" nations to test the effectiveness of the welfare state. Following the Second World War, Taiwan became an economic powerhouse, while Communist mainland China lagged behind. Before the fall of the Berlin Wall, West Germany dramatically outperformed East Germany, although both are peoples with the same background and history. Look at North Korea versus South Korea. Again, same people, same background, same history, yet South Korea dramatically outperforms the North. After Fidel Castro took over Cuba, many fled to Florida, creating engines of economic prosperity.

Today, Uncle Sam has spent more to "combat poverty" than it would have taken to purchase all of the Fortune 500 companies as well as all the available farmland in America.

Massive amounts of money failed to turn Appalachia, one of America's poorest regions. Over thirty-five years, the federal government's Appalachian Regional Commission spent $7.4 billion trying to improve this impoverished area.[17] Still the unemployment rate for those living in the Ohio part of Appalachia hovers at 6.3 percent—about 35 percent higher than the rest of Ohio—with some regions, like Morgan County, Ohio, registering a staggering 12 percent unemployment rate.[18] Guess no one suggested, I don't know, perhaps, like moving?

Nearly three million Americans live in public housing. But all too often public housing complexes serve as learning centers for Crime 101. Residents fear for their safety, with children serving as willing and unwilling pawns for teenage and adult criminals. Many people in public housing also fail to learn the kind of appropriate behavior and respect for property that makes them attractive to a private-sector landlord. And private landlords get deprived of income-producing properties as they compete with the public housing facilities, part of which landlords subsidized through their own taxes! This is nuts.

The Skinners live in my parents' Los Angeles neighborhood. Bob, a postal worker, and his wife, Ruth, a retired school librarian, decided to invest in a small apartment building around the corner from their home. After upgrading the property, and investing a lot of money and sweat equity, the Skinners kept the apartment building almost fully rented. A few years later, however, the government, through HUD, built a subsidized "affordable" public housing complex nearby. Soon, prospective tenants told them, "We're gonna wait and see if we qualify to move into public housing." This forced the Skinners to scramble even harder to find qualified tenants. Now the Skinners essentially compete against themselves. After all, their taxes helped to build the very housing project now robbing them of tenants.

Doing the Wrong Thing

The Republicans' and Democrats' answer to urban poverty? Programs, regulations, and government agencies.

When Democrats are not giving money directly to local politicians to "fight poverty," Republicans push for dead-letter "solutions" like enterprise zones, designed to encourage investment by lowering or eliminating taxes. But, low taxes, while important, remain just one variable a businessperson looks at in selecting a location for a plant, office building, or facility. A corporate head seeking relocation looks at the quality of the workforce, the eagerness of the workforce, the willingness of the workforce to work hard and accept responsibility for success or failure. Employers fear hiring those who may run to the EEOC or a civil rights lawyer should he or she get fired. In addition, a CEO looks at regulation, crime, and access to restaurants and other employee-friendly facilities.

And, if businesspeople choose not to invest in the inner city, why should taxpayers subsidize them to do so? Sooner or later, property values will decline enough to make it cost-effective for someone to buy and build.

Finally, people are starting to get it. One liberal-leaning magazine recently criticized the "federal program mentality" to rebuild Harlem: "A generation of black elected officials—Representative Adam Clayton Powell, Jr., and local Democratic leader J. Raymond Jones ("the Harlem Fox"), among others—pinned Harlem's economic hopes not on investment, but on federal antipoverty programs, which, instead of spurring growth, ended up mostly stifling it. Urban renewal projects took over large swatches of land and razed them, but, bogged down by political wrangling, they often failed to construct anything new."[19]

Who said that? Newt Gingrich? No. Trent Lott? No. Ronald Reagan? No. Tamor Jacoby and Fred Siegel, writing for the mostly liberal *New Republic*. And, on enterprise zones, often enthusiastically supported by government, they state, "The challenge for both Clinton and Congress is to design programs that minimize bureaucracy and political interference, leaving the market as free as possible—not so much for ideological reasons but because in the long run, only genuinely market-based investment will take root and connect places like Harlem to the mainstream economy."[20] Hello. Is anybody awake in the beltway?

The article quotes a veteran nonprofit investor, who said, "The government displaced the private sector and destroyed any semblance of a free market economy."

Labor lawyer Peter Kirsanow discusses the failure of jobs programs, despite taxpayer money exceeding $16 billion per year. Kirsanow says, "Federal job training programs have varying degrees of success. The effectiveness of many is marginal at best. Others simply compound the unemployment problem with a waste of taxpayer money. There is little evidence that the effect of government training programs upon employment is more than trivial."[21]

Of the Comprehensive Employment and Training Act (CETA), Kirsanow finds "no significant, sustained effect upon employment or earnings."[22]

What of the Job Training Partnership Act (JTPA)? Kirsanow says, "[Those] programs have been somewhat more successful. However, at least one study showed that the number of young JTPA trainees receiving food stamps and general assistance doubled after their involvement with the program. Furthermore, JTPA involvement may have actually reduced the earnings of male participants who are out of school."[23]

Kirsanow concludes, "A payroll tax on employers to fund yet another job training program is nothing more than a hiring tax. Taxing employers in this fashion reduces the amount an employer can spend on new hires, wages and its own specifically tailored training programs."[24]

The federal government subsidizes college education in the form of student loans. Yet, since the advent of direct student loans, the costs of attending college dramatically exceeded inflation. What incentive does a college administrator have to hold down costs when he or she knows the government guarantees a certain minimum?

Not content with the already substantial government involvement in higher education, President Clinton recently pushed for "hope scholarships," providing fifteen hundred dollars' worth of tax credits for education. And, get this, the secretary of education then wrote college administrators, asking that they refrain from hiking tuition in anticipation of the "hope scholarship" money! The secretary's letter, then, all but acknowledges the upward pressure on prices caused by "free" government money. Well, duh.

The government monopolizes public education. The result? Test scores that rank American students near the bottom in science, math, and geography. Excellence usually does not occur without competition. When three-fourths of inner-city kids cannot read, write, and compute at grade level, the answer lies in more competition. The government, through inefficiency, mismanagement, and lack of profit incentive, simply cannot perform as effectively, efficiently, and creatively, as can the private sector.

The government gives mortgage interest deductions to homeowners. Why? Owning a home, says the government, is a good thing. Well, if so, why do we need government subsidies to get people to do good things, things people should do to pursue their own self-interests. Besides, do renters contribute less to the health and well-being of society?

Through the Federal Emergency Management Administration (FEMA), government provides funds to victims of natural disasters. In some cases, FEMA gives monies to allow homeowners to rebuild homes in flood-prone areas. If a farmer lives in an area termed flood-prone, shouldn't that farmer carry insurance? Or, more shocking, farm elsewhere?

But Without Government, Won't the Rich Get Richer,
and the Poor Get Poorer?

Americans agree that a 100 percent welfare state—Communism—doesn't work. But, for some reason, we believe that we know just the appropriate blend of private enterprise and Socialism. We agree that too much is bad, but we somehow can't find ourselves to agree that as little as possible is best.

I recently had a conversation with a friend, Gwen, whom I've known for nearly thirty years. She said, "So, Larry, what should be done with the surplus?"

I said, "I think it should go back to the taxpayers."

"So, you believe in giving this windfall to the rich."

I almost lost it. "Oh, so you buy into that horse-bleep as well. Let me ask you this. Of the top 1 percent of taxpayers, what portion of the tax pie do they contribute?"

"What do you mean?"

"Let me rephrase that. Of the tax pie, the slice paid by the top 1 percent of taxpayers represents what percentage of the whole pie?"

Gwen got a little nervous. Obviously, the proportion, she thinks, must be high. Otherwise, Larry wouldn't be saying this. "I would guess," she said, "about 10 percent."

"No, Gwen, try more than 32 percent."[25]

"Wow!"

"Now, of the top 10 percent of taxpayers, what percentage of the tax pie do they contribute?"

"About 30 percent."

"No, the actual figure is 62.4 percent"[26]

"Wow!"

"Now, Gwen, what is the minimum amount of *money* you must earn to be among the top 10 percent of taxpayers?"

"Gee, I don't know. I, uh, uh . . ."

"C'mon, give me a number."

"Okay, two million dollars."

"Well, Gwen, you are slightly off. The minimum amount of money one must make to be in the top 10 percent wage of tax-payers is roughly seventy-five thousand dollars."[27]

"Wow."

"Gwen, 10 percent of the taxpayers pay 62.4 percent of the taxes. So, you're damn straight that a tax cut would benefit "the rich" as we define "the rich.""

"Wow."

Gwen's ignorance on who pays the taxes, what percentage they pay, how we define "rich," is typical. Articles on tax cuts versus debt reduction versus shoring up the safety net rarely discuss who pays the taxes and how much. Thus, the ease with which a liberal Democrat can accuse Republicans of pushing tax cuts for "the rich." Indeed, 40 percent of working Americans pay little or no taxes at all, a built-in constituency reliably opposed to or indifferent toward tax cuts since, after all, they benefit "the rich."

Of course, any tax cut would benefit "the rich." They're the ones paying the frigging taxes! My friend, Gwen, mind you, is nobody's fool. She is near retirement, raised a child, and worked in the legal field all her working life. She was, however, completely unaware of who paid the taxes, how much, and how the government defines "the rich." If someone like Gwen doesn't know, that puts all of us, to paraphrase George Bush, in "deep voodoo."

President Clinton says he refuses to support a tax cut that he "cannot pay for." That *he* cannot "pay for"? Get it? According to that line of thinking, it's the government's money, not ours. And, taxpayers, therefore, must "pay for" the privilege of getting some of it back!

A little history. Congress and the courts repelled the first attempt to impose an income tax, ruling it unconstitutional. Only after state legislatures amended the Constitution, in 1913, did Congress impose the federal income tax. The initial tax rate? One percent. And this was levied only on incomes greater than $20,000 (equivalent to $300,000 today). A maximum rate of 7 percent applied to incomes over $500,000 (equivalent to $7.5 million today).[28] Fast forward—today's top marginal rate stands at 39 percent with the state, local, and federal governments take, counting mandates, at nearly 45 to 50 percent—an all-time high.

President Clinton once said about welfare, "We are changing the rules so thousands of poor working families won't be denied food stamps, as they are today, just because they own a reliable car. We're also going to get rid of some of the old reporting rules and launch a national campaign to make sure that working people know there is no indignity in taking public assistance to help feed their children if they're out there working 40 hours a week."[29]

Really. Where does the Constitution say that you can have as many children as you want, whether or not you can afford them, and that taxpayers will pick up the slack?

Besides, the "poor" in America aren't really as "poor" as people think. The National Center for Policy Analysis tried to find out exactly how much money the poor spend. The poorest 20 percent, said the organization, reported receiving an average income of $6,395 in 1993. When tracking the expenditures of these poor, however, the analysis found that they spent an average of $13,957.[30] Now, how can you spend over $7,000 more than you receive? Well, "freebies" such as food stamps and public housing aren't counted as "income." And many poor may work under the table, doing work for cash to supplement their income, be it actual wages or public assistance.

According to a 1992 Census Bureau report, 92.2 percent of "the poor" own color televisions, 60 percent own microwaves, 7.4 percent have personal computers, and 41 percent own their own homes—70 percent of them with no mortgage. In fact, American "poor" live better than many non-poor in wealthy European countries: A greater percentage of American poor own more VCRs than the non-poor in all European countries except the United Kingdom, more dishwashers than the non-poor in the Netherlands,

Italy, and the United Kingdom, and more microwaves than the non-poor in every European country.[31]

But, are the rich getting richer and the poor getting poorer? While in junior high school, I ran the fifty-yard dash, in an anteater-slow time of 7.2 seconds. My friend Keith, one of the faster runners, came in at 6.5 seconds. As the semester progressed, I got faster, finally running the fifty in under 7 seconds, at 6.9. But Keith got even faster, beating me with a time of 6.1. So, the gap between Keith and me widened, even as I ran faster. But was I worse off, having run a 6.9 versus a 7.2, since Keith's times improved even more?

Our obsession with the gap between the rich and the poor is frequently an expression of envy and resentment. Poor people, by virtually any measure, are better off now than ever. Besides, when people talk about the gap between rich and poor, ask this question. What is the *appropriate* gap? Surely those that bemoan the "widening gap" must have some figure in mind.

Moreover, evidence suggests that the "gap" is overstated. Generally, surveys looking at this "gap" ignore the amount paid in taxes by the so-called rich, while ignoring the value of non-cash benefits received by the poor. Robert Rector and Rea Hederman of the Heritage Foundation examined the top fifth and the bottom fifth of households. First, they noted that the top fifth had more adult, working-age family members in it than did the bottom fifth. Thus, the top fifth seemed artificially more wealthy since more income-producing people existed in families in the top fifth. They adjusted for this, as well as deducting taxes from "the rich" and adding non-cash income to the poor. After adjustments, the income gap went from $13.86 earned by the rich, for every $1 earned by the poor, to $4.23 for the rich, for every $1 for the poor.[32]

The Welfare State and Education

Investment banker Ted Forstmann decided to do something about the dismal state of public education. He, along with others, put together a fund to allow some forty thousand poor, inner-city kids to apply for scholarships. The scholarships would enable the parents to remove a child from a dysfunctional government school and place the child into a private or parochial school of the parents' choosing. The program proved so popular that 1.2 million applied for the positions![33] What does this tell you about the dissatisfaction with the public schools?

The Cleveland School Board passed a limited voucher program in which, through a lottery system, a small number of "disadvantaged students" could use vouchers to opt out of government schools.

Unfortunately, the Cleveland Voucher Program proved so popular that more than 17,500 families applied for the 3,500 available positions.[34] The winners' joy didn't last long. On the eve of classes, a Cleveland judge issued an injunction temporarily banning the use of tax dollars for parochial schools. The appellate court removed the injunction, yet the entrenched public education establishment, especially the unions, remain a staunch opponent to vouchers.

On August 29, 1999, *Fortune* magazine editor Jeff Birnbaum discussed the Cleveland school voucher controversy on C-SPAN. Birnbaum chatted amiably about the case, and said, "Just the day before the school system was supposed to open up, a federal court judge initially said—but then reversed himself—originally said that that voucher program was unconstitutional because it was mixing church and state . . . that the public taxpayer-paid money should not go to supplement, to pay for parochial or religious educational institutions, and that was a problem that he thought was so bad that the whole program, at least initially, should have been tossed out. But he came to that choice so soon before school was opened . . . they decided on this compromise . . . that could be the beginning of the phasing out of that program, depending on what higher courts say."

Then, something extraordinary happened. A caller phoned:

"Good morning, how are you? Thank you very much for taking my call. I'm a Libertarian, so I'm calling on the Moderate line only because I'm neither liberal nor conservative and I read the *Pittsburgh Tribune Review*. I was struck by your comments regarding school choice with the Cleveland program and also money coming into charter schools now. Where in the United States Constitution do we authorize our federal government to be involved in education in any way, shape, or form? In fact, doesn't the Tenth Amendment prohibit our federal government to be involved in this and if so, how can both Liberals and Conservatives [Republicans and Democrats] continue to spend our money on something that the constitution clearly *does not allow?*"

What followed is the vintage, standard, conventional, current, "caring," "compassionate" beltway view of life.

Birnbaum, the *Fortune* editor, smiled with sort of an "Oh, it's one of those guys" kind of knowing smiles, then said, "Well, I'm not sure that the Constitution anywhere doesn't allow spending of money for education or for that matter for anything else. I think there's been a long history of federal assistance to education and a variety of other programs that states or localities could very well and do mostly fund, but the federal government is also involved and I think will be for a very long time." Hold the phone.

Grab your Constitution, dude. The Founding Fathers hated big government. The Founders hated King George. A tax revolt—the Boston Tea Party—sparked the nation's revolution. And that was over a tax of approximately 1 percent! The Constitution lists specific duties, responsibilities, and powers of the government. It enumerates them. Again, anything not enumerated flows to the states via the Tenth Amendment.

The point is not to ridicule people like Mr. Birnbaum. He

certainly seems intelligent, competent, and articulate. He likely feels that government involvement, if well intended, improves the quality of life and somehow levels the playing field. Of the federal government's role in education, Birnbaum says simply, "I think there's been a long history of federal assistance to education . . . and I think will be for a very long time." Some justification.

Rachel Scott was one of the teenagers killed in the Columbine High School shooting tragedy in Littleton, Colorado. Her brother, Craig, survived. Their father, Darrell Scott, addressed a House Judiciary Committee's subcommittee. He urged that the schools allow children to pray in school. "We do need a change of heart and a humble acknowledgement that this nation was founded on the principle of simple trust in God!

"As my son Craig lay under that table in the school library and saw his two friends murdered before his very eyes he did not hesitate to pray in school. I defy any law or politician to deny him that right!

"I challenge every young person in America and around the world to realize that on April 20, 1999, at Columbine High School, prayer was brought back to our schools. Dare to move into the new millennium with a sacred disregard for legislation that violates your conscience and denies your God-given right to communicate with Him."[35]

Assuming Mr. Scott seeks mandatory prayer in public schools, the Supreme Court ruled against this decades ago. But Mr. Scott is certainly right that he should have chosen where his children attended school. And if he preferred a school with mandatory prayer, he should have that option. Government schools force-match student and school, and are constitutionally prohibited from doing many things that parents think best for their children such as corporal punishment and prayer.

Many pundits offered reasons for the Columbine shooting tragedy. Here's another. Suppose parents picked their children's schools. Do you think the shooters, Eric Harris and Dylan Klebold, would have attended a religious school, the type Mr. Scott wanted for his children?

Perhaps under parental choice, Rachel Joy Scott and her killers would never have met.

For a PBS television special on public education, I interviewed Nobel laureate economist Milton Friedman. I asked whether government possessed the power to tax taxpayers for education. Friedman said, "Your question really is whether the *federal* government possesses the power to tax taxpayers." He then said, "No, the federal government has no power whatsoever to spend any tax dollars on education. Now, will any Supreme Court justice agree with me? No. But, based on how the Founders drafted the Constitution, with its doctrine of limited powers, as well as the reservation clause, the Constitution provides no basis for the federal government's role in education. None."

Teaching is hard, far more difficult than, say, delivering mail. Considering that the private sector outperforms the public sector in parcel delivery, why should we expect the federal government to demonstrate more effectiveness in education, a task far more complicated than sorting mail? Private schools, contrary to popular belief, are actually cheaper than public schools. Nationwide, we spend approximately six thousand dollars per child, with private schools spending a little more than half that. So, taxpayers spend twice the money for an inferior "product."

Furthermore, people who opt out of public education must, through taxes, continue to support the very school system they reject. And, even if you have no children, government still requires you to support this system.

As a percentage of the general population, more public school teachers have their kids in private schools than do the rest of us. As a percentage, members of the House of Representatives Black Congressional Caucus are more likely to have their kids in private schools than blacks not in Congress. And members of the Hispanic Congressional Caucus are more likely to have their kids in private or parochial schools than Hispanics who are not members of Congress. What does that tell you?

Think about it. Government lacks the profit incentive, the very spark that promotes efficiency. In the private sector, if things are not managed properly, people lose their jobs. Shareholders lose money. Shareholders don't *like* losing money. And no one has invented a better way to lose money than to fail to please customers. Yet the "customers" of public education, students and parents, suffer with virtually no recourse.

The Nanny State

For many, welfare means subsidies for the poor. Whether farm subsidies, mortgage deductions, college tuition loans, federal emergency funds, federal school subsidies, welfare for the non-poor vastly exceeds welfare for the poor. Government regulation increases the costs of doing business by mandating inefficient business practices.

Adolf Hitler launched a war against cigarette smoking and sought to confiscate all guns. In *Hitler, Great Lives Observed*, it says that if Hitler's "people had found that he intended after the war to prohibit smoking and make the world of the future vegetarian it is probable that even the SS would have rebelled."[36]

We quite properly call Hitler's regime totalitarian. But Americans accept government invasion in other areas of private conduct—cigarette smoking—as an example of enlightened big government intervention. In one Northern California city, laws bar people from smoking in public parks! What's next? Americans' intake of meat and sugar? Don't laugh. Yale University professor Dr. Kelly Brownell believes that government should tax fatty, unhealthy foods to discourage their consumption. Said Brownell, "To me, there is no difference between Ronald McDonald and Joe

Camel." He thinks the government should subsidize fruits and vegetables, to make them dirt cheap, but tax foods containing too many calories or grams of fat, so that people will think twice about their food purchases, knowing a Twinkie will hurt your wallet once you reach the cash register.[37]

To justify regulation, the government frequently flat-out lies. The Centers for Disease Control called AIDS an "equal opportunity" disease, capable of afflicting any of us. Ads showed middle-class white teens discussing AIDS, although they fall within the group least likely to contract the disease. The CDC admitted it exaggerated the extent to which those in non-high-risk groups could contract the disease. Still, they justified the lie because of good intentions. "The aim was, we thought we should get people talking about AIDS and we wanted to reduce the stigma," said the CDC's Paula Van Ness.[38] Since the government did not wish to "demonize" those in high-risk groups, the PR campaign misled the public into thinking AIDS an "equal opportunity" disease. It is not.

Dr. Walter Dowdle, a virologist who helped create the CDC's anti-AIDS office, conceded, "As long as this was seen as a gay disease or, even worse, a disease of drug abusers, that pushed the disease way down the ladder" of people's priorities. Thus, the Centers for Disease Control *admitted* deceiving the public. John Ward, chief of the CDC branch that tracks AIDS cases, said, "I don't see that much downside in slightly exaggerating [the AIDS risk]. Maybe they'll wear a condom. Maybe they won't sleep with someone they don't know."[39]

The government tells us that 400,000 people die each year from cigarette smoking. Really. Turns out the figure comes from a computer-generated model. If, for example, an eighty-year-old man who smoked dies, the government considers his death to be smoking related. If the eighty-year-old guy dies from a brain aneurysm but smoked, he goes on the 400,000 person pile. Fifty percent of the 400,000 dead live beyond age seventy-five, and another 70,000 live past age eighty-five. Did they "die too soon"?

Robert A. Levy is an expert in law and finance who teaches statistics at Georgetown University Law Center, and Rosalind B. Marimont is a retired mathematician and scientist who spent a 37-year career at the National Institute of Health and the National Institute of Standards and Technology. They studied the alleged 400,000 smoking death figure that the government claims result annually from cigarette smoking. Their conclusion?

"To be blunt, there is no credible evidence that 400,000 deaths per year—or any number remotely close to 400,000—are caused by tobacco. Nor has that estimate been adjusted for the positive effects of smoking—less obesity, colitis, depression, Alzheimer's disease, Parkinson's disease and, for some women, a lower incidence of breast cancer. The actual damage from smoking is neither known nor knowable with precision. Responsible statisticians agree that it is impossible to attribute causation to a single variable, like tobacco, when there are multiple casual factors that are correlated with one another. The damage from cigarettes is far less than it is made out to be.

"Meanwhile, do not expect consistency or even common sense from public officials. Alcoholism contributes to crime, violence, spousal abuse, and child neglect. Children are dying by the thousands in accidents, suicides, and homicides. But states go to war against nicotine—which is not an intoxicant, has no causal connection with crime, and poses little danger to young adults or family members."[40]

Similar research has shown the same sort of problems for the government's figures on secondhand smoke-related problems. The government tells us that thousands of people die each year through secondhand smoke. Ever read an obituary column or death certificate that says, "Old Joe died from secondhand smoke"?

A term describes the EPA's assertions about secondhand smoke: junk science. Federal Judge William Osteen, in an opinion, blasted the EPA's secondhand smoking death figures. "EPA publicly committed to conclusion before the research had begun: adjusted established procedure and scientific norms to validate its conclusion, and aggressively utilized its authority to disseminate findings to establish a de facto regulatory scheme to influence public opinion."[41]

For years after the energy crisis ended, government regulators insisted on maintaining—for safety reasons—a fifty-five-mile-per-hour speed limit. But careful study of the pluses and minuses of the fifty-five-mile-per-hour speed limit does not justify the government's euphoria. On a per capita basis, more Americans travel on the roads now than ever before. Yet, for a number of reasons, driving fatalities fell from 2.5 per 100 million vehicle miles in 1986 (when the fifty-five-mile-per-hour speed limit was in effect) to 1.7 in 1994. The fifty-five-mile-per-hour speed limit cost Americans a great deal of valuable, now wasted time.

Scientists disagree about the existence and significance of global warming, yet Vice President Al Gore, in his book *Earth in the Balance*,[42] flatly states, "Those who for the purpose of maintaining balance in the debate [over global warming] adopt the contrarian view that there is significant uncertainty about whether it's real are hurting our ability to respond."[43] The *New American* magazine[44] interviewed Dr. S. Fred Singer, head of the Washington, D.C., based Science and Environmental Policy Project. He teaches at George Mason University, in Virginia, and served as the first head of the U.S. Weather Satellite Service. An atmospheric physicist, Dr. Singer wrote *Hot Talk, Cold Science: Global Warming's Unfinished Debate*.

Q: Do you have a position regarding global warming?
A: I certainly do. The climate warms and cools naturally all the time. It changes from day to day, month to month, season to season, year to year, and so on. At times, there is global warming; at other times, there is global cooling. Some climate changes are predictable and some are not. We can predict that the winters are colder than the summers because we un-

derstand the mechanism. We cannot predict the climate from year to year, however, because we do not know why it fluctuates. When the climate warms, there could be a number of reasons for it doing so, including the sun. Another possibility is that human activities are adding greenhouse gases to the atmosphere, and this could produce warming.

The important question then is: How important is the effect of human activities? And that we cannot tell. We know the theory, which says that human activity could be important, but the theory cannot be trusted until it has been verified. Until now, this theory, which is based largely on a mathematical model, has not been validated against observations. If the theory becomes validated against observations, then we can be more confident about using it to predict the future. But we're not there yet, and nobody should be basing conclusions and remedies on an unverified theory.

Q: What do the scientific data really show about global warming?

A: Data from earth satellites in use since 1979 do not show any warming. But, eventually, they probably will because carbon dioxide and other greenhouse gases are increasing in the atmosphere. My personal guess, and I stress that this is only my guess, is that there is a greenhouse effect and that it is very small in comparison to natural fluctuations of the climate. We don't see this effect yet, but we may notice it in the next century. Even if we do notice it, it will be extremely small and actually inconsequential. It will be an interesting scientific curiosity but it won't be of any practical importance.

Republicans, despite their message of limited government and personal responsibility, happily invite the government to determine the contentious, religious, moral, spiritual, and personal issue of abortion. Based largely on religious views, opponents of abortion ask the government to stop a practice many deem not only offensive, but criminal.

Democrats, who largely support "a woman's right to choose," resent government intrusion and interference. This issue, they argue, turns on a woman's religious and moral convictions and with advice and counsel from her physician. Government, say the Democrats in this case, should butt out.

Neither party truly believes in maximum personal and financial freedom. Neither side comes to the argument with clean hands. How dare the government, say the Republicans, tell a businessman what to do. But it's perfectly O.K. for some pro-lifers to demand that government require a woman carry her unborn to term, no matter her financial condition, physical condition, ability and maturity, or, for some, whether the pregnancy resulted from incest or rape.

Democrats condemn the "Republican right wing" for holding that party hostage to its "pro-life zealots." But the same party ruthlessly condemns those who oppose affirmative action, campus speech codes, and hate crime legislation which requires delving into the private thoughts and opinions of the suspect.

My own view? Abortion remains the nation's most vexing issue since slavery. It is part religious, part spiritual, and part moral. I don't know the answer to the "question" of abortion. *But neither does the government!*

To those who dislike abortion, I say this: If you are opposed, don't have one.

And to the mostly pro-choice Democrats, I say this: Did you stand up when the government passed laws requiring motorcycle helmets, laws requiring seatbelt use, laws requiring smoke detectors, child safety locks on guns? Did you cheer when the government seized 50 percent of the country's health-care business? Did you high-five as the government successfully weakened legal business like the gun industry and the tobacco industry? If you did nothing, or cheered as the government seized rights and property, then you invited, indeed encouraged, the government to inject itself into the issue of abortion. Next time you wish to complain, seek out the nearest mirror.

A little experiment. Which of the following statements came from *The Communist Manifesto* by Karl Marx and Friedrich Engels and which from *It Takes a Village* by Hillary Rodham Clinton?

1. "Other developed countries, including some of our fiercest industrial competitors, are more committed to social stability than we have been, and they tailor their economic policies to maintain it."[45]

2. "As a society, we have a choice to make. We can permit the marketplace largely to determine the values and well-being of the village, or we can continue, as we have in the past, to expect business to play a social as well as an economic role."[46]

3. "Does wage-labor create any property for the laborer? Not a bit. It creates capital, i.e., that kind of property which exploits wage-labor, and which cannot increase except upon condition of begetting a new supply of wage-labor for fresh exploitation. Property, in its present form, is based on the antagonism of capital and wage-labor."[47]

The answer? Item 3 came from the *The Communist Manifesto*. The other two, well, you know.

Funny, the Soviet Union collapsed because of a command-and-control elitist-run economy. American politicians feel they intuitively know the "correct" mix of capitalism and command-and-control. Europe, in the last ten years, created virtually no new private sector job because of a rampant initiative-destroying welfare state. Yet, as mentioned, our smaller, but still significant, welfare state somehow, some way, has struck just the right balance between personal freedom and government control.

Again, politicians feel that a Communist government's 100 percent takeover is too much, but our 40 percent is j-u-s-s-s-t right. What nerve.

One could stock a library with shrill books predicting this or that apocalypse. An apocalypse, that is, unless government rides to the rescue to save us all.

Rachel Carson's *Silent Spring*[48] is one such book. Despite her wrongheaded warnings, based on a distrust of industry and capitalism, the environment continues to improve.

Professor Paul Ehrlich wrote *The Population Bomb*,[49] where he argued that more people meant less food. No, corrupt governments mean less food. Free markets, rule of law, and democratic principles create prosperity. What about *The Communist Manifesto* by Karl Marx and Friedrich Engels, or *Das Kapital* by the same distinguished gentlemen? The fall of the Berlin Wall in 1989 pretty much removed those books from any best-seller list. Earlier in this decade, Ravi Batra wrote *The Great Depression of 1990!* to which I say, "When?" Ditto Howard J. Ruff's *Survive and Win in the Inflationary Eighties*. People who ran out and bought gold because of Ruff's wild prediction of inflation got hosed.

Assume, for the moment, that I am right—that a market as free as possible, combined with low regulation and limited taxation leads to prosperity. Accept this, for the moment. Does this, then, necessarily translate into a society that is *happier*? Yes.

Happiness means different things to different people. More important, at any given moment in time, people may respond differently. If I have just had an automobile accident, and sustained a crushed vertebra, I'm not that happy. If I have just received a raise higher than expected, I might respond differently.

There's a better way to check. Watch people's feet. Are people leaving their country or staying put? Are others trying to get into that country? I know only a handful of people who have moved out of America to live somewhere else. Some retirees on fixed incomes have moved to places like Poland or Mexico, where they can live life very well. But did they move to Poland in their prime income-earning years? No. Did they move to Poland when they were in their twenties, thirties, forties? No.

Foreigners scale the walls to get into this country. Immigrants, both legal and illegal, dream about entering and "making it" in America.

Are people in socialist countries happy? No one says socialism is synonymous with unhappiness. People of inherited wealth in socialist countries might very well be happy. But excessive regulation and taxation clogs upward mobility. People at the top—especially those who did not earn their wealth and are, therefore, less angry when so much is taken away—have it pretty much made. A guy with an idea, a screwdriver, and some duct tape in a garage, a Steve Jobs or a Bill Gates type, does not nearly have the chance to "upset the establishment" and make a buck. But people like Jobs and Gates find an open market, shoot-'em-up wild, wild West, kill-what-you-eat culture invigorating and empowering.

As for those, however, at the bottom in those countries, their hopes, dreams, and aspirations get dampened by those protected at the top. When asked his definition of happiness, President Jack Kennedy offered what he called the Greek worldview: "The full use of your power along the lines of excellence."[50] Socialism stops this. In totalitarian countries, hopes, dreams, and aspirations get retarded, if not destroyed, by the protected elite class.

Bottom line. Does government possess the wisdom, maturity, power, right, and judgment to take money from some taxpayers and give it to others? Take your pick: government schools, Medicare, Small Business Administration, Head Start, DARE program, farm subsidies, food stamps, FEMA, direct student loans, public housing. They deliver services less efficiently and less humanely than the private business and private charitable sectors.

Still, the defenders of big government say, "Well, at least our hearts are in the right place." As for their heads . . .

Abraham Lincoln did not say the following, but he should have. Written by Reverend William J. H. Boetcke, it is often erroneously attributed to Honest Abe:

- You cannot bring about prosperity by discouraging thrift.
- You cannot help small men by tearing down big men.
- You cannot strengthen the weak by weakening the strong.
- You cannot lift the wage-earner by pulling down the wage-payer.
- You cannot help the poor man by destroying the rich.
- You cannot keep out of trouble by spending more than your income.
- You cannot further the brotherhood of man by inciting class hatred.
- You cannot establish security on borrowed money.
- You cannot build character and courage by taking away men's initiative and independence.
- You cannot help men permanently by doing for them what they could and should do for themselves.

Who knows? If we continue to ignore Boetcke's advice, someday we may wake up and pick up our morning newspaper to read:

A USELESS Law

Today Congress approved the three hundred billion dollar Universal Support Enablement Law for Evaders of Suitable Skills, known as the USELESS bill.

USELESS supporters call the measure's passage a statement to people with no work skills, bad attitudes, poor personal hygiene, that they, too, are Americans. The program is open to "any individual who can—but won't—work, whether due to laziness, self-pity, or bad attitude."

The USELESS passage delighted the chairman of the Democratic National Committee who, during the New Hampshire primary, called the measure a centerpiece of the year 2000 presidential campaign. "I know a lot of people who don't like getting up on Mondays. People who stay up too late, who drink too much, and sleep too little. We should honor those who refuse to submit to the Internet era."

USELESS seeks to close the gap between the rich and the poor, the skilled and the unskilled, the motivated and the unmotivated. "Many people," said the chairman, "lead lives of intellectual stupor. They watch Jerry Springer and smoke Winstons without filters. They think Picasso is something you order from Pizza Hut. They drink out of glasses that originally came with grape jelly. They eat at Sizzlers, bowl on Tuesdays, and say things like 'boo-yah' or 'what's u-u-u-u-p-p-p?' Somebody needs to be there for them."

A quarter of a million USELESS volunteers will be paid twenty-five dollars an hour, plus benefits, to search for and identify the indifferent, the lackluster, and the lazy. Volunteers are instructed to approach those not working and say, "Stand up. You count, too. That's why God invented microwave popcorn, the remote control, and the living room sofa."

USELESS participants will receive vouchers enabling them to purchase goods, products, and services they are simply not interested in working to acquire. Program sponsors say fraud will be kept to a minimum because the lazy and indifferent lack the energy and creativity to cheat the system. "It's the best of both worlds," said Hillary Rodham Clinton. "The critics say that giving money to the lazy, dumb, and stupid provides a disincentive to learn, grow, or educate. But every day contributions are made by those who are confused, disorganized, and dysfunctional. Except they call it Congress."

Even Republican George W. Bush yielded to the measure's popularity. "Life can be cruel to somebody who doesn't like working. We had a cousin, Irving, who didn't like to work. Gee, I remember in those long ago, less-sensitive days, we just hollered at him and told him to get a job. Oh, he did, but he held it against us for a really long time."

USELESS tax incentives will be awarded to employers who hire those with slovenly work habits, low self-esteem, and poor personal hygiene. Obsessive attention to profits and to corporate image, say USELESS sponsors, denies rights to those without taste, fashion sense, or social skills. "I was out of work a long time," said Ed Trucker, a former St. Louis airport baggage handler. "People complained that I smelled funny. I admit I never bathed or showered, but I don't trust the fluoride they put in the water. Makes me itch. But now, with this new law, there's a light at the end of the tunnel."

USELESS, which goes into effect on April 1, prevents landlords from requiring security deposits, mortgage lenders from seeking collateral, and employers from requiring employees to show up and perform as a condition of compensation. "We shouldn't create two classes of citizens—those who are punctual and those who are not," said Ms. Clinton. "Just because you come to work late, or don't show up at all, doesn't mean you can't contribute. What would have happened to the play, *Waiting for Godot*, if Godot had shown up on time?"

The measure also outlaws intrusive personal questions during job interviews, such as, "Did you bring a résumé?" "Have you worked before?" or "Why aren't you wearing pants?"

The measure excited Wally Dipstick of New Brunswick, Maine, who calls himself "an auto mechanic who's never actually worked on a car." Dipstick cheered after becoming USELESS eligible: "Finally, there's something for somebody like me. I graduated in the bottom half of my class. It's guys like me who make the top half possible. You get rid of unmotivated persons like me, how would you separate the winners from the losers?"

Said Ms. Clinton, "With this USELESS law, we can finally bridge the horrible gap between people with initiative and those who couldn't care less. Just because you're willing to get up early, stay late, and work harder does not entitle you to special privileges. For those of you out-hustled, outsmarted, and out-performed by money-motivated colleagues—USELESS says that you are not useless."

8

REPUBLICANS VERSUS DEMOCRATS—
MAYBE A DIME'S WORTH OF
DIFFERENCE

. . . I'm not part of the problem.[1]
—BILL CLINTON, PRESIDENT OF THE UNITED STATES

Republicans' favorite exercise is running for the hills.
—ECONOMIST THOMAS SOWELL

Same Difference

A phenomenon of today's electorate is the large number of voters who declare themselves "independent," or who refuse to identify with either party. A lot of people simply find that the differences between the two parties are so small as to be nearly irrelevant.

Oh, Republicans and Democrats do differ.

Republicans wish to take a pocketknife to a problem that requires a machete. The Democrats ask, "What problem?"

The Democrats see no problem—the "health-care crisis," the alleged gap between the rich and the poor, racism, sexism, the "crisis in childcare," falling educational standards—that cannot be solved with still more government. On social issues, they purport to believe in freedom—until someone says or does something politically incorrect. Then Democrats call for campus speech codes; laws against "hate crimes" (which, I think, punishes thought); and affirmative action, which insults the very concept of equal protection under the law.

Republicans propose less spending and typically call for less government than the average Democrat. Many Republicans, however, urge the Supreme Court to outlaw abortion; call for voluntary prayer in public schools; want flag-burning banned; refuse to allow gays to serve openly in the military; and call for, along with some Democrats, laws prohibiting the legalization of same-sex marriages.

The Democrats spend our money freely, while Republicans propose less spending, but not much less. Democrats distrust the private sector to act responsibly and thus call for active regulation by government agencies such as the FDA, the FAA, OSHA, and others. Republicans claim to exalt the private sector, but that party, too, embraces an activist government. Republicans control Congress, but subsidies for farmers still flow. Republicans routinely vote for ethanol subsidies. A Republican senator urges protectionist measures to shield steel industries in his state from cheap "dumped" foreign steel.

There is a word for "mainstream" Democratic ideology. It is *Socialism.* And "mainstream" Republicans ideology? *Socialism-lite.* Many GOP-ers are socialists as well, only with better PR. Republicans cringe at excessive regulations, but do not call for the abolition of those "offensive" regulatory agencies. Republicans whine about "irresponsible" or "vague" regulations without screaming for the shutdown of the "irresponsible" agency.

As for the creation, growth, and continued existence of the welfare state, both Democrats and Republicans have blood on their hands. Both believe in minimum wage, farm subsidies, the

Tennessee Valley Authority, the Department of Education, the Department of Energy, FEMA, Medicare, Medicaid, Social Security, government schools, "enterprise zones," government-backed college loans, block grants, urban renewal, and the income tax.

The Constitution created a government intended to stay out of our bedrooms and out of our wallets. How do Republicans and Democrats stack up against a true ten-point contract with America, a contract that calls for maximum personal freedom built on a foundation of personal responsibility?

The Ten-Point Elder Plan

1. **Abolish the IRS—Pass a National Sales Tax**—Also known as the "Let's Make Tax Lawyers and Lobbyists an Endangered Species Act." A simplified tax code gives lobbyists little to lobby about. A low tax rate spurs people to work harder without resorting to schemes to "shelter" income. At the turn of the century, government took about 10 percent of the national income. Now, it takes nearly 40 percent. Low taxes means higher productivity and greater job creation. Let's welcome *any* move to reduce our tax burden, whatever form it takes.

2. **Reduce Government by 80 percent** Less than 2 percent of Americans are farmers, yet the Department of Agriculture adds still more bureaucrats. And what exactly does the Department of Commerce do? Do we need the Small Business Administration? Amtrak? The Tennessee Valley Authority? Department of Education? Before 1950, the government largely stayed out of the housing business. Now we have housing projects in all of our major cities. They have become sewers of crime and drugs. The government, an absentee landlord, couldn't care less. The private

sector can build housing more cheaply, with an incentive to maintain the property and screen tenants.

3. **End Welfare, Entitlements, and Special Privileges**   Welfare for the poor works out to a national average of $12,000 to $13,000 a year (cash and non-cash) per recipient. Why work at minimum wage? Why worry about impregnating someone when the government shields you from financial responsibility? But welfare for the non-poor, or entitlements, are five times as bad. This includes Social Security (the average recipient has put in fifteen cents for every dollar he or she takes out), Medicare, tuition tax credits, farm and dairy subsidies, tobacco subsidies, as well as government ownership or control of airports and utilities.

4. **Abolish the Minimum Wage**   A low-paying job remains the entry point for those with few marketable skills. The minimum wage hurts the so-called hard-core unemployable by forcing an employer to pay more than the fair value of labor. Every time the government raises the minimum wage, thousands of entry-level jobs get destroyed.

5. **Legalize Drugs**   Legalization does not mean approval. America spends at least $20 billion a year to fight a losing battle against drugs. (Research by William F. Buckley places America's direct *and* indirect costs of this "war" at more than $200 billion a year.) Experts say that worldwide, the annual drug trade may be as high as $500 billion! "Just say no" ain't gonna stop that. The drug trade provides an economic incentive for children and teens to drop out of school and earn fast money. It accounts for 50 percent of all street crimes and perhaps 30 percent of the prison population. Tax drugs, and use the money for drug treatment and additional police protection. Drug legalization would free up prison spaces, vacancies that could be used to lock up violent criminals. What about the harm to society? Drug abuse would have to in-

crease well over fivefold to match the deaths caused by cigarette smoking (allegedly 400,000 a year).

6. **Take Government Out of Education** Before the mid
1800s, elementary and secondary education (except for
slaves) was largely parent financed. Today, taxpayers spend
more than $6,000 a year per student, more than virtually
any other country, including Japan. With what result? Poor
test scores, high dropout rate, kids incapable of filling out
employment applications. Why can't the private sector assume this responsibility? Let's cheer anything, including
vouchers, that takes us in this direction.

7. **Drop the Davis-Bacon Act** This little-known act compels
contractors bidding on government jobs to pay union
wages. This cuts out competent, non-union workers willing
to work for less. This hurts minorities, many of whom were
for years discriminated against by unions.

8. **Eliminate Corporate Taxes** The government taxes corporate profits and re-taxes the dividends, taking money
otherwise used to reduce prices, pay higher dividends, pay
higher salaries, or invest in research and development.
More corporate investment means more jobs.

9. **Charity from People—Not Government** During the
1980s, the "decade of greed," charitable contributions by
corporations and private citizens increased by at least 30
percent! Why? People had more disposable income, paid
fewer taxes, and therefore gave more away. Americans are
among the most generous people on Earth. But people
want their money to go to people and organizations that
they choose and trust.

10. **End Protectionism** How many people know that Japanese
trucks and minivans cost $2,000 more due to import tariffs?
Government-mandated "price supports" force consumers

to pay more for milk. Government goodies for the tobacco and sugar industries stiff consumers. Congress imposes a mind-boggling array of rules and regulations to protect declining, inefficient businesses, while taking money away from new ones.

Our government gets bigger and bigger, and spends more and more of our money. This destroys the incentive of the hard-working, while creating a class of people dependent on government, many of whom could become productive, contributing members of our society.

So-called liberals no longer demand equal rights, but equal results. Thus the call for affirmative action, set-asides, and race- and gender-based schemes to "level the playing field." Discrimination as an antidote to discrimination.

The question is not whether we should help those who, through no fault of their own, cannot cope. The question is *how* should we help. The libertarian-minded believe that individuals can and will help other individuals with more efficiency and compassion than can the government. But how do you expect people to be generous when the government already takes away 40 percent of the earnings of a typical middle-wage earner?

It isn't necessary that you be in perfect agreement with this plan. Alert, engaged minds will never be in 100 percent agreement. But I'm willing to bet that you agree with my philosophy more than with either the Democratic or the Republican Party.

We *can* agree that a good government is a small one and that government's most important function is to protect its citizens. One look at both the tax and crime rates tells us that the government has failed in its most essential responsibility. Incumbent politicians obviously don't get it. Let's clean 'em out and elect those who do.

The Welfare State Crime Blotter

Democrats and Republicans frequently talk about "common ground" and "working together." All too often, the ultimate goal remains the same. Take money from one person, and give it to another. Regulate. Tax. Subsidize. Control.

Some examples: "Staunch conservative" Dan Quayle teamed up with Ted Kennedy to create the Job Training Partnership Act (JTPA) out of the ashes of another failed government make-work program, the Comprehensive Employment Training Act (CETA). At the time, Quayle talked about the importance of "working together" with Democrats.

And "staunch conservative" Orrin Hatch teamed up with the almost pathologically liberal Ted Kennedy to propose a fifty-cent tax on cigarettes to create a fund for "uninsured children."

Senator Mike DeWine (R-Ohio) complained about "a crisis of historic proportions": the "dumping" (selling below production cost) of foreign steel. Senator DeWine told the Senate Steel Caucus, "Hundreds of jobs have already been lost, and tens of thousands more remain in danger." Domestic steel officials warned lawmakers of the great harm facing their industry if immediate action was not taken, while foreign producers said the national steel oversupply was caused by General Motors strikes and other economic conditions. Meanwhile, the unsuspecting consumers who got "dumped on" benefit from paying less rather than more for steel.[2]

Remember, Nobel laureate economist Milton Friedman called minimum-wage laws "perhaps the most anti-black law on the statutes." How many Republicans recently joined with Democrats to propose hiking minimum wage? When the House last voted to hike minimum wage, the measure passed 354 to 72. What does this mean? A boatload of Republicans voted for the price hike, a measure that 90 percent of economists claim damages the employment prospects of women, teens, and minorities. Principles, anyone? Someone remind the GOP that even President Clinton once said, "I'll say it again. The era of big government is over."

The perception is that Republicans loathe affirmative action. But, again, who was the first president to institute an affirmative action plan with goals and timetables? Answer: Richard Nixon, who, in 1969, authorized the Philadelphia Plan, the nation's first true affirmative action plan.

Richard Nixon also created the Woman, Infant, and Children Program, government monies for health care for women and children on welfare. He imposed a wage and price freeze to combat inflation. Wage and price freeze! Not, mind you, imposed by Fidel Castro, Mao Tse-Tung, or Josef Stalin—but by Republican Richard Nixon.

Republicans can't seem to get straight whether or not they want the market to work. During President George Bush's term, oil prices plummeted dramatically. Good news for consumers? Not according to this "conservative" Republican president. Bush publicly questioned whether oil prices could continue to fall "like a parachutist" without doing damage. Damage to whom? To his buddies on Wall Street who invested in oil futures? To the concerned oil company shareholders who fear that lower prices may depress the stock? Or to the millions of consumers who benefit from cheaper auto fuel, cheaper oil products, and cheaper energy costs?

George Bush also signed the Clean Air Act, the Americans with Disabilities Act, and reregulated the cable television industry. Of course, he famously declared "no new taxes," only to break the promise by raising taxes.

Both Democratic and Republican state attorneys general filed lawsuits against legal products, such as tobacco and guns. Never mind that since the '60s, cigarette packages have contained warning labels or that the government taxes cigarettes even while it subsidizes the production of tobacco. Still, the federal government, along with several states, now sues tobacco manufacturers to "recoup" costs spent on health care. Never mind that many economists argue that because many smokers die sooner than they otherwise would, the taxpayer actually *saves* money otherwise spent on Medicare, Medicaid, and Social Security. W. Kip Viscusi, a Duke University economist, calculated the societal costs of smoking (medical care, sick leave, life insurance, fire, secondhand smoke, lost taxes on earnings) against the societal benefits (nursing home savings, pension and Social Security saving, excise tax paid). The net result? We gain 58 cents on every pack of cigarettes smoked.[3] Still the lawsuits pile on.

Who is among those leading the charge against tobacco? Arizona Republican John McCain, who ran for his party's presidential nomination in 2000.

On affirmative action, Republicans talk the talk but fail to walk the walk. Ward Connerly, the black man who led the fight to repeal California's race- and gender-based preferences, rightly feels betrayed by the Party. The Republicans, the "Party of Merit," gives lip service to abolishing race- and gender-based preferences. But Republicans, fearing a backlash from women and minorities, did little to assist Connerly's effort to defeat preferences in California.

Following his successful effort in California, Ward Connerly went to Florida to place a similar initiative on the ballot. Florida's governor Jeb Bush dissed him. Said Bush, "He's about war, we're about love." Instead Governor Bush sought a "third way." He offered spots in the University of Florida system to those high school students finishing in the top 20 percent of every high school, no matter the quality of the school. The result? Protesters picketed, and called him "racist." Oh, well.

What about principle, Governor? What about the proposition that race- and gender-based preferences are

a) unfair,
b) suggest certain people are too inferior to compete in an open field, and

c) continue the misguided notion that the government should make "people whole" because of racial and sexual discrimination done to previous generations.

Spending, Spending, Spending

All too often, the Republicans and Democrats represent dueling versions of "big government." An editorial from *Investors Business Daily*[4] on the health-care debate between Republicans and Democrats shows us how it works:

1. Democrats who support a government-run health-care system begin to push a health-care reform proposal they say is absolutely necessary.

2. They find a prominent Republican—names like Kassebaum, Hatch, Domenici and D'Amato come to mind—who is willing to carry their water.

3. The Democrats stand back while the issue divides Republicans.

4. Democrats then lure moderate Republicans to the Democratic bill (no difficult task, that).

5. Moderate defections force the Republican leadership to craft its own bill similar to the Democrats' legislation.

6. Republicans throw in some conservative provisions intended to mollify conservatives.

7. Democrats demand provisions and restrictions that gum up the real reforms so they can't work.

8. Republicans pass their modified bill and claim credit.

9. Democrats protest that the legislation doesn't go far enough.

10. Finally, when the Republican bill doesn't work as prom-

ised, Democrats say, "I told you so" and call for a government-run system.

Since 1994, Republicans have controlled both houses of Congress. They faced a Democratic president, severely weakened by impeachment. If Republicans were sincere about downsizing government, could they have asked for a more propitious time? Yet, nothing happened.

The Republican Senate, in the last budget, voted $7.4 billion in increased emergency farm aid. And the $7.4 billion comes in addition to nearly $16 billion in farm subsidies already approved by Congress. The vote in the Senate for the $7.4 billion was 89 to 8! And Republican House Speaker Dennis Hastert said that the House, too, intends to follow suit and do its part. Oh.

Of the multi-billion-dollar aid bill, Victor Davis Hanson, a professor (also a farmer), wrote in the *Wall Street Journal,* "Republicans, who say they wish to reduce government, cut taxes and end welfare, now intend to increase government, restore welfare and give money to purportedly independent growers. Democrats, who rail against corporate welfare, attempt to outdo Republicans in upping the ante to agribusiness."[5]

For thirty-five years, my dad operated a small café near downtown Los Angeles. Through good times and bad times, he never received a "snack-bar subsidy" to get him through either a recession, a shutdown of a nearby plant whose workers he fed, or stormy days when business fell off. Farming, like other industries, grows more efficient and productive, rendering unnecessary many so-called Mom-and-Pop farms. In the eighties, Hollywood produced three "save the family farm" movies—such as *Places in the Heart*—all extolling the virtues of the family farm. It is, after all, a "way of life." In one movie, the coldhearted banker said to a loan-seeking farmer with poor collateral, "No, it's not a way of life. It's a business."

Yet, both Democrats and Republicans continue to pay millions of dollars in farm subsidies, most of which go to the least needy, wealthiest farmers. The rationale: Why, it's to keep farmers in business, because, well, you never know when there, like, might be, you know, Armageddon or something.

The ongoing debate in Congress over how to spend the so-called surplus provides an interesting illustration of the lack of differences in the parties.

The president wants to use the surplus to shore up Social Security and to pay down the national debt. Republicans feel that surpluses mean the government overcharges the taxpayers, and wish some of it returned.

Well, by 50 to 49, the Senate passed a tax cut bill. The *Los Angeles Times* called the bill "sweeping." A headline from a *New York Times* story read: "Congress Approves Massive Tax Cuts." Well, the "sweeping" and "massive" bill provides exactly for a reduction in the personal income tax rate of one percentage point in each of the five tax brackets. That's right. One percentage point. The bill does reform the estate inheritance tax, but the "tax cut" is marginal to nonexistent. The bill reduces the capital gains rate from 20 percent to 18 percent, when many economists argue the actual rate should be zero. The Republicans again took a pocket-knife to a problem requiring a machete.

Republican Speaker of the House Dennis Hastert got a $30 million tax break for the Plano Molding Company, headquartered in his district. Representative Jennifer Dunn (R-Washington) got $166 million for shopping malls in her district. Senator Frank Murkowski (R-Alaska) got $3 million to help Native Alaskan whaling captains. Senator William V. Roth, Jr. (R-Delaware) got a tax credit for those burning chicken manure in his state.[6]

Do Republicans believe the federal government should play no role in our nation's health care? No. Do Republicans believe the federal government should play no role in education? No. Do Republicans believe that the government has no right to take part of someone's check for Social Security and that, if so, people should invest 100 percent of it? No. Do Republicans believe the government should butt out of assistance to the needy, allowing people to help people through religious organizations and other nonprofit organizations? No. Do most Republicans demand the abolition of the IRS, and that the government, at all three levels—state, local, and federal, should take no more than 10 percent of the American's income in taxes? No. Do Republicans, for the most part, call abortion, drugs, prostitution, and gambling all "personal matters," about which the government ought not be involved? No.

If Republicans truly feared a monstrous federal government, why support minimum wages, rent control, subsidies for Amtrak, subsidies for the Tennessee Valley Authority, the Post Office monopoly on first-class mail, public ownership of airports, public financing of sports stadiums, and taxpayer subsidies for American corporations to promote their products overseas? Indeed, many Republicans objected to NAFTA and GATT, on the grounds that "jobs will be taken from the American people." Never mind lower tariffs provide more choices at less cost.

Republican congressman David Dreier, head of the powerful Rules Committee, is a friend. He and I have heated discussions about where Republicans are versus where they should be. Congressman Dreier finds the American people unready to accept dramatic reductions in taxes, spending, and regulation. He feels that "purists," like me, fail to appreciate the practical difficulties in moving the center to accept radical changes in the role of citizen and government. He's wrong.

Why aren't the American people screaming for lower taxes and less government? Americans keep electing statist and collectivist Democrats and Republication. Doesn't this say that we want the welfare state? Answer: No, and I believe America awaits the right messenger with the right message.

How else to explain Ross Perot? His seemingly fresh and candid appearances on *Larry King Live* revealed an American responsive to what appeared to be a call for a no-nonsense, efficient, and small government. He bought television time, where he simply and methodically held up charts and graphs showing the nation's deficit and rising debt. Never before had so many Americans tuned in to watch a lecture on something as dry as the economy, the budget, and deficits and their significance. The next day, I attended a business meeting. While waiting for the elevator, I overheard two janitors discussing the "danger" of our growing debt and deficit. Ross Perot, single-handedly, put this issue on kitchen tables all across America, and received 21 percent of the vote.

Why Not a Libertarian?

The Democratic and Republican parties have differences, although comparatively small. The difference between a Republican and a libertarian is massive. The difference between a Democrat and a libertarian, gargantuan. Libertarians believe in the Henry David Thoreau motto: a government that governs least governs best. Libertarians believe the Constitution, as drafted, represents *restrictions* on the powers of the federal government.

Libertarians believe Americans smart enough, wise enough, mature enough, capable enough to manage their own affairs to the fullest extent possible. Libertarians believe the welfare state diminishes the incentive of both the giver and the given. Libertarians, too, believe in the "social safety net," but with the proviso that support should be in the form of people to people, and private charity to people.

Libertarians reject so-called conservative Republicans like Texas senator Phil Gramm. Gramm brags that he helped stop the Hillary Clinton–led move toward a completely nationalized health care. "I stood up and said the Clinton health care plan is going to pass over my cold, dead, political body."[7] He likes to remind us that he stood tall during the battle over Hillary-care. Fine. But does Senator Gramm call for the complete abolition of the Medicare Act of 1965, an unbelievably horrible government invasion of the private sector. He, too, wishes to "preserve" Medicare, instead of completely rejecting the government role in this aspect of our lives.

Similarly, the difference between a Republican and a libertarian Supreme Court justice is massive. A libertarian judge would find farm subsidies unconstitutional. A libertarian judge would find public housing unconstitutional. A libertarian judge would find unconstitutional the federal government's efforts to fight the "war on drugs."

As mentioned, during the Clinton-care debate, more than five hundred economists—liberal, moderate, and conservative—wrote the White House. Abandon this attempt to nationalize one-seventh of the nation's economy, the letter said. A libertarian judge would not need a letter from economists to understand the unconstitutional and corrosive effect of a national health-care system.

But, by voting for libertarian candidates, doesn't the voter run the risk of electing more Democrats? After all, Democrats spend more money than Republicans. So, wouldn't voting libertarian increase the likelihood of Democrats getting elected? In the short run, it might. And the president in the first term of this millennium may have the opportunity to appoint three or four Supreme Court justices. The current Supreme Court rules 5 to 4 on many decisions, frequently coming down on the side of a smaller role by the federal government. Won't a Democratic president reverse this course? Again, in the short run, yes.

But Americans need to take a stand. Richard Nixon once said that for a Republican to win the presidency, he must run to the right to get nominated and run to the center to get elected. A libertarian says, *stake out a persuasive, principled position, and the center will find you.* As a minister once put it, "If you want to lead the choir, sometimes you gotta turn your back to the audience." OSHA mandates, sugar price supports, milk price supports, federal subsidies for Archer-Daniels-Midland to produce ethanol,

Title I educational money. A libertarian president, appointing libertarian judges, would say, "No, no, no."

If Americans understood the benefits of less government, they would sign on. But "leaders" refuse to make the case. Former Speaker Newt Gingrich, who talked the talk of small government, took a pounding from the media. He retreated, becoming less aggressive and less ideologically pure. In the end, before he resigned, Gingrich urged his colleagues to take tax cuts off the agenda! Can you say "retreat"?

Didn't the massive Ronald Reagan tax cut demonstrate the benefits of low taxes? Yes, but most Republicans today, at best, only meekly push for still lower taxes. All too often, they read the polls, showing that a booming economy makes the public "less concerned about tax cuts." Republicans then retreat because the same polls show Americans concerned about securing the "social safety net." "Appeal to the center," say the advisers, and Republicans march along.

Minnesota governor Jesse "the Body" Ventura's election signals what could happen. Lots of new voters, especially young voters, voted for the first time, having been presented with a true alternative. Although not a true libertarian, Ventura asked simple questions, making his Republican or Democratic candidates look downright dense. Why should a government with a surplus not return the money to its overtaxed citizens? said Ventura. An art college student once asked Ventura what government aid she could expect in order to pursue her interests. Ventura suggested she make some art, and sell it. "Hallelujah," said the voters of Minnesota, "this is what I've been thinking, feeling, and saying over the dinner table and at the water cooler." Since his election, Ventura has retreated on many libertarian-sounding proposals. Still, his election demonstrates what can happen when voters see a refreshing true alternative.

Democrats: Avenging Angels

Dick Morris, the former aide to Bill Clinton, says that Clinton denounced his Republican opponent Bob Dole. The president, said Morris, attacked Dole not merely for his positions but for his motives. "Let me tell you something," the president said, according to Morris, "Bob Dole is not a nice man. Bob Dole is *evil*. The things he wants to do to children are *evil*. The things he wants to do to poor people and old people and sick people are *evil*."

Other anti-Republican remarks by "compassionate" Democrats include the following:

Democratic California Congressman George Miller proclaimed, "It's a glorious day if you're a fascist," when railing against Republicans' HHS labor appropriations bill in July 1995.

According to *USA Today*,[8] Representative John Dingell (D-Michigan) made statements on *Nightline* in April 1995 "comparing the new Republican-controlled House to 'the Duma and the Reichstag'—that is, respectively, the legislature set up by Czar Nicholas II of Russia and the Parliament of the German Weimar Republic that brought Hitler to power. In fact, comparing Republicans to Nazis has become a favorite pastime of Democrats. . . .

"Among those who have used the tactic are Democratic Reps. Charles Rangel and Major Owens, both of New York.

"In a speech to a group of black and Puerto Rican activists, Rangel said that Republican budget cuts were worse than what happened in Nazi Germany: 'Hitler wasn't even talking about doing these things.'

"Owens agreed: 'These are people who are practicing genocide with a smile, they're worse than Hitler.' "[9]

"A wave of scapegoating is sweeping the country. . . . Just like under Hitler, people say they don't mean to blame any particular individuals or groups, but in the U.S. those groups always turn out to be minorities and immigrants," said Representative Charles Rangel in a press release, declaring that "for political gain,

GOP blames the poor, minorities and immigrants for America's problems."

"In South Africa we'd call it apartheid. In Nazi Germany we'd call it fascism. Here we call it conservatism. These people are attacking the poor," said the Reverend Jesse Jackson, in the *Fort Lauderdale Sun-Sentinel.*

Charming.

These ugly remarks by the holier-than-thou Democrats aside, neither party truly has faith in the intelligence and industry of the American people.

President Clinton and Jesse Jackson "Feel Our Pain"

Men of great skills, both Bill Clinton and Jesse Jackson overcame extremely difficult childhoods. Both came from poor, financially insecure broken homes.

Recall that in Jesse Jackson's case, his mother had Jesse with the married man next door. The man never publicly claimed Jackson, causing him an insecurity that some believe still exists.

And President Clinton's biological father died in a traffic accident while Clinton's mom was pregnant with Bill. His stepfather drank, worked only intermittently, and physically abused Clinton's mother.

Jackson went on to become a star quarterback for a black North Carolina college, married the campus beauty, and, through hard work, charisma, and boldness, became the preeminent civil rights leader in America. He ran credibly for the presidency in 1984 and, again, in 1988, this time winning the second-highest number of delegates at the Democratic National convention.

The president went to Georgetown and then to Yale Law School, where he met and dated an upperclassman, Hillary Rodham. He became a Rhodes scholar and spent time studying in Oxford, England.

In 1976 Clinton ran for governor of Arkansas and won, becoming the youngest governor in the history of the United States.

These men have both displayed remarkable talents. But Americans duplicate their stories in smaller ways, day in and day out, and have done so since the founding of the Republic. Leaders like Clinton and Jackson do not practice what they preach. They preach victimhood—"you wuz robbed," "you're entitled,"—but they *personally* practice focus, hard work, drive, and energy. This is condescension: *we* overcame adversity, but without big government, *you* cannot.

In his classic book on the libertarian philosophy, *The Road to Serfdom*,[10] F. A. Hayek attacks the emotional feel-good thinking that justifies today's welfare state. Never mind studies, surveys, and experience showing the bigger the state, the less free and less prosperous the people. Emotional toe-tag liberals still insist on things like "the social safety net." Economist Milton Friedman, in his introduction to Hayek's book, asked this question: Why do so many otherwise bright people believe in a collectivist, statist, socialistic government? "The argument for collectivism is simple if false; it is an immediate emotional argument," Friedman said that "the argument for individualism is subtle and sophisticated; it is an indirect rational argument. And the emotional faculties are more highly developed in most men than the rational, paradoxically or especially even in those who regard themselves as intellectuals."[11]

1994 Republicans AWOL

For one shining moment in 1994, Republicans had a shot. They captured a majority of seats in Congress, and analysts attributed their victory, in part, to revulsion over Clinton-care. The people thought they had elected a moderate Democrat, but Clinton, at least at first, came across as liberal as previous Democratic presidential nominees such as Michael Dukakis and Walter Mondale.

So the Republicans had an opportunity. To prove to the American people that Republicans who attack "big government" meant it, the GOP leadership could have and should have gone after corporate welfare. They should have attacked tax subsidies paid to corporations like McDonald's and Carnation to advertise their products overseas. They should have eliminated farm subsidies, most of which go to wealthy agribusiness. They should have eliminated special tax breaks and loopholes "targeted" for specific industries and companies who just happened to make substantial campaign contributions.

Why didn't the Republicans take this tack? After all, former Republican House Speaker Newt Gingrich once accurately called Bob Dole "the tax collector for the welfare state." America would have bought a broad-based attack on this welfare state. But, again, the Republicans took out a pocketknife.

Talking the talk is one thing. Walking the walk, yet another.

Rush to Legislate

Statist "activists" of both parties frequently make absurd statements to accomplish the same goal—more government.

Following the Littleton, Colorado, massacre at Columbine High, House representative Bob Barr (R-Georgia) urged legislation allowing school districts to post the Ten Commandments, saying that if high schools were allowed to display the Ten Commandments "we would not have the tragedies that bring us here today."[12]

Hillary Rodham Clinton called for more gun control legislation, despite the killer's having violated numerous laws already on the books.

Both politicians used illogical leaps of faith to justify their own vision of a nosy, interventionist, activist government, a government at odds with the Founding Fathers' vision of the Constitution as a document that limits government.

A friend stayed a couple of weeks in a hotel in Cleveland. During that time, both the National Republican and National Democratic Parties sponsored functions a week apart. The Republicans were orderly, neat, and created little disturbance. When, however, the Democrats came, the party was on. Beer bottles littered the halls. Loud music and yakking all through the night.

Both parties conspire to maintain and expand the inefficient, freedom-sapping welfare state. But, face it, Democrats sure have a lot more fun doing it.

We need to wake up and understand that a big activist government, however well intentioned, creates damage to the very populace it purports to help. High taxes destroy jobs, suppress innovation, and create less prosperity. Corporate welfare and individual welfare create dependency and lethargy. Feel-good and entrenched institutions such as rent control ultimately reduce the incentive to build low-cost housing, and have a direct impact on creating more homelessness.

Interfering with the principles of supply and demand creates unintended negative consequences. Gun control legislation helps the black market, while doing little to prevent criminals from getting their hands on guns.

Americans must ask whether the Republican and Democratic parties' embrace of the welfare state and social safety net makes us less or more secure? Has Social Security, collected and "managed" by government, caused retirees to end up with less or more financial security in their old age? Has the government monopoly on education produced a less literate and productive workforce than would have been produced by the private sector?

THE WAR AGAINST DRUGS
IS VIETNAM II:
WE'RE LOSING THIS ONE, TOO

If I never do anything else in this career as a member of Congress—
I'm gonna make somebody pay for what they've done to my com-
munity and to my people.

—MAXINE WATERS (D-CALIFORNIA), ON THE ALLEGED
INVOLVEMENT OF THE CIA IN THE INNER CITY DRUG TRADE

Clinton spent more federal money on drugs in his first four years
than was spent during Reagan's and Bush's 12 years combined.[1]

—DR. THOMAS H. HAINES, CITY UNIVERSITY OF NEW YORK
MEDICAL SCHOOL PROFESSOR AND CHAIR OF THE PARTNERSHIP FOR
RESPONSIBLE DRUG INFORMATION

In any war, the first casualty is common sense, and the second is
free and open discussion.[2]

—JAMES RESTON

Nothing is more destructive of respect for the government and the
law of the land than passing laws which cannot be enforced. It is
an open secret that the dangerous increase of crime in this country
is closely connected with this.[3]

—ALBERT EINSTEIN

"Why?"

Once while I was visiting a friend, a drug dealer came over. Not getting an opportunity like this very often, I asked Mr. Dealer a question, "If you were in charge of stopping drugs, what would you do?" When his laughter died down, he said, "Are you serious, or are you [expletive deleted] me?"

He then said, "Ain't nothing you can do to stop this [expletive deleted]. I've seen women sell their children for drugs. I've seen people steal from their mamas. The only thing you can do—and you ain't gonna do that—is legalize this [expletive deleted]."

The war against drugs is wrong both tactically and morally. It assumes people are too stupid, too reckless, and too irresponsible to decide whether and under what conditions to consume drugs. *The war on drugs is morally bankrupt.*

Certainly the potential for drug abuse exists, but isn't that also true of alcohol? Why is it OK for my neighbor to come home and have a martini or two but not for his neighbor to smoke a joint? The short answer from most people is that drugs kill. But so does alcohol.

In *Ending the War on Drugs*, Dirk Chase Eldredge writes, "When compared to the annual number of "premature" deaths from tobacco (allegedly 400,000) and from alcohol (100,000), drug deaths lag far behind. It would be difficult to support a figure of more than 30,000 deaths from illegal drug use, even if the assumption were made that half of all homicides are drug-related."[4] Counting lost days at work, automobile accidents, and medical care, alcohol costs the American economy far, far, more. As far back as September 1986, the U.S. Department of Health and Human Services determined alcohol to be a contributing factor in workplace injuries (10 percent), suicide and suicide attempts (40 percent), and traffic deaths (40 percent).[5]

The government allows the sale, distribution, and use of cigarettes, an act that, according to the feds, claims 400,000 lives per year. Yet drugs, accounting for one-twentieth of the number of fatalities, are illegal and their usage punishable by jail or fine or both.

But the real reason to oppose the war on drugs is moral. Who owns your body, you or the government? If the answer is you, then what right does the government have to say "We will stop you, a grown adult, from engaging in an activity we deem unsafe to you. Not unsafe to others, but unsafe to *you*."

Some people say, "Well, drugs hurt others, too. What about family members?" Well, this can be said about many sanctioned activities. We allow people to enter into marriage without noting the maturity or financial self-sufficiency of either party. An "irresponsible" marriage certainly damages others, including present and future children. But the government does not stop that.

Many Americans wile away their daytime and nighttime hours watching television rather than reading, exercising, or engaging in enlightening conversation. We don't stop this. Excessive television can damage as well. Why doesn't the government call parents irresponsible if they choose to watch *Ally McBeal* or *Friends*, rather than assist their children with homework? We allow (at least for now) people to consume as much food as they wish, no matter how much weight they gain. This certainly damages not only the individual but loved ones. Yet, we don't stop this.

Short of war, the most important task an individual can assume is that of becoming a parent. Irresponsible parenting certainly affects others. Yet we do not prevent "unqualified" people from breeding children.

A free government allows maximum personal freedom, liberty, the power to come and go, to make our own choices, and to experience life as *we* choose to. In exchange for this freedom, we must accept that others will make bad choices. This is the price of liberty.

Where does it say that the federal government is empowered to stop people from smoking, drinking, or, for that matter, consuming drugs? Our born-again drug warrior, President Clinton, joked on MTV about his attempt to inhale marijuana. When asked whether he would inhale if he had another shot at it, Clinton said, "Yes, I tried before." Al Gore admits experimenting with marijuana, as does the secretary of Health and Human Services, Donna Shalala. Former press secretary Dee Dee Myers admits having used marijuana, and many of Clinton's White House appointees could not get security clearances because of recent, prior drug use.

Why not ask Al Gore or George W. Bush at what point in their young lives should the police have arrested them for allegedly engaging in the same conduct for which they now wish to arrest others? Yet, somehow, these people survived their "experimentation" with drugs to go on to become productive members of the public sector.

Former Health, Education, and Welfare Secretary Joseph Califano, Jr., now heads the National Center on Addiction and Substance Abuse (CASA) at Columbia University. He recently released a study labeling marijuana a "gateway" drug. In the study, most hard-core drug users, he found, start out with marijuana, and that a kid who smokes marijuana before age 12 is 79 times more likely to end up on harder drugs.[6]

This "conclusion" is not only sloppy and misleading, it insults intelligence. Certainly, marijuana is a *gateway* if this expression means that the act of smoking tells us something about the smoker. For the same person who smoked marijuana might have sassed mom and dad, skipped school, failed to turn in homework, stayed out late, and started smoking cigarettes at age eleven.

In their book, *Marijuana Myths, Marijuana Facts,*[7] Dr. John P. Morgan and Lynn Zimmer blow away this silly "gateway drug theory." "People using uncommon drugs have almost always used common drugs first," said coauthor Zimmer. "If you wanted to stop motorcycle riding, you wouldn't start by stopping people from riding bikes." The Substance Abuse and Mental Health Services Administration says that nearly 80 million Americans used an illegal drug at least once in their lifetimes. Why don't we have 80 million crackheads and smackheads? Furthermore, because of the illegality of drugs, a marijuana purchaser must sometimes interact with unsavory characters, exposing the buyer to a broader array of drugs than he would like.

President Nixon established a commission to study the impact of marijuana use. The commission's recommendation? Legalize it.

In April 1997, *Atlantic Monthly* in an article called "More Reefer Madness,"[8] said, "President Nixon felt betrayed by the commission and rejected its findings. A decade later the National Academy of Sciences studied the health effects of marijuana and concluded that it should be decriminalized, a finding that President Reagan rejected."

Legal for most of this nation's history, marijuana is now classified by the government as a "Schedule I drug." This translates to no known medicinal value and highly addictive. Both assertions are false. As far as marijuana being highly addictive, try taking it away from a habitual user. He or she will survive without the severe physiological symptoms of withdrawal related to, for example, heroin. Now try and take away the same person's cigarettes or thrice-daily cup of coffee and see what happens. Yet, extremely habit-forming cigarettes remain legal. So does coffee, even though excessive caffeine may be unhealthful, and withdrawal can cause headaches and other physical symptoms.

As for medicinal value, study after study proves marijuana beneficial for many conditions, including the nausea associated with chemotherapy. Marijuana helps stimulate the appetite. For that reason, some doctors quietly urge cancer patients to smoke marijuana to combat loss of appetite and the resultant weight loss. California passed Proposition 215 to allow the use of marijuana for medicinal purposes. But President Clinton, ignoring the wishes of California voters, threatened federal prosecution against any doctor who prescribed this drug. Medical literature overwhelmingly confirms the beneficial use of marijuana in minimizing the adverse reaction to chemotherapy *and* in treating glaucoma.

Of the twenty thousand drug-related deaths mentioned earlier, guess how many are attributable to marijuana? Zero. In fact, there is no such thing as a marijuana overdose.

The War Against Drugs Versus the War Against Alcohol

English philosopher John Locke profoundly influenced the Founding Fathers. Locke believed that a person's body belonged to that person, not to the state. However counterproductive the consumption of alcohol might be, the Constitution, properly interpreted, allows for the right of an individual to abuse his or her own body.

But in 1919, Congress passed the Volstead Act, which led to a change in the Constitution, outlawing the sale and distribution of alcohol.

Immediately after Prohibition, thousands of so-called speakeasies, where people could go to purchase and consume liquor, sprang up seemingly overnight. Organized crime took root. Violent crime exploded. So, by the way, did alcohol consumption (after an initial decline). During Prohibition, the murder rate increased 54 percent; after its repeal, the murder rate fell for the next eleven years.[9]

During Prohibition, people often watched others stumble down the street, drunk, since the imbiber had to leave home to purchase alcohol and most often to consume it, as well. After Prohibition's repeal, visibly stumbling drunkards disappeared almost overnight.

The same applies to the current war on drugs. Many experts estimate that 50 percent of all crime directly or indirectly relates to robbing, maiming, and stealing to support a prohibitively expensive drug habit. In testimony before the House Subcommittee on Criminal Justice, Drug Policy, and Human Resources, David Boaz, executive vice president of the Cato Institute, said, "Drug prohibition creates high levels of crime. Addicts are forced to commit crimes to pay for a habit that would be easily affordable if it were legal. Police sources have estimated that as much as half the property crime in some major cities is committed by drug users."[10] Legalize drugs, crime falls. Nearly one-third of the prison population consists of drug traffickers, many of whom committed no violent offense. Clearing prisons of these offenders would leave vacancies for violent criminals, some of whom now get released early because of overcrowding.

The Profit Incentive Insures Defeat in the War on Drugs

Marijuana is the number one cash crop in Kentucky and is one of California's most important agricultural products. If America allowed the legal growth, transportation, and consumption of marijuana, the price would fall, saving millions of Americans money. Police would spend less time busting people for marijuana and more time pursuing serious crimes. The product could be taxed with a fund established for addicts. Self-help organizations like Cocaine Anonymous exist to help abusers.

No one truly knows the amount of the worldwide drug trade. Some estimate as much as a trillion dollars a year, an amount that is approximately 20 percent of America's GDP. The American demand for drugs creates a virtual narcotics-based economy in Colombia, Burma, and other countries. Official corruption runs from the very lowest to the very highest levels, with judges, politicians, and prosecutors on the take, and others are menaced if they avoid corruption. Yet our country brazenly demands that the "drug-producing countries" aggressively police drug lords when our own country's demand for drugs created the problem in the first place. How incredibly arrogant!

The War Against Drugs Compromises Freedoms

To fight the war on drugs, the Clinton administration authorized more FBI wiretaps than during the Bush and Reagan eras combined. The goal: to fight the war on drugs. State and asset forfeiture laws pop up, allowing, for example, an apartment building owner to lose his investment because a tenant, unbeknownst to him, dealt drugs. The Coast Guard confiscates boats should someone, not necessarily the owner, leave a minute amount of marijuana on board.

To fight this war, the government must use informants. After all, drug trade consists of two willing parties—the seller and the buyer. So when something bad happens, who calls the cops? No one, since both sides have engaged in an illegal act. Hence, the need for informants.

But what about the informant's incentive? Many trade information, often false, to benefit themselves. Many informants, drug dealers themselves, lie in order to cut a better deal for themselves. As with alcohol, the drug war creates unintended negative consequences. The drug trade tempts children into dropping out of school to pursue lucrative, if short-lived, careers as drug dealers. Drug laws encourage drug dealers to "employ" children, because the dealers know that should children be apprehended by the law they will be prosecuted less severely than would an adult. And, to children, drug dealers become "role models" of flash and dash in their impressionable minds.

The drug trade frequently takes place in the inner city, where there is all too often an absence of fathers to help serve as positive role models or authority figures. The drug war also hurts property values, as crack houses pile up like speakeasies in the inner city, making neighborhoods less safe and prospective buyers wary. The drug war creates a criminal class, often consisting of people who never committed violent offenses. AIDS is rampant in prison. When released, some ex-inmates pass along AIDS, helping to create an AIDS epidemic within inner-city minority communities.

Time to Reconsider

Conservative William F. Buckley estimates that the drug war's indirect cost—higher prices, loss of sales tax, higher insurance premiums to prevent theft, cost of break-ins and property theft, loss of work time to pursue property claims, emergency room-related expenses—and direct government expenses like prison costs, Coast Guard and Border Patrol—is more than $200 billion a year, or about the same as our recent average annual deficit.

Legalization does not mean lawlessness. We expect cops to bust someone driving high on drugs just as though he were driving drunk. We should not sell drugs to children any more than we do cigarettes or alcohol. Employers may require drug-testing upon hire, and may impose random drug test policies.

A varied cross-section of prominent Americans such as Abigail Van Buren (Dear Abby), prosecutor Vincent Bugliosi, Walter Cronkite, former secretary of state George Shultz, and William F. Buckley all suggest the decriminalization, if not legalization, of most drugs.

Drug czar Barry McCaffrey recently slammed the Dutch approach to drugs. In Holland, the government gives heroin to addicts. Their premise: that addicts steal to get drugs, so a drug giveaway program reduces harm to society. McCaffrey asserted that the program caused an increase in Holland's murder rate, a rate McCaffrey claimed was twice that of America's. Uh-oh. McCaffrey claimed 17.58 murders per 100,000 people, compared to 8.22 for the United States. But according to a Dutch spokesman, "The figure [McCaffrey is using] is not right. He is adding in attempted murders." Official Dutch data put the murder rate at 1.8 per 100,000 in 1996.[11] Busted. Not only is Holland continuing its program, but other European states are now following suit. Sweden, for example, is considering introducing a heroin giveaway program patterned after the one in the Netherlands.

Many screamed foul when former surgeon general Jocelyn Elders suggested studying the possibility of legalizing drugs. Yet, for a few weeks, the American people paid attention as the pundits debated the issue. Poll numbers began to show some support for, at least, consideration of this issue.

Former Baltimore mayor Kurt Schmoke stood virtually alone among politicians with the courage to publicly state what many privately believe—that the war on drugs is a failure, and that we ought to consider drug addiction a health problem, not a criminal justice problem.

Texas libertarian-in-Republican-clothing Ron Paul also urges legalization, as does outgoing Republican New Mexico governor Gary Johnson. That's a start.

But all drugs? Yes, all drugs. Unlike the current situation, legal drug retailers would be able to guarantee quality and would have to promise the consumer a level of reasonable care. Unreliable retailers, unlike now, could be held accountable. It goes without saying that warning labels would apply. But aren't soft drugs like marijuana one thing, and hard drugs like heroin and cocaine another? Of course. Still, the individual must decide. It is his body to use. And to abuse.

Won't consumption increase? Common sense, say prohibitionists, dictates that more people will consume who previously did not if only for fear of getting caught. But, remember, after the repeal of Prohibition, alcohol consumption fell. Apparently, many were attracted to and intrigued by booze simply because of its illegality, the delicious "getting away with something" feeling that many get when they step over the line.

Pollsters ask children who abstain from drugs, "Why not you?" Here's how they respond: "My parents and my peers would disapprove." They were saved by their values—parental, personal, and spiritual.

Princeton professor Ethan Nadelmann examined the number

of drug users in America. He concluded, "It is impossible to predict whether or not legalization would lead to much greater levels of drug abuse."[12]

Professor Michael S. Gazzaniga, professor of neuroscience at Dartmouth Medical School, was asked the effect of drug consumption if drugs were made legal. In the book *Ain't Nobody's Business if You Do*,[13] he says, "Drug-consumption rates will bounce around, related as they are to environmental factors, fads, and a host of other factors. Drug-abuse rates will not change much, if at all. Yet many of the negative social consequences of keeping drugs illegal will be neutralized. The health costs of drug abuse will always be with us. We should try to focus on those problems with more serious neurobiologic and neurobehavioral research and help where we can to reduce the percentage that fall victim. I am an experimental scientist, and like most people can see that the present system doesn't work. We need to try another approach. If, for whatever reason, legalization doesn't improve the situation, it would take five minutes to reverse it."

Ben Franklin said, "They that can give up essential liberty to obtain a little temporary safety deserve neither liberty nor safety."[14] The government convinces Americans to give away their personal freedom in order to fight this senseless war on drugs. When "conservatives" wish to impose waiting periods and parental notification on the right to abortion, pro-choicers screamed foul. An intrusion on women's rights! When liberals demand campus speech codes to reduce sexism and racism, First Amendment supporters scream foul. Intrusion! Invasion of the right to privacy and free expression!

But when the government seeks to invade the freedom to do what one will with one's own body, we say nothing. But what about freedom?! When we sentence criminals, we don't inject them with some bacterium. We don't dismember a limb. We incarcerate them, restrain them, remove them from society. We take away their most precious gift of all: freedom. And, in the end, this is the most compelling argument of all to halt the war on drugs.

Hollywood: Another Casualty in the War on Drugs

Two hundred eighty-six million dollars last year. This year, $1.6 billion goes from the United States to Colombia to fight the "war on drugs."

"Clinton spent more federal money in the war on drugs in his first four years than was spent during Reagan's and Bush's twelve years combined," said Dr. Thomas H. Haines, City University of New York medical school professor and chair of the Partnership for Responsible Drug Information.[15]

And now the most recent bombshell. In 1997, Congress authorized the White House Office of National Drug Control Policy (ONDCP) to spend $1 billion to buy time for anti-drug public service announcements on the major networks. But the law forces networks to sell the government this time at half price, a practice understandably balked at by bottom-line-oriented Hollywood execs.[16]

So the White House came up with a classically Clintonesque "third way." Here's the deal. The White House, having purchased network time, gives networks "credit" for that time. How does a network earn credit? By including an anti-drug message in the content of its programs.

The ONDCP determines whether it finds the script's "anti-drug message" strong enough to allow credit. Once granted credit, the networks can sell the ONDCP's previously purchased time to another advertiser at *fair-market value*. So far, NBC, ABC, CBS, Fox, and WB netted nearly $25 million using these "anti-drug credits."[17]

The Drew Carey Show, Seventh Heaven, ER, Beverly Hills, 90210, and *Chicago Hope* all received credit, according to the online magazine *Salon*, which spent six months investigating this practice.

The government did not tell the taxpayers about the arrangements, and the networks did not inform the writers and producers. The entire arrangement may violate anti-payola laws requiring disclosure of any financial or proprietary interest in content or programming.

President Clinton denies the White House exercised any control over scripts and did not participate in any altering of material. But, WB CEO Jamie Kellner conceded that his network altered scripts of *Smart Guy* and *The Wayans Brothers* as a result of suggestions by government personnel. "We submitted the scripts," said Kellner, "to get their input and make sure we were handling the stories in the most responsible way."

Congressman and chairman of the House Rules Committee David Dreier [R-California] condemned the practice. But why did Congress authorize such a law in the first place? Demanding that networks "sell" time at 50 percent off is a taking of property, a violation of the Fifth Amendment. The interference with programming content directly attacks the First Amendment. The ONDCP calls the program voluntary. Right. Pity the network executive who refuses to go along while other networks rake in millions of dollars, placing a non-participant at a competitive disadvantage.

Suppose the next occupant of the White House feels as strongly about the pro-life cause as the Clinton White House does about the anti-drugs crusade? What about a Republican White House crusade against, say, affirmative action or mandatory prayer in public schools? And why stop at only dramas and sitcoms? What about a financial reward for including anti-drug messages in news magazine shows or, for that matter, the nightly newscast?

When New Mexico governor Gary Johnson courageously called for the legalization of drugs, his popularity rating fell from 60 percent to 49 percent. Politicians do read polls. So, the war continues, largely because a politically compliant media keep the American people ignorant about the war's true cost.

In the end, public ignorance remains the White House's biggest ally.

Blacks and the War on Drugs

Nearly one-third of all young black men are involved in the criminal justice system: either in jail, on parole, or on probation. Consider the effect of the war on drugs on an inner-city youth. He gets involved in the drug trade, gets busted, goes to prison. There, he interacts with hard core criminals, broadening his criminal horizons. He gets out of prison with a record. Depending upon the state he lives in, he may or may not be able to vote. In addition, his "marriage value" has now declined, making it less likely that a woman would find him a good long-term marriage prospect. Because he has a record, he may not be able to get a job, with employers understandably reluctant to hire an ex-con. While in prison, he may have engaged—forcibly or willingly—in unprotected sex, possibly contracting an STD, up to and including AIDS. (AIDS, on the decline in America as a whole is on the rise among young black men and women.) The young black man now has no pension, no 401k, no stock options, no money, no spouse, lots of enemies, and is possibly ill. And for what? So that a bunch of cops can stack a bunch of drugs on a table, have their pictures taken, and declare that we've "turned the corner" on the war on drugs.

And the war on drugs is the primary reason for the DWB stops that black men are subject to. Call off the war on drugs, and the incentive for police to stop motorists plummets. But our "leaders" simultaneously urge the police to back off, to insure that no motorist gets his or her feelings hurt. Yet the very same politicians urge stiff penalties for drug users and demand that the police do something about the drug trade and its attendant violence.

Sher Horosko, formerly Connecticut's director of Addiction Services, talked about the disproportionate effect of drug prohibition on American blacks. In 1995, Horosko said, "Today in this country, we incarcerate 3,109 black men for every 100,000 of them in the population. Just to give you an idea of the drama in this number, our closest competitor for incarcerating black men is

South Africa. South Africa—and this is pre–Nelson Mandela and under an overt public policy of apartheid—incarcerated 729 black men for every 100,000. Figure this out: In the land of the Bill of Rights, we jail over four times as many black men as the only country in the world that advertised a political policy of apartheid."[18]

The drug war requires that the government lie to the population.

As mentioned, Joseph Califano called marijuana a "gateway" drug. The government provides millions of dollars in grant money to colleges and universities willing to research the bad effects of drugs. The argument is not that drugs—except for medicinal purposes—are good for you. But, in order for the government to fight the war, it must demonize all drugs, while acting as if all are equally problematic. Think of the famous egg and skillet commercial with the ominous voiceover: "This is your brain on drugs."

But researchers at Baltimore's Johns Hopkins University conducted the first study on the long-term effects of marijuana on mental ability. Johns Hopkins published the results in the May 1, 1999, issue of *American Journal of Epidemiology*. For twelve to fifteen years, researchers followed nearly thirteen hundred adults, from the ages of eighteen to sixty-four. Mental agility tests were given at the beginning and at the end of the study. The researchers divided the studied group between heavy users, light users, and non-users of marijuana. Researchers noted, "The results . . . seemed to provide strong evidence of the absence of a long-term residual effect of cannabis use on cognition."[19] And, as between the three categories of users, the report found "no significant differences in cognitive decline between heavy users, light users and nonusers of cannabis."[20]

Incidentally, the report received very little media coverage. But, if you've read Chapter 3, you already know why. But isn't the media liberal and, therefore, likely to be receptive to the libertarian idea of drug legalization? You would think so. Most journalists are probably schizophrenic on this issue. On the one hand, as baby boomers and younger, they may have experimented with drugs. And many reporters probably object to long, harsh sentences for some drug-related offenses. But reporters also work for sometimes large, mainstream organizations. And, most Americans want the war fought, many blissfully ignorant about the war's true cost and consequences. Once brave politicians and others explain the war on drugs' true cost, the American people will scream for a cease-fire. Bring the troops home, people will urge. Treat drugs as a health problem, not as a matter for the criminal justice system.

10

GUN CONTROL ADVOCATES—GOOD GUYS WITH BLOOD ON THEIR HANDS

I'd rather be judged by twelve than carried out by six.

—Elderly inner-city waiter

Gun Control's Ultimate Goal: Confiscation

Reactionary. Gun control "advocates" often use this term to describe defenders of the Second Amendment. After all, say the advocates, who can quarrel with child safety locks? Or waiting periods? Or "sensible" registration and licensing requirements? Or training sessions before gun purchases?

But these "reactionaries" have reason to fear. Because the ultimate objective for many so-called gun control "advocates" is simple, if unstated: the complete abolition of firearms in the hands of private citizens.

In a *New Yorker* article dated July 26, 1976, the magazine's Richard Harris interviewed Nelson Shields, who then served as director of the National Council to Control Handguns, an organization that became Handgun Control, Inc. Shields commented, "Our ultimate goal—total control of handguns in the United States—is going to take time. My estimate is from seven to ten years. The first problem is to slow down the increasing number of handguns being produced and sold in this country. The second problem is to get handguns registered. And the final problem is to make the possession of *all* handguns and *all* handgun ammunition—except for the military, policemen, licensed security guards, licensed sporting clubs, and licensed gun collectors—totally illegal."

He continued, "The pro-gun crowd keeps arguing that people like me want to take *all* guns away from Americans. That's just not true. Sporting rifles and shotguns have their place. But the handgun has no purpose except to kill somebody. While it's true that criminals would still manage to get hold of handguns even if there were strict laws against their possession, the gradual reduction of handguns in general would make it much harder for them to get hold of guns. . . ." Subtle.

The more restrictions the government places on guns, the fewer citizens will be willing to jump through the hoops necessary to purchase a gun. The end result—fewer gun owners, and, therefore, fewer people to protest even further restrictions.

Don't laugh. On December 12, 1993, the *Los Angeles Times* published an editorial: "Get Rid of the Guns—More Firearms Won't Make America Safer, They Will Only Accelerate and Intensify the Heartache and Bloodshed."

A rash of shootings prompted this editorial. It was not subtle, it was not discreet, it was blunt:

> You will not feel safe, your children will not be safe, until there are almost no guns on the streets and in the homes. No guns, period, except for those held by law enforcement

officers and a few others, including qualified hunters and collectors. . . .

Why should America adopt a policy of near-zero tolerance
for private gun ownership? Because it's the only alternative
to the present insanity. . . .

Can Congress impose such a ban? Federal courts, including
the U.S. Supreme Court, have consistently upheld a variety of
firearms restrictions, even prohibitions, over the last 60 years.
In practice, the Second Amendment has not been an imped-
iment to tighter gun laws, nor should it be in theory, given
the amendment's origins in the colonists' desire for an organized state militia. . . .

We must begin thinking differently about guns: Instead of
assuming, as we have for too long, that all but a few demon-
strably dangerous citizens are presumptively entitled to own
a gun, we must, as a nation, move toward a very different
model, one that presumptively bars private citizens from owning a firearm unless they can demonstrate a special need and
ability to do so.

Many things are curbed—why not firearms? Thus we must
act. As a society, we have already agreed that many things are
simply too dangerous to be left in unrestricted private possession. . . .

After the bloodshed in this region and this nation in the
last two months alone, who can still argue compellingly that
Americans can be trusted to handle guns safely?

We think the time has come for Americans to tell the truth
about guns. They are not for us; we cannot handle them.
They kill people, our children included. It's time to get rid
of them. Period.

"Who can still argue compellingly that Americans can be
trusted to handle guns safely?" I can.

Did Gun Control Save George Harrison?

In 1999, British authorities arrested a man who entered former Beatle George Harrison's house. Armed with a knife, the man stabbed Harrison four times. Harrison and his wife fought off the attacker, the wife striking the assailant with a lamp. Harrison survived his injuries, but a knife wound in a slightly different area of his chest could have killed him.

Predictably, a *Los Angeles Times* columnist wrote an editorial, headlined, "Thank My Sweet Lord for Gun Laws,"[1] in which he argues that Harrison remains alive because of Great Britain's tough anti-gun laws.

Columnist Mike Downey wrote, "Because the attacker carried nothing worse than a knife, Harrison's wife, Olivia, apparently was able to save her husband by picking up a lamp and striking [the assailant] with it. A lamp would have done little good against a gun." Well, a knife would have done little good against a gun. Suppose Harrison kept a gun in the nightstand next to his bed. He might well have avoided four puncture wounds, in addition to the slight injury sustained by his wife. Suppose the assailant, casing Harrison's house, knew that Harrison possessed a gun. Even if the assailant had armed himself with a gun, do you suppose he would have entered knowing that Harrison possessed a gun?

The *L.A. Times* columnist reacted in a typical knee-jerk, emotional, liberal way. Guns, bad. No guns, good.

University of Chicago professor John R. Lott, Jr., however, has written an important book called *More Guns, Less Crime: Understanding Crime and Gun Control Laws.*[2] Few emotional, liberal journalists bothered to read it—or any other anti-gun-control books—which explains this journalist's appalling ignorance of the "NRA side" in the gun control debate, and it explains the journalist's irresponsible and certainly negligent handling of this issue.

Professor Lott, the recipient of death threats following the publication of his book, earlier wrote an article on gun control to be published in the *Journal of Legal Studies*. He offered Susan Glick, research director for the anti-gun Violence Policy Center, a chance to review the article. According to Lott, she refused to even read it! Later, when reporters asked her to comment on Lott's writing, she trashed his work, its data, and its conclusions—all without ever having bothered to read it. Typical.

L.A. Times columnist Downey continued, "John Lennon never stood a chance in 1980, when he was ambushed by a gun-wielding Mark David Chapman outside a New York apartment building and assassinated. Had his brother Beatle been living in America rather than on a 34-acre compound near London, it is entirely possible that a candlelight vigil would be carrying on this morning just outside the gates of that estate." Really.

Thirty-one states in America allow citizens to carry concealed weapons, nearly all, first requiring both a permit and training. In *all* thirty-one states, the murder rate declined.[3] True, most categories of crime in America are declining, but the states that allow citizens the right to carry concealed weapons saw even bigger decreases in homicide. By columnist Downey's logic, the opposite should have happened.

Downey also perpetuates the warm, fuzzy, romantic image we have of the British—that the island nation is populated by gentle, civil souls revealing a streak of violence only, perhaps, at the occasional rugby game or soccer match. But here are the facts. Overall crime in Great Britain is rising faster than that in America.[4] The per capita burglary rate, robbery rate, car theft rate, is higher, repeat, *higher* than that in America. More important, their per capita rate of so-called hot burglaries—in which an intruder enters an occupied home—is greater than that of America. Why? Bad guys know that people at home possess no weapons. In America, the bad guys know that the occupant may have a gun. The National Institute of Justice surveyed two thousand felons in state prisons and asked ex-cons whether "one reason burglars avoid houses when people are home is that they fear being shot during the crime." Seventy-four percent of the felons said yes. The survey also asked these felons whether they had abandoned at least one crime because they feared the intended suspect might be armed. Thirty-nine percent said they abandoned at least one crime; 8 percent had abandoned such a crime "many" times; 34 percent admitted being "scared off, shot at, wounded, or captured by an armed victim"; and nearly 70 percent knew a "colleague" who had abandoned a crime, been scared off, been shot at, wounded or captured by a victim packing heat.[5]

Furthermore, England's murder rate is also rapidly increasing. America's murder rate is affected because of the disproportionately high amount of minorities who kill or are killed. We can attribute a large number of America's murders to gang-related violence, a phenomenon Americans are plagued with far more so than those in other industrialized countries. American society is simply more violent. When compared to other nations, our murder rate, whether by knife, handgun, or baseball bat, exceeds that of many other nations. The issue is whether government restrictions on handguns help or hurt, since guns used for self-defense save lives and avoid injuries.

On January 16, 2000, the *Times* (London) published a story headlined "Killings Rise as Three Million Illegal Guns Flood Britain." And on January 14, 2000, the *Manchester Guardian* published a story stating that, among machine-gun-toting criminals, guns are now "almost a fashion accessory."[6]

And on June 20, 1999, the UK's *Sunday Express* wrote, "In recent months there have been a frightening number of shootings in Britain's major cities, despite new laws banning gun ownership. . . . Our investigation established that guns are available through means open to any criminally minded individual."[7]

Beyond this, the genie is out of the bottle. There are more than 200 million firearms in America, or nearly one for every man, woman, and child. Contrary to popular perception, guns are harder to obtain than they were a generation or two ago. But now we have more laws, more regulations, and stiffer penalties for misusing guns than in the past. Yet less than 1 percent of all guns are ever involved in crimes.

The real question is this: Suppose all law-abiding citizens gave up their weapons. Would America be safer, less violent, with fewer murders and aggravated assaults?

So, Who Needs a Gun, Anyway?

Carl Rowan, respected newspaper columnist, hated guns. He wrote passionately and often about his opposition to guns. In a January 21, 1981, column, Rowan wrote that "anyone found in possession of a handgun except a legitimate officer of the law goes to jail—period," and, in 1985, he called for a "complete and federal ban on the sale, manufacture, importation, and possession of a handgun (except for authorized police and military personnel)."[8]

In June 1988, an intruder entered Carl Rowan's property, and decided to help himself to Rowan's swimming pool. Enraged, frightened, or both, Mr. Rowan got a gun, later determined to be unregistered, and shot and wounded the trespasser. When pundits asked Mr. Rowan, whom some dubbed "the Jacuzzi Gunman," to explain his apparent inconsistency, Rowan remarked, "I am for gun control, but I am not for unilateral gun control, in which I leave my family naked to the druggies and the crooks out there."[9]

NRA president Charlton Heston says that during the Los Angeles Riots of 1992, his liberal Democratic friends called and sheepishly asked if Heston could train them to use a firearm. Heston replied, "Not this quickly." Remember the old line, "A conservative is a liberal who's been mugged"?

Actress Sharon Stone, cameras in tow, made a big pronouncement of "turning in her firearms and relying on the police." Too many guns, says Stone.

Yet, this is the same Sharon Stone who, in a *Movieline* interview, admitted that, years ago, an intruder tried to break into her home. "I called 911 and no one came," she said. "I called 911 again about ten minutes later and still no one came. Then he started to climb the gate. I called 911 a third time, and said, 'This [expletive deleted]'s on the gate.'" Yet, no one arrived. Finally, as the man began climbing over her gate, Stone got a firearm, stepped out her front door, and hit the button that opened her automatic gate. "As [the gate] swung open I pumped my shotgun and said, I'm gonna blow your ass all over the street.'"[10] The next thing she heard was the sound of his footsteps running away.

Let's analyze this. Sharon Stone, not exactly living in Shantytown, called 911 several times. If the cops did not arrive for Sharon Stone, what do you think your or my chances are? Secondly, she saw the guy climbing over her fence through her security camera. This means, she has video security and a fence high enough that someone has to climb over it. Assets most of us don't, and will never, have.

Now, she gives up her guns. Does she also give up her home in an undoubtedly crime-light area? Did she tear down her fence, a fence so high that it requires an intruder to scale it to enter? Did she give up her armed guard security, where her home alarm, which she undoubtedly possesses, sends not only security guards, but armed security guards? Did she give up the private security patroller, who drives up and down the streets, a feature enjoyed by affluent neighborhoods?

So, I imagine Ms. Stone feels fairly safe, with or without her trusty musket. But, as for the rest of us. . . .

Senator Dianne Feinstein [D-California] opposes laws allowing responsible, trained citizens to apply for permits to carry concealed weapons. Yet, Feinstein herself holds such a permit! In 1978, Feinstein (then president of the board of supervisors) became mayor of San Francisco after former supervisor Dan White entered city hall and murdered Mayor George Moscone and Supervisor Harvey Milk. As a senator, Feinstein, of course, can get taxpayer-provided security. As one of the richest members of Congress, she can afford private security, but she nevertheless feels sufficiently fearful to have a permit allowing her—an opportunity she would deny others—to carry a concealed weapon.

Is Senator Feinstein less safe than, say, a black woman with two kids who has to take the 2:30 A.M. bus across town to get to her job as an office maintenance worker? Yet, this woman who may live in a crime-ridden area would find it difficult, if not impossible, to obtain a permit to carry a concealed weapon.

New York, like California, also prevents citizens from carrying concealed weapons. However, New Yorkers with "juice" somehow, some way, manage to get a CCW (a permit to *c*arry a *c*oncealed *w*eapon). Donald Trump has one. William F. Buckley has one. Laurence Rockefeller has one. Howard Stern has one. But the baker from Queens who gets up at four o'clock in the morning to open his shop early. . . . fuggedaboutit!

According to Professor John Lott, ". . . if all states had adopted nondiscretionary concealed-handgun laws in 1992, about one thousand, six hundred fewer murders and four thousand, eight hundred fewer rapes would have been committed."[11]

By now, Americans are beginning to ask, "How many more laws do we need to pass?" Polls show that Americans no longer want more gun control legislation. They want current laws enforced.

In 1994, Congress passed the Brady Bill. The law provides for a five-day waiting period, a national background check, and makes it illegal for a felon to purchase a gun.

And, since the passage of the Brady Bill, what has been the result? According to President Clinton, in his 1999 State of the Union speech, "The Brady Bill has stopped a quarter million felons, fugitives, and stalkers from buying handguns."[12]

This is, quite simply, a crock. It is illegal for a felon to attempt to purchase a gun *in the first place*. So, according to Clinton, there should have been a quarter of a million prosecutions. How many prosecutions have there been? By June 1997, when the Supreme Court found the background-check provision was unconstitutional, only four people had gone to jail for violations.[13] Where are the rest of the prosecutions, Mr. President?

Long before the Brady Bill, most states had laws as far-reaching—if not more so—than those imposed by the Brady Bill. What sane, or, for that matter, semi-sane felon walks into a gun store, signs his name on a registration form, and purchases a gun?

Some argue that gun purchases should be limited to, for example, no more than one gun per month. Why impose limits on a legal product? Should we limit Americans to the purchase of one automobile per month? Or one VCR per month? What is the policy objective sought with such a structure? After all, one is enough to commit a crime, isn't it? Rarely are crimes committed with an arsenal.

Should there be some sort of registration for people who wish to purchase a gun? No, for under the Second Amendment of the Constitution, citizens have the right to keep and bear arms. While virtually no right is unlimited, why impose counter-productive conditions, restrictions, and other requirements for Americans to exercise this Constitutionally protected *right*?

There is no evidence to support the argument that registration decreases crime. Registration will impose yet another burden on the law-abiding citizen seeking to purchase a handgun. The greater the burdens imposed, the fewer the people willing to jump through hoops to purchase a gun. The fewer guns in the hands of citizens, the easier for politicians to impose even further restrictions.

Moreover, under the United States Supreme Court decision, *United States vs. Haynes,* 1968, registration only affects the law-abiding. In fact, it is a violation of the Fifth Amendment against self-incrimination to *force* a felon to register a gun, because the very act of doing so causes him to admit the commission of a crime!

What About the Mentally Unstable?

Everybody agrees crazy people shouldn't own guns. But how do you define "crazy"?

There is no national roster of people diagnosed with mental disorders. Are gun control advocates claiming that the government should compile such a list?

Should the owner of a gun shop hand a No. 2 pencil to an applicant and ask that he fill out a test to determine his mental suitability?

Following the Columbine tragedy, Hillary Rodham Clinton urged Congress to do more to keep guns out of the hands of the mentally unbalanced. She did not, however, tell us how to accomplish this.

What about people suffering from depression? Should we bar them from purchasing a gun? President Abraham Lincoln suffered from melancholia. Should he have been banned from owning a gun?

And what about suicides? In 1997, 10.6 Americans per one hundred thousand killed themselves.[14] England's rate of suicide? Twelve per one hundred thousand.[15] Not a lot different from America's. According to John Lott, "The evidence for suicides indicate that people will commit suicide whether a gun is present or not. It might change the *way* someone commits suicide, but it seemed to have no impact on the total number of suicides."

In 1999, a day trader at an Atlanta brokerage went on a shooting spree, killing nine and wounding twelve.[16] Hillary Rodham Clinton, preparing for her New York Senate run, said, "I think it does once again urge us to think hard about what we can do to make sure that we keep guns out of the hands of children and criminals and mentally unbalanced people. I would hope that Congress would take action on the legislation that is now pending before it as soon as possible."[17]

Unfortunately, this day trader failed to fit any of Ms. Clinton's categories. He was neither a child, a criminal nor diagnosed as "mentally unbalanced." But whenever tragedy strikes, the legislative response is to "do something." This usually means more restrictive legislation.

The media also show complete indifference when a civilian uses a gun to defend himself or even to ward off widespread carnage.

The day following the Atlanta day trader shootings, there was a little-reported story in the same town. In this case, a civilian used a gun to *stop* more carnage.

Rick Carr, who runs an automotive parts store, fired an employee. Carr, not a handgun proponent, nevertheless felt concerned enough following the day trader massacre to go to a local gun store. He passed the state's instant background check and purchased a 9mm handgun.

Sure enough, the wife of the disgruntled ex-employee ran to the store, warning the workers that her husband intended to kill everybody. Eighteen people in the store attempted to leave, but the disgruntled ex-employee had already shown up with a 12-gauge shotgun. He put the gun to the head of a woman and then ordered everybody into a storeroom. Carr gave a gun to an employee who pointed it at the assailant, then ultimately grabbed the assailant's gun and wrestled it away. The police chief said, "This could've been a lot worse, since alcohol was involved."[18]

And, nearly a month earlier, a San Jose, California, man took several gun club employees hostage. A shooting club employee, however, shot the suspect twice. No one else was injured, but the assailant had left a suicide note stating his determination to take several lives as well as his own. Again, little newspaper coverage.

What About Self-Defense?

A guy goes to a baseball game. When he returns home, his wife says, "Who won?" The guy answers, "Well, the Cleveland Indians scored four runs." Hubby, of course, failed to answer wife's question. For, without knowing how many runs the Indians' opponents scored, the winner of the game is unknowable.

Similarly, gun control "advocates" rarely seem to ask the question, "How often do Americans use handguns for self-defense, to prevent rape or other serious injury or death?" On my radio show, I interviewed LAPD chief Bernard Parks, a proponent of still more gun laws, including the ban of the sale of so called "cheap" Saturday night specials. I told the chief how I felt it was astounding that he was ignoring the fact that two million people each year use guns for defensive purposes—usually just having to brandish them to deter crime—and how I felt that he was saying to poor people, "I don't care how little money you have. I'm not gonna allow you to buy a cheap gun. If you buy a gun, it must be an expensive gun, whether or not you can afford it. The very people that need the guns the most are the people living in the inner city, who have the least amount of money, and they are the ones who buy Saturday night specials."

Chief Parks replied, "It's interesting that we're only concerned about people that have no money and that they are poor when we want to give them an object that will injure them or injure other people. We're not concerned with a lot of other issues. . . ."

"Well, you just ignored what I said about two million people a year using guns for defensive purposes," I said. "Can you address that?"

"Well, I don't know where you got that figure."

"I got it from John Lott [the author of the book *More Guns, Less Crime*]," I replied.

"Well, Larry, let me say this," Chief Parks said. "If that is true, we don't see that in the city of Los Angeles. What I would think people would be reporting to us when we make over two hundred thousand arrests a year—"

"Oh, please, Chief Parks, the reason people don't do it is because you may arrest *them*." After dancing around the defensive purposes of guns issue for a while longer, I finally asked him, "Are you telling me that if I gave you evidence that guns were used for defensive purposes every year over a million times, you would alter your position?"

His response? "I would not alter my position, because I see the end result."

I asked the chief to comment on the fact that countries like Switzerland and Israel, which have far more guns per capita than we do, have a much lower rate of gun-related deaths. He said, "You know, Larry, I don't know if I could explain that, because I don't have that information and I've never studied it. I can only talk to you about what we know in the United States."

"Chief, with all due respect," I said, "You don't seem to know how many times guns are used for defensive purposes, you don't seem to know about other countries . . . even in Australia, they had a turn-in program—"

"Let's talk about the United States," said Chief Parks. "That's where we live, that's where guns are killing people."

"No, it's relevant, Chief, to know other countries' experience, too, because there are lots of variables, and guns are just one of them."

In looking at guns, why not look at the benefits as well as the costs? Professor John Lott, author of *More Guns, Less Crime*,[19] estimates that over two million Americans each year defend themselves and thwart violent crime with a handgun. Others place the figure at a million or less. If Americans do, in fact, use guns for defensive purposes well over a million, and perhaps over two million times, damn right this is relevant. If brandishing a gun prevents the death of a small percentage of handgun brandishers, lives saved by guns outweigh lives lost! The honest answer is that no one knows for sure, but evidence suggests that the benefits of guns outweigh their cost.

There's a reason no one knows. Assume an intruder enters your home, and you shoot with an unregistered weapon. Authorities may arrest *you*, especially if they feel you shot without fear of imminent risk to yourself or to others. That's right. An intruder can enter your home, perhaps with children inside, and, if the homeowner acts "too precipitously," he or she could be in trouble. Thus, many civilians, after brandishing a gun to stop a crime, simply refuse to call the cops, obscuring the numbers of innocent Americans who may have protected themselves with a gun.

On my radio show, I asked those who, in the last few years, used a gun for defensive purposes to call or write. The following letter is typical of those I received:

"I wanted to share my personal story of a defensive gun use. This occurred in January or February of 1995. At about 1:00 A.M., we were awakened by a loud noise, and a dog's barking. I got up to investigate, and, when nothing inside the house seemed amiss, I went outside. Just as I was about to step out the door, I decided to take my friend, 'Herr Glock.' Nothing seemed out of place either. I did hear something rustle in the bushes up the street, but thought nothing of it. The next week, I noticed that our security screen door wasn't working quite right.

"I looked at the latchplate, and saw scratches from a pry tool. At that point, I realized what that odd noise was. It was my noisy screen door slamming shut after the guy's pry tool slipped. Next, I realized that the sounds coming from the bushes weren't a cat as I thought. The guy was watching the house and probably planning to make another attempt to get in. The sight of me with that big, ugly Glock sent him scurrying."

Economist Thomas Sowell writes, "The media present gun control issues solely from the perspective of a battle of the good guys who want to get rid of dangerous weapons versus the National Rifle Association that wants to keep guns around. Most mainstream journalists have an almost total lack of interest in either the facts or the fates of a quarter of a billion Americans who do not belong to either the anti-gun lobby or the NRA."[20]

On the issues of guns, gun control, and violence, the media consistently mislead Americans, underreport or fail to report data contradicting their preconceived notions. The media, therefore, mislead the American people into thinking that the presence of guns causes far more social damage than their absence. It is a lie, placing millions of Americans at greater risk of harm than had the truth been told.

How ignorant are people about the extent to which Americans use guns for defensive purposes? Consider the following letter I received from a well-educated man who considers himself well-informed.

Dear Larry:

A couple of years ago after another "shooting tragedy," my friend and I were having a discussion on the issues of the day (as we often do) and the topic of gun control came up. Neither of us owns a gun, nor really cares to, but we tried to be unbiased and base our opinions on logical thought. We were discussing how often a gun is actually used for self-defense compared to how many accidental deaths there were.

Based on the data (i.e. frequency of newspaper and network news reports), do you know how many times a year we thought guns were used for defensive purposes?

Fifty!!!!!!

Our 1300-SAT-scoring well-read engineering-graduate-degree logical minds came up with fifty !!!!!!

We figured that if they were used more often, we'd hear about it!

Based on a number of fifty, the argument to ban guns makes sense (at least more sense). When you quoted that the actual number was around two million, I was shocked! I haven't read *More Guns, Less Crime*, but I've read excerpts and some other material describing how that data was obtained. I can't argue with those stats.

Now when I tell my friends that guns are used for defensive purposes two million times annually, they don't believe me. That number is so far beyond what they can possibly conceive, they think I'm crazy, even my conservative "pro-gun" friends. *However, being reasonably intelligent individuals, they all concede that if it really was that high, they'd have to rethink their view.* See, many people aren't basing their views on gun control merely on emotion, but on a lack of facts.

Now I'm angry. I feel lied to. If there's one thing that really irks me, it is withholding information. How can I, or anybody, form a reasonable opinion on something if the data presented is so overwhelmingly skewed? The story of the eighty-three-year-old man using a gun to defend himself appearing in only two of three hundred newspapers really infuriated me. I don't need a newspaper to tell me what to think (or what not to think). I need a newspaper to present the facts so I can form my own opinions.

Another Mass Shooting

UCLA professor emeritus James Q. Wilson, a respected expert on crime, police practices, and guns, says, "People who . . . defended themselves with a weapon were less likely to lose property in a robbery or be injured in an assault than those who did not defend themselves."[21] Two things to note: self-defense works, and all the gun control laws in the world don't matter if authorities fail to do their jobs.

These are the two most profound lessons from the 1999 shooting at the North Valley Jewish Community Center in Los Angeles, a shooting that resulted in five wounded. Also that day, the alleged gunman, Buford Oneal Furrow, a white supremacist, shot and killed a Filipino letter carrier.

The suspect allegedly cased and rejected the three most visible L.A. Jewish "targets"—the University of Judaism, the Museum of Tolerance at the Simon Wiesenthal Center, and the Skirball Cultural Center. Why? Too much security.

What about more anti-gun laws? The guns-kill-people crowd call for more gun regulation, from registration, to banning the sale of handguns, to their confiscation. But people who live in the real world know that bad guys abound and take measures to minimize tragedy. Furrow had apparently planned the crime for many months. So lengthening the waiting period for purchasing a firearm would not have prevented the tragedy.

In 1998, Furrow spent one month in the psychiatric unit of a Seattle hospital. Following his discharge, he then tried to commit *himself* into a different facility. There he bluntly stated his desire to kill people and even pulled a knife on two workers. Furrow had apparently cut a finger deep enough to expose bone, and had about a half a dozen knife slashes on his arm. For threatening the mental hospital workers, the police arrested him, charging him with second-degree assault.

After his arrest, Furrow wrote, "I'm a white seperatist [sic]. I've been having suicidial [sic] and homicidial [sic] thoughts for some time now. Yesterday, I had thoughts that I would kill my ex-wife and some of her friends, and then maybe I would drive to Canada and rob a bank. I wanted the police to shoot me. I own a 9-millimeter semiautomatic handgun made by Taurus. I always carry it in the glove box of my car. I also have several knives." He also wrote, "Sometimes I feel I could just loose [*sic*] it and kill people."[22]

His defense attorney initially filed a motion for an insanity defense, and the prosecution called Furrow a threat to himself and others, the standard for involuntary commitment. The court sentenced him to eight months in jail, but he served only five, getting credit for time served, and for good behavior. Then, he walked free. The judge ordered Buford to surrender his guns, but the probation officer, in violation of department policy, never checked to determine whether Furrow complied. And the *Seattle Post-Intelligencer* says that a psychologist made several calls to the police. He wanted them to file charges against Furrow so that he could begin the process of involuntary civil commitment. Somebody dropped the ball.

Following the shooting in L.A., Attorney General Janet Reno urged testing for prospective gun buyers, "I'd have them take a written and manual test demonstrating that they know how to safely and . . . to lawfully use [a weapon] under state law."[23]

Would that have stopped Furrow? As a convicted felon, he already violated the law by possessing handguns of any sort. Also, California law outlaws carrying a firearm within a thousand feet of a school. His probation officer violated policy by failing to make any in-home visits. And, as a mechanical engineer, Furrow could likely have passed any written test about gun operation without much difficulty.

The predictable political response is, "Let's do something." This usually means pass more laws, push more regulation, spend more money. Let's get real. This country contains "nut cases," some with murderous, evil intentions. We must enforce laws already on the books and urge mental health professionals to do their jobs. Let's also keep things in perspective. A recent poll by the Anti-Defamation League calls 12 percent of Americans anti-Semitic, an all-time low. Crime is down. Shootings are down, including school shootings, although you wouldn't know it from "news" coverage.

But, we must also examine why this shooter failed to pick on bigger, more symbolic targets. They armed themselves. They were prepared. The Bible, the Torah, and the Talmud make numerous references to the importance of preparedness and self-defense.

We must remain vigilant, acutely aware that bad guys exist. For the Bible says, ". . . and you must surely guard your life. . . ."

At Columbine High in Colorado, two student outcasts, Eric Harris and Dylan Klebold, opened fire on their classmates. At the end of the carnage, fifteen people lay dead, including the two teenage gunmen. Authorities found sixty-seven bombs,[24] including a powerful twenty-pound propane tank bomb, six- to eight-inch pipe bombs, and explosives rigged to timing devices, strategically planted throughout the school. Only three of the bombs went off, but Harris and Klebold intended on death on a massive scale.[25]

Immediately, Congress "seeks answers" and "debates solutions." And, of course, this leads to the typical reaction—pass more laws, spend more money.

But Harris and Klebold had already broken seventeen state and federal weapons control laws.[26] Besides, "the system" ignored warning signs. Harris sent one of his friends a threatening letter. The letter so alarmed the friend's dad, he contacted the police several times and complained about Eric Harris's instability and threats. Little happened. The police did put Columbine High security on alert, and for one year security paid extra attention to Harris. No one intervened.

After the shooting, Harris and Klebold's classmates also spoke of Harris's statements of violence and revenge, but the students had failed to take the remarks seriously.

Polls of street cops show that most of them support laws allowing responsible, trained citizens to apply for permits to carry concealed weapons. Polls show that police chiefs feel otherwise. But, think about it. Since the public largely remains emotionally in favor of more gun control, and since politics play a large role in a police chief's job, small wonder few will publicly declare support for concealed weapons permits. But the men and women in blue on the street—those who know—know.

I recently argued with a man who talked about the large numbers of accidental homicides committed by guns. According to economist John Lott, only seventeen children under the age of five in 1997 died from an accidental gunshot. Not bad, considering the nearly two hundred million firearms in America. Outlawing guns makes about as much sense as outlawing swimming pools, since three hundred accidental drownings take place each year. Why not outlaw automobiles, since forty thousand motorists die annually?

Nationwide, law books contain some twenty thousand gun laws.[27] What good are gun laws if they are in place and not in force?

On March 30, 1981, John Hinckley shot President Ronald Reagan. Two law enforcement officers were shot, the president was wounded, and press secretary James Brady received a near-fatal shot to the head.

James Brady, who miraculously survived, became a staunch proponent for gun control legislation. Brady blamed the gun.

In the hospital, Reagan said of his attempted assassin, "What's that guy's beef?" Reagan blamed Hinckley.

Both men received serious wounds, and Reagan unbeknownst to many, nearly died, and suffered far more than reported.

One of Reagan's many great strengths is that he appeared to live by the motto: I believe what I see, I don't see what I believe. The facts about guns, the Second Amendment, and self-defense did not change despite the near-tragedy of yet another presidential assassination. Because facts are facts. So many variables contribute to crime, the "availability of guns" being but one of them.

After the Columbine High School shooting tragedy, Rachel Scott's father addressed the House Judiciary Committee's subcommittee. He blamed the shooter for killing his daughter. He said, "In the days that followed the Columbine tragedy, I was amazed at how quickly fingers began to be pointed at groups such as the

NRA. I am not a member of the NRA. I am not a hunter. I do not even own a gun. I am not here to represent or defend the NRA because I don't believe that they are responsible for my daughter's death. Therefore I do not believe that they need to be defended. If I believed they had anything to do with Rachel's murder I would be their strongest opponent.

"I am here to declare that Columbine was not just a tragedy—it was a spiritual event that should be forcing us to look at where the real blame lies! Much of the blame lies here in this room. Much of the blame lies behind the pointing fingers of the accusers themselves.

"And when something as terrible as Columbine's tragedy occurs, politicians immediately look for a scapegoat such as the NRA. They immediately seek to pass more restrictive laws that contribute to eroding our personal and private liberties.

"We do not need more restrictive laws. Eric and Dylan would not have been stopped by metal detectors. No amount of gun laws can stop someone who spends months planning this type of massacre. The real villain lies within our own hearts."[28]

For years, the National Rifle Association urged the government to enforce laws already on the books. Richmond, Virginia, has had a severe high crime problem. The NRA contributed $100,000 toward a $400,000 program called Project Exile. Under this program, the authorities used federal laws to prosecute those found with illegal handguns. Now, I believe crime control, for the most part, remains a state, not federal, function. But, under Project Exile, federal laws were used because, if convicted, criminals went to a federal penitentiary. Criminals hate federal pens because they are frequently out of state, far from their homes. So fearful of federal prosecution, Richmond, Virginia, criminals began saying to prosecutors, "Can we stop this thing from going federal?" Within a couple of years, Richmond's murder rate fell in half, this without new gun laws.[29]

Enforcing current laws works. Crime goes down once you increase the fear of capture, conviction, and incarceration. The NRA put up, and others shut up.

Guns and the Second Amendment

The Founding Fathers left us with a little something called the Second Amendment:

A well regulated Militia, being necessary to the security of a free State, the right of the people to keep and bear Arms, shall not be infringed.[30]

Some scholars claim that this simply means that a citizen may carry a gun only as a part of a "well regulated Militia." That is, the government can regulate, or completely outlaw, firearms for any purpose other than serving in a "well regulated Militia." In other words, the Second Amendment confers a collective, and not individual, right of gun ownership. The Supreme Court has not taken up a Second Amendment case since 1939. Then, the Court implied that the Second Amendment conferred a collective but not individual right to keep and bear arms. And Chief Justice Warren Burger once accused the NRA of badly misleading the American people about the Second Amendment. Burger said, "One of the greatest pieces of fraud, I repeat the word fraud, on the American public by special interest groups that I have ever seen in my lifetime."[31]

But we rightly regard the Founding Fathers as learned and articulate men, certainly possessing the ability to specifically restrict the right to bear arms to those serving in the "well regulated Militia." The Constitution contains many other instances where the Founding Fathers did, in fact, make such restrictions. Not here.

Thomas Jefferson wrote in a letter to a friend in England, "The constitutions of most of our states assert, that all power is inherent in the people; . . . that it is their right and duty to be at all times armed."[32] In a letter to George Washington, he said that a model state constitution guaranteed that "[n]o free man shall be debarred the use of arms in his own lands."[33]

Patrick Henry declared that, "the great object is that every man be armed." James Madison stated that tyrants were "afraid to trust the people with arms," and lauded "the advantage of being armed, which Americans possess over the people of almost every other nation."[34]

Thomas Paine realized that the criminal element would always have weapons, and that decent people should be able to defend against them: "The peaceable part of mankind will be overrun by the vile and abandoned while they neglect the means of self-defense. . . . [Weakness] allures the ruffian [but] arms like laws discourage and keep the invader and plunderer in awe and preserve order in the world. . . . Horrid mischief would ensue were [the good] deprived of the use of them. . . . The weak will become a prey to the strong."[35]

Respected liberal Harvard law professor Laurence Tribe recently came out of the closet and conceded that, yes, a plain reading of the Constitution as well as writings by the Founding Fathers point one way. The right to keep and bear arms is an individual, not collective, right. Tribe writes that the Second Amendment is subject to "reasonable regulation," but calls gun control advocate extremists wrong when they say the Second Amendment restricts the right to only a "state militia" like the National Guard. Tribe said that "the Fourteenth Amendment, which makes parts of the Bill of Rights applicable to the states, reflected a broad agreement that bearing arms was a 'privilege' of each citizen."[36]

Liberal attorney Alan Dershowitz agrees, "Foolish liberals who are trying to read the Second Amendment out of the Constitution by claiming that it's not an individual right or that it's too much of a safety hazard don't see the danger of the big picture. They're courting disaster by encouraging others to use the same means to eliminate portions of the Constitution they don't like."[37]

Is the Second Amendment absolute? No. No more than is the First Amendment. There are boundaries, one of which prevents possession of weaponry that threatens national security (nuclear weapons, for example). The government outlawed certain "assault" rifles, such as tommy guns, nearly fifty years ago. It's difficult to argue that owning a tommy gun is necessary for self-defense. On the other hand, many clamor for the outlaw of so-called assault-style weapons. The term sounds, big, bad, and ugly, but no precise definition for it exists. And, however Congress defines "assault-style weapons," agile manufacturers modify, alter, or redesign guns to fall outside of any definition.

Of the nation's firearms, less than 1 percent will ever be used in any crime. Of that 1 percent, only a tiny fraction involve so-called "assault weapons," or "assault–style weapons." Most criminals wish to avoid detection, finding it difficult to hide and carry such a large weapon, whether an Uzi, AK-47, or hunting rifle. The weapon of choice for criminals is a handgun. So, while a ban on "assault weapons" or "assault-style weapons" allows politicians to stand and say they "did something," the impact on crime remains negligible.

Handgun control "advocates" call for the licensing of all guns. But since, as explained, the Second Amendment grants individual citizens the "right" to keep and bear arms, requiring licensing for a "right" is a contradiction in terms.

The "Facts"

Many in the medical profession lead the fight for more gun control legislation. Doctors, especially emergency room physicians, see the blood and the gore and instinctively call for more gun control. Since doctors are people of statistics, logic, and reason, one would think they would know better. But, when applied to issues like gun control, the structured, scientifically oriented logic goes AWOL.

Dr. Edgar A. Suter, national chair for Doctors for Integrity in Policy Research, Inc., wrote a paper on doctors and guns called "Guns in the Medical Literature." He said, "Errors of fact, design, and interpretation abound in the medical literature on guns and violence. . . . [The] medical literature has virtually ignored all of the comprehensive scholarly evaluations of guns, violence, and gun control . . ."[38]

In short, Dr. Suter argues that most doctors, like many members of the public, viscerally dislike guns, and tailor research conclusions to reach their own personal beliefs. Dr. Suter wrote that medical literature on guns consist of "prejudicially truncated data, non-sequitur logic, correct methodology described, but not used," and that doctors "deceptively understated the protective benefits of guns."

For example, a famous study published in the *New England Journal of Medicine* by Drs. A. L. Kellerman and D. T. Rea, noted that a gun owner is forty-three times more likely to kill a family member than an intruder.[39] Newspapers widely reported this figure.

The Kellerman-Rea study ignored the protective uses of guns each year. When, however, researchers carefully examined the data, the "43 times" number became "2.7 times."[40]

Dr. Suter writes that "guns were next to last in importance of the 'risk factors' studied. Alcohol, living alone, family violence, and renting one's home held more risk than guns" according to other studies.

Another study authored by Kellerman says, "When women killed with a gun, their victim was five times more likely to be their spouse. . . ."[41]

But Kellerman left out the fact that, according to FBI data, when women kill with a knife, the victim was also more likely to be their spouse. In short, when women kill with anything, the victim is four or five times more likely to be the spouse. Well, duh.

Dr. Suter blasts the medical literature for failing to apply scientific rigor to the study of guns and violence in America. Doctors discard contradicting data and, like reporters, allow biases to create foregone conclusions. Says Dr. Suter, "The responsible use and safe storage of any kind of firearm causes no social ill, and leaves no victims. In fact, guns offer positive social benefit in protecting good citizens from vicious predators. The overwhelming predominance of data we have examined shows that between 25 to 75 lives may be saved by a gun, for every life lost to a gun. Guns also prevent injuries to good people, preventing medical costs from such injuries and protect billions of dollars of property every year. In view of the overwhelming benefits, it is ludicrous to punitively tax gun or ammunition ownership. They save far more lives than they cost.

"The peer review process has failed in the medical literature. In the field of guns, crime, and violence, the medical literature—and medical politicians—have much to learn conceptually and methodologically from the criminological, legal, and social science literature."

And, as mentioned in Chapter 3, the media go berserk about gun control. The Media Research Center studied the Brady Bill debate coverage by NBC, ABC, CBS, and CNN from July 1, 1997, to June 30, 1999, and found the coverage blatantly slanted toward the anti-gun crowd:[42]

- **TV News Has Chosen Sides** Stories advocating more gun control outnumbered stories opposing gun control by 357 to 36, or a ratio of almost 10 to 1. (Another 260 were neutral.)
- **Evening News Shows Favored the Anti-Gun Position by 8 to 1** Almost 60 percent of stories (184) favored one side. While 89 percent of those (164) pushed the liberal, anti-gun position, only 11 percent (20) promoted the pro-gun position. ABC's *World News Tonight* (43 anti-gun stories to 3 pro-gun)

and CNN's *The World Today* (50 to 7) were the most slanted evening shows.

- **Morning News Shows Favored the Anti-Gun Position by 13 to 1** More then half of morning news gun-policy segments (208) tilted away from the balance. Of those segments, 93 percent (193) pushed the liberal, anti-gun position, while only six percent (15) promoted the pro-gun position. ABC's *Good Morning America* (92 to 1) was the most biased morning show.

Also, the networks repeatedly called those opposing the Brady Bill "lobbyists," while reporters called supporters of the Brady Bill "advocates." Remember, gun "lobbyist," bad. Gun "advocate," good.

Bob Kahn owns B&B Sales, one of the largest firearms dealers in the West. He is a noted expert on firearms, and averages at least one request per week for an interview by the print or TV media. He told me that "the media edits out not only reasonable arguments, but also provocative statements that support our side." The media, he maintains, seems uninterested in things like the frequency of the defensive use of handguns. He added, "We are the company that supplied firearms and ammunition to the police in the 1997 North Hollywood bank shoot-out. The media attacked us for our efforts and never reported that we auctioned off the firearms we loaned the LAPD, and donated the proceeds to the Police Memorial Fund." Can't let good things "bad guys" do get in the way of a good story about a "bad guy."

In Gun Control "Debates" Emotion Rules

A recent gun debate I had with a friend—a liberal Democrat—is typical. I told her that all too often people who don't like guns respond in an emotional fashion without the facts. Many are people who don't know the information or who, if given the information, dismiss it, finding it inconsistent with a preconceived belief.

My friend denied that she based her opposition to guns on emotion, "I'll give you my biggest reason. Guns are likely, if you have them in your house, to be used on a family member, more so than the guy who breaks into the house."

I said, "Where'd you get that statistic?"

She said, "Oh, it's commonly known."

Right, and commonly false. This notion comes from that famous *New England Journal of Medicine* article which reached that conclusion. Here's what this "scientific" study did:

Suppose an intruder came into the house with a gun, and there was a gun in the house. The gunman shot somebody. This study would attribute this shooting, or any shooting, to the gun possessed by the owner! So a gun in the house becomes a gun that fired, even when the actual shot was fired by the intruder's gun. *More Guns, Less Crime* author Lott says that few cities give a real breakdown on "acquaintance killings." "Only one U.S. city, Chicago," Lott writes, "reports a precise breakdown on the nature of acquaintance killings, and the statistic gives a very different impression: between 1990 and 1995, just 17 percent of murder victims were either family members, friends, neighbors or roommates of their killers."[43] The overwhelming majority of gun deaths that take place within the house are between somebody who has a gun and somebody who has intruded. My friend, like many, was simply, flatly wrong.

She then said, "Forget about inside the house. Let's talk about outside the house. What about the fact that a gun is more likely to end up killing a friend or an acquaintance than killing a bad guy?"

I said, "Who told you that?"

My friend is misled, as are many Americans, because of the way the FBI defines the word "acquaintance." They define it extremely broadly, to include a cab driver, pimp, prostitute, drug dealer. So, if a guy uses his gun because of a bad drug deal, the

FBI considers it an "acquaintance killing." But, if they define "acquaintance killing," the way normal people do, to include friend, family member, mother, father, sister, brother, neighbor, co-worker, the picture changes dramatically.

Lott says that when "domestic violence" murders between family members are excluded, the number of actual "acquaintance killings" falls even lower. "The Chicago Police Department . . . finds that just five percent of all murders in the city from 1990 to 1995 were committed by non-family friends, neighbors or roommates. This is clearly important in understanding crime. The list of non-friend acquaintance murderers is filled with cases in which the relationships would not be regarded by most people as particularly close: for example, relationships between drug pushers and buyers, gang members, prostitutes and their clients, bar customers, gamblers, and cab drivers killed by their customers."[44]

Other myths about guns: that a large number of children innocently die through the misuse of handguns; that closing "gun acquisition loopholes" will affect bad guys' abilities to acquire guns; and that trigger locks are a good idea.

The reason so many Americans feel that a lot of "children" die from guns is, again, based on how the government defines "children." Many "children" are, in fact, teenagers who are gang members and who use guns in gang-related fights. According to John Lott, "The normal claim is that 13 children die every day from guns. This is arrived at by including all gun deaths (murder, suicide, accidents, and justifiable homicides) for people under 20 years of age. Nine of those 13 are for 17-, 18-, and 19-year-olds and primarily involve murder in high crime urban areas (most likely gang members). Eleven of the 13 deaths per day are for those ages 15 and up. 1.9 per day involve those under age 15, and less than .25 per day involve those under age ten."

A mass shooting took place in 1999 in Hawaii, a state with extremely restrictive gun laws. Similarly, violent cities like Washington, D.C., and New York City have very restrictive gun laws. In

Vermont, a citizen need not even apply for a permit to carry a concealed weapon. Yet Vermonters enjoy a very low homicide rate.

Former Manhattan assistant district attorney David P. Koppel, who completed a study of gun control for the Cato Institute, cites a 1979–85 study by the National Crime Survey: "[W]hen a robbery victim does not defend himself, the robber succeeds 88% of the time, and the victim is injured 25% of the time. When a victim resists with a gun, the robbery success rate falls to 30%, and the victim injury rate falls to 17%. No other response to a robbery— from drawing a knife to shouting for help to fleeing—produces such low rates of victim injury and robbery success."[45]

Guns and the Inner City

Once, after I gave a speech, an elderly black service worker came up to me and patted his waist. "I live in South Central," he said, "and the cops busted me once for carrying my piece. I told them, 'I'd rather be judged by twelve than carried out by six.' They told me to 'Have a nice day, Mr. Johnson.' " The street cops know.

A black friend said that manufacturers conspire to "put" guns in the black community. "Larry, guns, like drugs, are brought in from the outside. There's no gun manufacturer in Compton or in Watts."

"Yes," I said. "And there are no pig farms or egg hatcheries there, either. But I had ham and eggs this morning. Grow up."

Enter the NAACP. Various city attorneys, along with the cities of Chicago and New Orleans, threaten to sue gun manufacturers. The NAACP, too, claims that those who make guns negligently supervise the sale and distribution of those guns, and show indifference when guns fall into the hands of bad people.

And many, like the LAPD chief, wish to ban Saturday night specials, arguing that they "saturate" the inner city with guns. Strange argument. If the argument is that cheap guns are poorly manufactured, that's why we have lawyers. All manufacturers owe their customers duty of care. Failing that, call a lawyer. Others argue that "cheap guns" enable firearms to "flood" the streets. Again, a bizarre argument. If, for example, we banned "cheap" cars, who gets hurt? The poor. That's who. Saturday night specials are merely inexpensive weapons available for people unable to afford premium ones. By banning Saturday night specials, politicians disarm inner-city residents, the most vulnerable of all to crime. This is, quite simply, nuts.

But this propaganda—that guns cause crime—is extremely effective. Polls show blacks, a group more likely to be victimized by gun violence, support gun control measures more so than less vulnerable whites.

NAACP president Kweisi Mfume acknowledges other contributing factors to urban violence but says, "It's got to end. They [manufacturers] must stop dumping firearms in oversaturated communities and markets, because the obvious result is those guns are not going to legally authorized gun dealers. They are getting in the hands of criminals for criminal use."[46] "Oversaturated communities"? Do the gun manufacturers go door to door, leaving Glocks in mailboxes? Does the company that manufactures Colts enter inner-city homes, down the chimney à la Santa Claus, quietly leaving revolvers in the hands of sleeping residents?

The *Wall Street Journal* quotes the vice president and general manager of the Austrian company that manufactures Glocks on the NAACP proposed lawsuit, "I love it." He calls the NAACP "racist." "That's what they are, blaming the inner city problems on white gun manufacturers."[47]

More striking is the "black leadership's" ignorance of the history of gun control. Gun control regulation started as a means to prevent black slaves from getting their hands on guns and exacting escape from and revenge on their white oppressors.

Remember the Dred Scott Case, in which the Supreme Court decreed that blacks must be returned to slave owners, since they were not persons, but property? Well, the chief justice of that case,

Roger Taney, stated that if blacks were "entitled to the privileges and immunities of citizens. . . . [i]t would give persons of the [N]egro race, who were recognized as citizens in any one state of the union, the right . . . to keep and carry arms wherever they went. And all of this would be done in the face of the subject race of the same color, both free and slaves, and inevitably producing discontent and insubordination among them, and endangering the peace and safety of the state . . ."[48]

Slave owners' fear of blacks owning guns no doubt rivaled the Nazis' fear of Jews owning guns. The Fascists were staunch proponents of gun control and decreed that citizens ought not own handguns.

Would the Holocaust have turned out differently had innocent civilians owned guns? In his 1979 movie, *Manhattan,* Woody Allen not-that-facetiously said, "Has anybody read that Nazis are gonna march in New Jersey? You know, we should get down there—get some guys together . . . get some bricks and baseball bats and really explain things to them. . . . A satirical piece in the *Times* is one thing, but bricks and baseball bats really get straight to the point."

Frankly, the most accurate definition of "gun control" appears in an old "B.C." comic strip: "Gun control: Hitting what you aim at."

11

THE LAST WORD ON THE "STOLEN" 2000 ELECTION AND THE NEW ADMINISTRATION—WILL EVERYBODY PLEASE QUIT WHINING?

Uh-oh, somebody get the victicrats some Prozac.

During the "stolen" 2000 presidential election, the hysterics put on quite a show. For the third time in our nation's history, the winner of a presidential contest went to the candidate who failed to win the popular vote. When the dust settled, some Democrats not only wanted to take their football back, but attempted to get the game itself declared invalid!

On the eve of the Supreme Court decision that "handed" the election to George W. Bush, Reverend Jesse Jackson led a rally in

Florida to protest: "Today we stand surrounded, Jeb Bush on one hand, Miss Harris on the other, George W. and Cheney comin' from behind, the Supreme Court of Florida. But we will not surrender. Our hopes are alive. Our dreams are alive. Our faith is alive. God will see us through. It's dark, but the morning comes. Don't let them break your spirit."[1] Good Lord.

Black Florida congressman Alcee Hastings said, "There's outrage out there. This isn't something I'm making up. I go to the grocery store and the cleaners, and folks are totally outraged. There's serious frustration, serious disillusionment."[2]

How interesting to receive a lecture in integrity from Congressman Hastings. According to *The Almanac of American Politics 1998* after Hastings' appointment to the federal bench, ". . . He was impeached by the House of Representatives by a vote of 426–3 in 1988 and convicted and removed from office by the Senate by a vote of 69–26. The impeachment arose from allegations that Hastings conspired with a friend to accept $150,000 for giving two convicted swindlers a break in sentencing. . . . In the House, the case for impeachment was made by John Conyers, senior member of the Congressional Black Caucus. Removed from the bench, Hastings was unapologetic."[3] After suffering this indignity, Hastings ran for Congress, and played victim, arguing that his impeachment and conviction resulted from a government vendetta against a powerful black public figure. Blah, blah, blah. But we digress.

The National Organization for Women president, Patricia Ireland, acted as if an asteroid threatened the earth's existence, "I thought first as I listened to Bush, claiming that he won and that Gore was trying to steal the election, and I thought it must be *Alice Through the Looking Glass* down there. And then I thought, no, upon further reflection I think it's really *The Wizard of Oz*. Because, you know, Bush and Cheney, they need a brain and a heart."[4] (Never mind that shortly after the election, but before the courts ultimately decided the outcome, vice-presidential candidate Dick Cheney suffered a heart attack. Nice.)

Lawyer Alan Dershowitz, whom one wag called a "wholly owned subsidiary of the Democratic Party,"[5] pronounced George W. Bush's election legal victory "a legal coup d'etat in suit and tie."[6]

To summarize one of the most dramatic, crazy, topsy-turvy elections in U.S. history, here's what happened. Despite cries of a "stolen" election, Republican candidate George W. Bush carried more states than did Democratic candidate Al Gore, thirty to twenty. Yet, Al Gore won the "popular vote," meaning that Gore received more votes than his rival. But presidential elections go to the electoral college winner.

In the end, Florida became the battleground; its twenty-five electoral votes were enough to put either candidate over the top. Before the historic Supreme Court decision, the electoral college count stood at Bush–246, Gore–268.

The day after the polls closed in Florida on November 7, 2000, the Florida Division of Elections reported that Bush won the popular vote, 2,909,135 to Gore's 2,907,351. By Florida law, the close margin triggered an automatic machine recount. Florida law, however, allows a candidate to contest the vote by demanding a *manual* recount. Within seventy-two hours of the election, the candidate who wishes a manual recount must make a request. Gore did so. Yet, in one of the most monumental decisions in presidential election history, Gore demanded a manual recount in only four counties—Volusia, Broward, Miami-Dade, and Palm Beach.

Why those counties? Al Gore carried those counties by a lopsided margin. The Gore camp theorized that those counties contained "under-votes," ballots where the voter intended a Gore vote, but somehow made an error which the machines couldn't count. Perhaps the voter misunderstood the ballot, or possessed weak hand-strength and was unable to properly punch the ballot. Some of the precincts used the so-called punch-card method, where the voter picks up a stylus or a peg and punches a hole through the card, dislodging a "chad." The Gore camp assumed that many voters failed to push the chad completely through, yet had intended to vote for Gore. The Gore camp decided those four counties contained a motherlode of pro-Gore votes. And Palm Beach County used a so-called "butterfly ballot," with the candidates' names on either side of the ballot, arguably confusing voters. (Yet a Democrat designed the ballot, and anyone objecting had ample time before the election to do so.)

Under a manual recount, a counter literally holds up the voter's ballot card and searches for some sort of identifying mark, an indentation, or partially pushed-through "hanging" chad, demonstrating that the voter tried to register a preference for, say, Gore, but made a mistake.

Never mind that each voter received instructions, clearly and boldly printed on the instruction page of their sample ballot. The instructions read, "After voting, check your ballot card to be sure your voting selections are clearly and cleanly punched and there are no chips left hanging on the back of the card."[7]

Hold the phone, said the Bush camp. Yes, Florida law does allow for automatic manual recounts in close elections, and the initial manual recounts which were completed showed that Bush remained ahead. And, yes, Florida law allows any candidate to demand an additional manual recount, but that recount must take place and be completed within seven days following the vote. Bush argued that Gore lacked the time to complete the recount within the time frame set forth by the Florida legislature.

The Gore camp asked the Florida Secretary of State, Katherine Harris, a Republican appointee and Bush campaign supporter, to grant additional time. Surely, argued Gore, the Florida legislature anticipated providing sufficient time for the likely lengthy and tedious manual recount process. No, said the Bush camp. The law allows only a specific time frame for the manual recounts, and your request for a time extension violates the law.

Harris, the Secretary of State, sided with Bush, and refused

Gore additional time for his manual recounts. Lawsuit followed lawsuit, charges followed counter-charges.

Even if the authorities had granted Gore's request for additional time for manual recounts, counties used varying standards to determine voter intent. Some counties, Bush argued, allowed a more generous standard, counting every mark, however slight, that might indicate voter intent. Other counties used rigorous standards, counting only ballots with dislodged, nearly dislodged, mostly dislodged, or "hanging" chads. Confusing? Judge Charles Burton, head of the Palm Beach County canvassing board, publicly expressed his confusion and exasperation: "It has been my hope that somewhere along the way, a judge, a government body, or somebody else was gonna say, 'This is how it's done,' and having sat here for a week I'm convinced that they can't tell you how to do it. You gotta look at it, you gotta feel what's in your heart and you gotta feel what you're observing and try and decide if that's what the voter wanted."[8] Got that?

In a 5–4 decision, the United States Supreme Court ruled in Bush's favor. The court ruled that since different counties used different standards for discerning voters' intent, such a manual recount process violated the equal protection clause of the Constitution because some votes counted more in some counties than in othters. Seven justices agreed that the Florida county procedure violated the equal protection standard, although two of those justices argued that election officials possessed sufficient time to correct the procedure. Five justices, however, found an equal protection violation and an inadequate amount of time to cure the problems. In its majority decision, the court said, "The right to vote is protected in more than the initial allocation of the franchise. Equal protection applies as well to the manner of its exercise. Having once granted the right to vote on equal terms, the state may not, by later arbitrary and disparate treatment, value one person's vote over that of another."[9] In other words, the equal protection clause of the Constitution cannot allow dimpled chads to be counted as a vote in one county and not in another.

Before the ink dried on the decision, the crying commenced: "George W. Bush, President-Select!" and "Bush Stole the Election!"

Until the Supreme Court decision, Gore supporters continuously chanted the false and misleading line, "They didn't count every vote!" On *60 Minutes*, Gore tried to peddle this nonsense. Correspondent Leslie Stahl asked him, "Make your best case for why you should go on with the recounts, assuming these court decisions do go against you and you want to proceed. What's your best argument?"

Gore replied, "Well, it's not a recount. We want a first count. There are thousands of ballots that were legally cast that have never been counted at all. When people go to the polls and cast legal ballots, we count them. We don't arbitrarily set them aside and refuse to count some of them, but count others."

His twisting of the facts became too much for Stahl, "You make it sound like they never were counted. They did go through the machine count, and it came up that there was no vote. That doesn't mean that they didn't go through the process."

Gore responded, "They were never counted. It means that the computer . . ."

"You don't know that. There could have been votes that weren't cast," said Stahl. "The experts," replied Gore, "including those called by Governor Bush in the court hearing, said the only way you can count ballots is to count them by hand."[10]

The Supreme Court blocked the count! If no Supreme Court—whose conservative majority sided with Bush—Gore wins!

Okay, let's play that game. If every vote "had been counted," Al Gore wins, right? Wrong. The *Miami Herald*, along with a consortium of the nation's major news organizations, each hired outside consultants to examine the "uncounted" ballots—those that never underwent a manual recount, and which were machine-rejected as "overvotes" (where the voter marked more than one candidate for president) or "undervotes." But according to the *Miami Herald*, had the manual recounts continued in Gore's hand-picked counties, he still lacked enough votes to overcome the 537 vote margin of Bush's victory.

As of this writing, the media's counting of all the so-called Florida undervotes continues, but it appears that Bush would likely have won, no matter how you cut it. And even if it doesn't, the reality is this: Of properly cast votes on November 7, 2000, and given the need for the winner to achieve 270 electoral college votes, George W. Bush won this election. As someone once put it, "Can't we all just get along?"

Gore Versus Bush—Major Differences?

Considering the relatively modest differences between the two parties, the 2000 election is much ado about not all that much.

During the election, Bush positioned himself as a "compassionate conservative." But unlike Ronald Reagan, Bush didn't campaign to shut down the Department of Education, but rather to expand it! In 1965, Congress created Title I, a program designed to close the performance gap between affluent public school districts and less affluent, often inner-city districts. Thirty years and more than one hundred twenty billion dollars later, the gap between the affluent and non-affluent districts is much larger than it was at the beginning of the program![11] What to do? George W. Bush proposed spending $25 billion in over five years on an education initiative to expand Title I.

Yes, Bush did propose a ten-year $1.6 trillion tax cut. The president and Congress ultimately settled on a $1.35 trillion cut, but the tax cut gets phased in over a period of years, and reduces the top marginal tax rate a mere four percentage points from 39.6 percentage points to 35 percent. Big deal. Contrast Bush's tax cut plan with that of Ronald Reagan's, when The Gipp lowered the top marginal tax rate from 70 percent to 28 percent, a whopping difference of 42 percent. Or, contrast Bush's plan with the fiscal policy of Republican presidential candidate Alan Keyes, who argued for the abolition of the Internal Revenue Service.

During his first address to the nation, the new president reiterated his campaign position that no American should pay more than one-third of his income to the federal government. *One third*?! How about abolishing the Internal Revenue Service? How about funding the essential functions of government by duties and tariffs, as intended by the Founding Fathers?

The "compassionate conservative" also wishes to divert federal funds to so-called faith-based initiatives, non-profit organizations that assist the needy while preaching religious values. Great—except one thing. Government funds invite government imposition of rules and regulations, blurring yet again the line between church and state. Bush says he "trusts the people." Trusts the people? Then give the people their money back! A government subsidy provided by a Republican president remains a government subsidy.

The attacks against George W. Bush for nominating "extremists" make the differences between the parties seem larger than reality. For example, Bush nominated the "extremist" former Republican governor of Missouri, Senator John Ashcroft, for attorney general. What makes Ashcroft an extremist? Two things. His opposition to affirmative action, and his pro-life stance.

First, many *blacks* oppose affirmative action. Depending upon how the term gets defined, some polls show increasing black opposition. In Chapters 1 and 2, we discussed California's controversial Proposition 209, a voter-passed initiative that eliminates considerations of race and gender in public hiring, contracting, and admissions into colleges and universities. Three in ten black voters supported the initiative. Booker T. Washington argued that one should make it through hard work and the pursuit of excellence, rather than requesting government handouts. He even eerily predicted the emergence of people like Jesse Jackson, who exaggerate the significance of racism. "There is [a] class of colored people who make a business of keeping the troubles, the wrongs, and the hardships of the Negro race before the public. Having learned that they are able to make a living out of their troubles, they have grown into the settled habit of advertising their wrongs—partly because they want sympathy and partly because it pays. Some of these people do not want the Negro to lose his grievances, because they do not want to lose their jobs."[12]

Ashcroft also caught hell for his "extreme" pro-life position. Ashcroft opposes abortion even in cases of rape or incest—an "extremist" position. But think about it. Why is this extreme? Assuming a pro-lifer believes in the protection of an "innocent" third party, of what relevance are the circumstances under which the "unborn" was created? Whether of rape or of incest, the innocent third party remains innocent, say pro-lifers. A truly "extreme" position—one that Ashcroft does not share—would insist upon no abortion ever, even where it literally threatens the life of the mother. And let's remind the John-Ashcroft-opposes-civil-rights forces that according to the National Right to Life Committee polls find blacks are more pro-life than whites, with black men even more pro-life than black women!

For chief of staff, Bush appointed Andrew Card, whom pro-lifers consider "soft" on abortion. As EPA head, Bush appointed former Republican New Jersey governor Christine Todd Whitman, who is pro-choice. This means the "ideologue" Bush demonstrates more inclusiveness for the pro-choice position than Clinton showed for those on the pro-life side. Did Clinton have *any* pro-life cabinet members or high-level appointments?

Still, George W. Bush's election caused NAACP Chairman Julian Bond to practically froth at the mouth: "They selected nominees from the Taliban wing of American politics, appeased the wretched appetites of the extreme right wing, and chose Cabinet officials whose devotion to the Confederacy is nearly canine in its uncritical affection."[13] Devotion to the Confederacy?

Never mind that Bush also nominated Colin Powell and Condoleeza Rice, the first black secretary of state and national security advisor, respectively. Never mind that Bush nominated Alberto Gonzales, a Latino, as White House counsel, or Elaine Chao, the first Asian-American cabinet appointee. Nevertheless, Ashcroft became the lightning rod for many of those who call Bush "President-Select."

Never mind that Ashcroft approved twenty-six of twenty-seven black nominees for judicial positions.[14] Or that when Ashcroft appointed Judge David C. Mason to the state bench in 1991, Mason became one of six black judges in the St. Louis circuit who had been appointed by Republican governors, while only one black had been appointed by a Democrat.[15] Or that Ashcroft's wife worked for several years as an instructor at Washington, D.C.'s historically black college, Howard University.

Democrats attack the GOP's "lack of sensitivity" concerning race. During his primary debate, Al Gore, as usual, positioned himself as Friend of the Black Man, promising action on racial profiling: "If you elect me to the presidency, the first civil rights act of the twenty-first century will be a federal law outlawing racial profiling."[16]

But during the vice presidential debates, "cold, mean-spirited" Republican candidate Dick Cheney sounded positively Gore-like. CNN's Bernard Shaw asked, "Imagine yourself an African-American. You become the target of racial profiling, either while walking or driving. What would you do about it?"

Cheney's response? "Bernie, I'd like to answer your question to the best of my ability, but I don't think I can understand fully what it would be like. Try hard to put myself in that position, imagine what it would be like, but, of course, I've always been part of the majority and never been part of a minority group. But it has to be a horrible experience.

"It's the sense of anger and frustration and rage that would go with knowing that the only reason you were stopped, the only reason you were arrested was because of your color of your skin. It would make me extraordinarily angry. And I'm not sure how I would respond.

"I think that we have to recognize that while we've made enormous progress in the U.S. in racial relations, and we've come a very long way and we still have a long way to go. That we still have not only the problems we're talking about here tonight in terms of the problems you mentioned of profiling, but beyond that, we still have an achievement gap in education, income differentials, differences in life span.

"We still have, I think, a society . . . where we haven't done enough yet to live up to that standard that we'd all like to live up to, I think, in terms of equality of opportunity, that we judge people as individuals. That, as Martin Luther King said, we ought to judge people on the content of their character instead of the color of their skin. I would hope that we can continue to make progress in that regard in the years ahead."[17]

And on the issue of racial profiling, Attorney General John Ashcroft also sounded Gore-like. As one of his three priorities, Ashcroft announced his goal to eliminate racial profiling.[18] Not exactly a call for the re-enactment of slavery.

Differences? On the issue of the war on drugs, both parties trumpet the same theme. As one of his last official acts, President Clinton pardoned, or commuted the sentences of, several people convicted of drug-related offenses, including his half-brother Roger. Yet, during his Presidency, after suffering accusations of being soft on drugs, Clinton became a staunch drug warrior.

Because of the war on drugs during the Clinton era, the rate of blacks going to prison exceeded the rate of blacks imprisoned under the administrations of President Ronald Reagan, and his successor, President George Bush. According to the Justice Policy Institute, during the Clinton administration, the incarceration rate of blacks increased by an average of 100 percent per 100,000 per year[19] over his Republican predecessors' rates.

Are things any different now with a Republican president? Not according to new Attorney General Ashcroft, who announced as another of his top three priorities the reinvigoration of the war on drugs. Blame Colombia. Blame Mexico. Blame the Border Patrol. Blame everybody except the "real culprit"—the U.S. demand for drugs. Rather than urge intelligent reconsideration of this nation's war on drugs, Ashcroft said he wanted to "escalate the war on drugs, relaunch it if you will."[20]

Media Bias, Anyone?

The election also provided a nice laboratory to observe media bias. News anchors described Democratic "workers" that attempted to disqualify absentee military ballots for technical, procedural reasons. (So much for the every-vote-must-count Gore position.) But the same journalists spoke eerily of Republican "operatives," who performed the same tasks for the Republican side.

After the election, the network anchors described George W. Bush's early days as president. But note the treatment the same media gave Bill Clinton's first days.

In 1993, Clinton, in his first executive initiative, reversed "anti-abortion" policies by former presidents Ronald Reagan and George Bush.

At CBS, anchor Dan Rather reported, "On the anniversary of Roe vs. Wade, President Clinton fulfills a promise, supporting abortion rights. It was twenty years ago today, the United States Supreme Court handed down its landmark abortion rights ruling, and the controversy hasn't stopped since. Today, with the stroke of a pen, President Clinton delivered on his campaign promise to cancel several anti-abortion regulations of the Reagan-Bush years."[21]

At NBC, Tom Brokaw said, "Today, President Clinton kept a campaign promise and it came on the twentieth anniversary of Roe vs. Wade legalizing abortion."[22]

And ABC's Peter Jennings stated, "President Clinton keeps his word on abortion rights. President Clinton kept a promise today on the twentieth anniversary of the Supreme Court decision legalizing abortion. Mr. Clinton signed presidential memoranda rolling back many of the restrictions imposed by his predecessors."[23]

As his first initiative, George W. Bush reversed a "pro-abortion" initiative by Bill Clinton. Bush cut off federal funds to international groups that counsel abortion. How did the Big Three anchors handle this news?

At CBS, Dan Rather said, "This was President Bush's first day at the office and he did something to quickly please the right flank in his party: He reinstituted an anti-abortion policy that had been in place during his father's term and the Reagan presidency but was lifted during the Clinton years."[24]

NBC's Tom Brokaw said, "We'll begin with the new president's very active day, which started on a controversial note."[25]

And according to ABC's Peter Jennings, "One of the president's first actions was designed to appeal to anti-abortion conservatives. The president signed an order reinstating a Reagan-era policy that prohibited federal funding of family planning groups that provided abortion counseling services overseas."[26]

Catch the drift? Clinton "delivered on his campaign promise."

Bush, on the other hand, knuckled under the "right flank" of his party. He "appeased" his supporters. And the anchors stamped Bush's initiative "controversial," yet Clinton's counter-measure suffered no such value judgment.

Republicans—Not Exactly Libertarians

Certainly Gore and Bush staked out different positions, but their similarities overwhelmed their differences. Both candidates, for example, called to expand Medicare, a program that, from its inception, dramatically exceeded its cost estimates. The next goodie dangled before voters: prescription benefits for seniors. This continues the practice of putting more and more treats in the Medicare basket, an entitlement program on automatic pilot to appease aging voters. Yet seven out of ten seniors spend less than $500 a year on prescription drugs,[27] while the average senior citizen spends $1,160 on restaurants, $1,093 on clothing, and $1,141 on entertainment.[28]

Notice anything during the Bush candidacy? Name one single agency, bureaucracy, or department targeted for extinction. Just one. The National Taxpayers Union says, "Bush, while addressing issues not usually associated with Republicans such as education, health care, and low-income housing, would like to increase spending by over $42 billion a year, or $425 billion over ten years."[29] Indeed, Bush's first budget calls for spending *increases* of five percent.

Under George W. Bush, will workers get to invest 100% of their Social Security funds? No. Will the Departments of Education, Energy, Housing and Urban Development, and Agriculture get closed? No. Will we abolish the Internal Revenue Service? No.

For the first time in nearly fifty years, Republicans briefly controlled the White House and both chambers of Congress. Oh, they talked the talk, but did they walk the walk? Republicans do not need a single Democratic vote to enact an aggressive plan for tax cuts and a downsized government. Not one. Yet, almost immediately, "moderate," "centrist" Republicans like Arlen Specter of Pennsylvania, James M. Jeffords of Vermont (who later left the GOP to become an independent), and Lincoln Chafee of Rhode Island warned the new president against excessive aggressiveness.

Chafee said the proposed tax cuts were "too big, too early,"[30] and threatened to vote against Bush's plan if necessary. Senate Budget Committee Chairman Pete Domenici [R-New Mexico] warned Bush about the possible shortfall in votes needed to pass his tax cut in the Senate. "Right now," said Senator Domenici, "it would appear there are a number of senators who are undecided and there are between forty-seven and forty-nine that are absolutely committed and we're still working."[31] Same old, same old.

Bottom line, the differences between Al Gore and George Bush border on minor. A slowdown in the rate of government growth does not take the place of a reversal.

As of this writing, two high school shootings took place near San Diego, California. In response, the Los Angeles City Council banned so-called "pocket rocket" guns, small, easily concealable firearms. The council also now requires any gun purchaser to submit to a thumbprint, so the police may have a record. Years ago, the city banned the sale of so-called "Saturday night specials." But what about Saturday night parents?

In a report on deterring teen drug use, a government study outlined the biggest deterrent—hands-on parents.[32] What is a hands-on parent? Hands-on parents monitor their kids' television viewing, watch what they do on computers, restrict the types of CDs they purchase or listen to, are aware of their children's whereabouts at all times, including after school and weekends, watch their academic performance, have advised them on drug use, impose a curfew, eat dinner with their children several times a week, turn off the TV during dinner, give them regular chores, and have an adult present when a teen returns from school. Basic stuff. But tell me, how do we accomplish this with a tax burden twice as high as that faced by families in the 1950s? And don't we create incentives for irresponsible or absentee parenting by providing welfare and other programs that reward irresponsible breeding?

Blame both the Democratic and Republican parties for the

construction and continued expansion of the welfare state. Voters must reject tax-spend-and-regulate, and must recognize the damage done to our personal and financial freedoms. With government out of the way, free people make better, wiser, and more productive citizens.

After the election, pundits repeatedly told us about our "divided" country—divided down the center between Democrat and Republican. No. Draw the line of division between Americans who believe in personal responsibility and self-reliance, versus those who choose to remain victicrats. The battle is on.

APPENDIX

1. Blacks Are More Racist than Whites

Chart 1.1 (see page 71)

What a Single, African–American Low–Income Male Aged 25 Can Expect in Lifetime Returns from Social Security and Various After–Tax Private Investments of His Payroll Taxes (1997 Dollars)

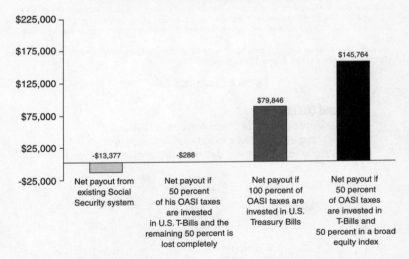

NOTE: Individual is assumed to earn an amount equal to 50 percent of the average earnings as defined by the Social Security Administration ($12,862 in wage, salary, and self-employment income in 1996). Rate of return is based on OASI taxes, benefits, and is net of income taxes. The worker is assumed to annuitize his retirement savings over 15 years, receiving a real rate of return of 2.7%. Assumes the individual places contributions in a tax-deferred IRA–type account (but with initial contributions not tax-deductible).

SOURCES: *1997 Trustees Report*, Social Security Administration; and National Center for Health Statistics, *Vital Statistics of the United States*, 1992 Life Tables, 1997.

2. White Condescension Is as Bad as Black Racism

Chart 2.1 (see page 71)

Real Rate of Return from Social Security for a Single Low-Income African-American Male (1997 Dollars)

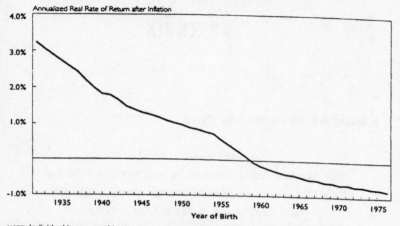

NOTE: Individual is assumed to earn an amount equal to 50 percent of average earnings as defined by the Social Security Administration ($12,862 in wage, salary, and self-employment income in 1996). Rate of return is based on the Old-Age and Survivors portion of taxes and benefits only and is net of income taxes.

SOURCES: *1997 Trustees Report,* Social Security Administration; and National Center for Health Statistics, *Vital Statistics of the United States,* 1992 Life Tables, 1997.

Figure 2.1 (see page 84)

Race and the Enviroment

A 1995 EPA analysis of the communities around polluted "superfund" sites found that whites were just as likely to be affected as other racial and ethnic groups:

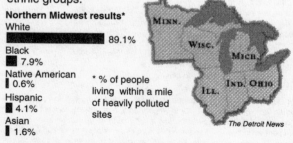

Northern Midwest results*

White
89.1%

Black
7.9%

Native American
0.6%

Hispanic
4.1%

Asian
1.6%

* % of people living within a mile of heavily polluted sites

The Detroit News

SOURCE: Enviromental Protection Agency.

3. The Media Bias—It's Real, It's Widespread, It's Destructive

Figure 3.1 (see page 103)

It's Conclusive
Most Media Elite Identify Themselves as Liberal in Anonymous Polls

Year	Survey	Journalists surveyed	Sample size	Liberal	Conservative
1962	Columbia Journ. Review	Wash. Press Corps	273	57%	28%
1971	Nat'l Opinion Research Cntr.	Elite journalists	363	53%	17%
1976	Harvard/Washington Post	Wash. Press Corps	150	59%	18%
1978	Stephen Hess/Brookings Inst.	Wash. Press Corps	178	42%	19%
1980	Rothman/Lichter	Media elilte	240	54%	17%
1982	California State University	Top 50 newspapers	1000	50%	21%
1983	Weaver/Wilhoit	Prominent outlets	126	32%	12%
1985	Los Angeles Times	600 newspapers	3290	55%	17%
1995	Times Mirror Center	National media	248	22%	5%
1996	U. of Conn./Freedom Forum	Wash. Press Corps	139	61%	9%

SOURCE: Center for Media & Public Affairs.

Figure 3.2 (see page 104)

Top J-Schools

U.S. News & World Report asked academics
to rank the top graduate programs in
print journalism in '96

1. University of Missouri, Columbia
2. Columbia University
3. Northwestern University
4. U. of North Carolina, Chapel Hill
5. Indiana University, Bloomington
6. University of Florida
7. Ohio University
8. University of Wisconsin, Madison
9. University of California, Berkeley
T9. University of Kansas
11. University of Maryland, College Park
T11. University of Texas, Austin
13. Syracuse University
14. Arizona State University
15. University of Minnesota, Twin Cities

SOURCE: *U.S. News & World Report.*

Figure 3.3 (see page 111)

Unemployment Rates Before and After the Increase in the Minimum Wage

	3RD Q. 1996	1ST Q. 1997
Teenagers	16.6%	17.0%
Blacks	10.5%	10.9%
Women heading families	8.5%	9.1%
TOTAL	**5.3%**	**5.3%**

SOURCE: *Monthly Labor Review.*

4. The Glass Ceiling—Full of Holes

Figure 4.1 (see page 139)
Estimated Earnings of Women Ages 16–29 as a Percentage of Men's Earnings, Controlling for Demographic and Job Characteristics
1974–1993

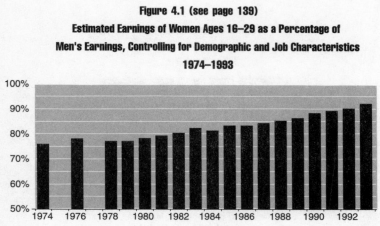

NOTE: This estimate accounts for education, race, age, part- or full-time, public- or private-sector status, production or nonproduction occupation, and union status. Data for 1975 and 1977 are not available.
SOURCE: David A. Macpherson and Barry T. Hirsch, "Wages and Gender Composition: Why Do Women's Jobs Pay Less?" *Journal of Labor Economics*, vol. 13 (July 1995): p. 466, table A1.

5. America's Greatest Problem: Not Crime, Racism, or Bad Schools—It's Illegitimacy

Chart 5.1 (see page 156)

Percentage of illegitimate births

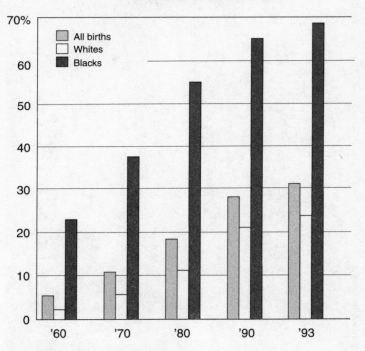

SOURCE: National Center for Health Statistics.

Table 5.1 (see page 156)		
Percent of Births Out of Wedlock, by Race, 1960–1994		
	Black	**White**
1960	22	2
1970	38	6
1980	55	11
1994	70	25

SOURCES: Figures for 1960–1980 from Donald J. Bogue, *The Population of the United States: Historical Trends and Future Projections* (New York: Free Press, 1985), 275; 1994 figures from June 1996 National Center for Health Statistics press release.

Figure 5.1 (see page 157)

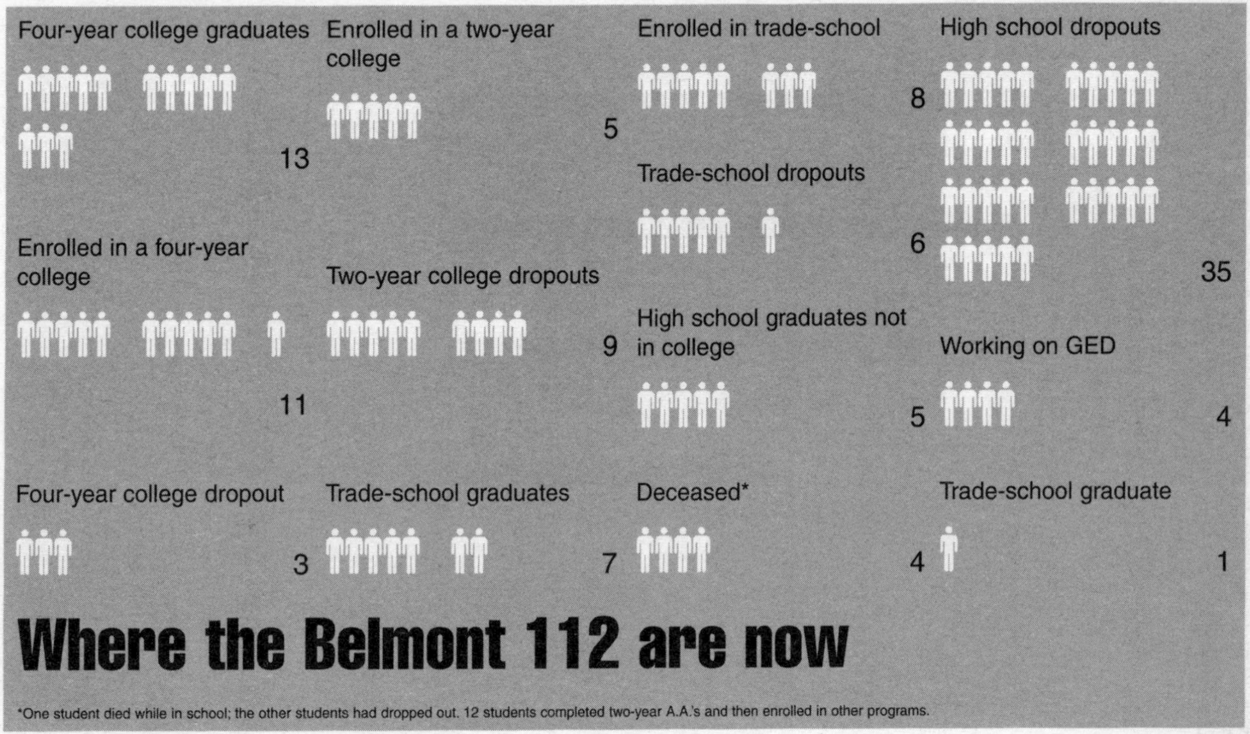
Four-year college graduates
13
Enrolled in a two-year college
5
Enrolled in trade-school
8
High school dropouts
35
Trade-school dropouts
6
Enrolled in a four-year college
11
Two-year college dropouts
9
High school graduates not in college
5
Working on GED
4
Four-year college dropout
3
Trade-school graduates
7
Deceased*
4
Trade-school graduate
1
Where the Belmont 112 are now
*One student died while in school; the other students had dropped out. 12 students completed two-year A.A.'s and then enrolled in other programs.

SOURCE: *The Philadelphia Inquirer.*

Chart 5.2 (see page 159)

Growth of Illegitimacy

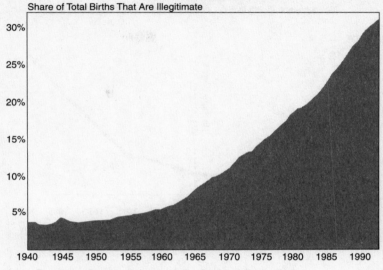

Share of Total Births That Are Illegitimate

SOURCE: The Heritage Foundation's *Issues '96: The Candidate's Briefing Book.*

Chart 5.3 (see page 164)

Births to Unmarried Women

Year	All Races Number	%	Whites Number	%	Blacks Number	%
1960	224,300	5.3	82,500	2.3	138,744	23.0
1965	291,200	7.7	123,700	4.0	162,215	27.9
1970	398,700	10.7	175,100	5.7	215,100	37.6
1975	447,900	14.2	186,400	7.3	249,600	48.8
1980	665,747	18.4	320,063	11.0	325,737	55.2
1985	828,174	22.0	432,969	14.5	365,527	60.1
1989	1,165,169	27.1	593,911	19.0	457,480	64.2
1990	1,165,384	28.0	647,376	21.0	472,660	65.2

SOURCE: U.S. Bureau of Census; U.S. House of Representatives, Committee on Ways and Means.

6. There Is No Health-Care "Crisis"

Chart 6.1 (see page 175)

Medicare and Rising Health-Care Costs per Patient Day (1982 dollars)

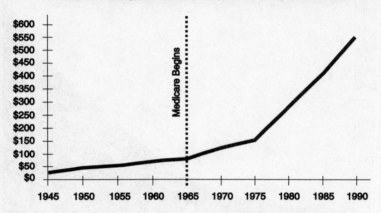

SOURCE: Milton Friedman, "Gammon's Law Points to Health Care Solution," *Wall Street Journal*, November 12, 1991, p. A1.

7. America's Welfare State: The Tyranny of the Status Quo

Chart 7.1 (see page 193)

	Wage Equivalent of Welfare, 1995		
Rank	Jurisdiction	Pretax Wage Equivalent ($)	Hourly Wage ($)
1	Hawaii	36,400	17.50
2	Alaska	32,200	15.48
3	Massachusetts	30,500	14.66
4	Connecticut	29,600	14.23
5	District of Columbia	29,100	13.99
6	New York	27,300	13.13
7	New Jersey	26,500	12.74
8	Rhode Island	26,100	12.55
9	California	24,100	11.59
10	Virginia	23,100	11.11
11	Maryland	22,800	10.96
12	New Hampshire	22,800	10.96
13	Maine	21,600	10.38
14	Delaware	21,500	10.34
15	Colorado	20,900	10.05
16	Vermont	20,900	10.05
17	Minnesota	20,800	10.00
18	Washington	20,700	9.95
19	Nevada	20,200	9.71
20	Utah	19,900	9.57
21	Michigan	19,700	9.47
22	Pennsylvania	19,700	9.47
23	Illinois	19,400	9.33
24	Wisconsin	19,400	9.33
25	Oregon	19,200	9.23
26	Wyoming	19,100	9.18
27	Indiana	19,000	9.13
28	Iowa	19,000	9.13
29	New Mexico	18,600	8.94
30	Florida	18,200	8.75
31	Idaho	18,000	8.65
32	Oklahoma	17,700	8.51
33	Kansas	17,600	8.46
34	North Dakota	17,600	8.46
35	Georgia	17,400	8.37
36	Ohio	17,400	8.37
37	South Dakota	17,300	8.32
38	Louisiana	17,000	8.17
39	Kentucky	16,800	8.08
40	North Carolina	16,800	8.08
41	Montana	16,300	7.84
42	South Carolna	16,200	7.79
43	Nebraska	15,900	7.64
44	Texas	15,200	7.31
45	West Virginia	15,200	7.31
46	Missouri	14,900	7.16
47	Arizona	14,100	6.78
48	Tennessee	13,700	6.59
49	Arkansas	13,200	6.35
50	Alabama	13,000	6.25
51	Mississippi	11,500	5.53

This table may actually understate the hourly wage equivalent because it is based on a 52-week (2,080-hour) work year and assumes no vacation.

Chart 7.2 (see page 193)

Value of Welfare in Selected Cities, 1995			
City, State	**Welfare Benefit Level ($)[a]**	**Local Income Tax Rate (%)[b]**	**Pretax Income Equivalent ($)[c]**	**Hourly Equivalent ($)[d]**
New York, NY[e]	23,743	4.20	30,700	14.76
Philadelphia, PA	19,949	4.96	25,900	12.45
Baltimore, MD[f]	19,543	2.50	23,600	11.35
Detroit, MI[g]	18,580	3.00	22,700	10.91
Indianapolis, IN	18,260	0.70	21,100	10.14
Akron, OH	17,679	2.00	20,100	9.66
Toledo, OH	17,619	2.25	20,100	9.66
Cleveland, OH	17,631	2.00	20,000	9.62
Cincinnati, OH	17,463	2.88	20,000	9.62
Columbus, OH	17,343	2.00	19,800	9.52
Pittsburgh, PA	17,189	2.10	19,800	9.52
Lexington, KY	17,037	2.00	19,500	9.38
Kansas City, MO	16,428	2.20	18,600	8.94
Louisville, KY	16,389	1.00	17,700	8.51
St. Louis, MO	16,308	1.00	17,450	8.39
Birmingham, AL	14,945	1.00	15,300	7.36

SOURCE: Advisory Commission on Intergovernmental Relations, "Significant Features of Fiscal Federalism: Budget Processes and Tax Systems, 1994," June 1994.

NOTE: Chart 7.2 gives the 16 cities of the 80 largest (by 1990 population) that impose either a city or a county income tax.

[a]Includes fair market housing benefit for the respective counties.

[b]Rate is imposed on adjusted gross income with no exemptions or deductions, except in Indianapolis and New York City where the tax base is state taxable income.

[c]Includes federal, state, local, and FICA taxes.

[d]Based on a 2080-hour work year.

[e]New York City's income tax has graduated rates, starting at 2.5 percent. The 4.2 percent listed is the top marginal rate paid by a taxpayer whose after-tax income would equal welfare benefits.

[f]In Baltimore the tax is 50 percent of state income tax liability. The 2.5 percent listed is half of the top marginal state rate paid by a hypothetical taxpayer.

[g]In Detroit a portion of city income tax liability is deductible from the state income tax.

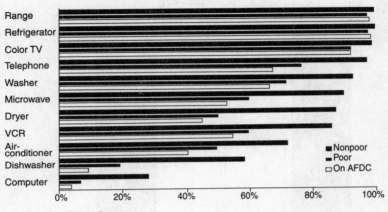

Chart 7.3 (see page 213)

Percent of Families with Access to Consumer Durables

- Nonpoor
- Poor
- On AFDC

SOURCE: Census Bureau.

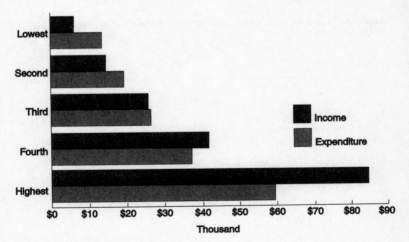

Chart 7.4 (see page 214)

Average Household Income and Expenditures by Quintile, 1993

- Income
- Expenditure

SOURCE: Bureau of Labor Statistics.

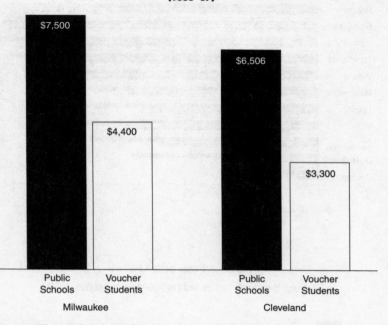

Chart 7.5 (see page 215)

Education Spending per Student

(1996–97)

$7,500

$6,506

$4,400

$3,300

| Public Schools | Voucher Students | | Public Schools | Voucher Students |

Milwaukee   Cleveland

SOURCES: Wisconsin State Budget Office, Ohio Department of Education, Cleveland Scholarship and Tutoring Program.

Figure 8.1 (see page 238)

Smoke Math

Costs and benefits to American society, per pack of cigarettes smoked in 1993

Medical care (total)	$0.55
For those under 65	*$0.37*
For 65 and older	*$0.18*
Sick leave	$0.01
Group life insurance	$0.14
Fires	$0.02
Second-hand smoke	$0.25
Lost taxes on earnings	$0.40
Total cost to society	**$1.37**
Nursing home savings	$0.23
Pensions, Social Security	$1.19
Excise taxes paid	$0.53
Total benefit to society	**$1.95**

SOURCE: W. Kip Viscusi, professor at Duke University.

9. The War Against Drugs Is Vietnam II: We're Losing This One, Too

Chart 9.1 (see page 253)

Leading Causes of Death in the USA in 1996

According to the Centers for Disease Control, National Center for Health Statistics, and the *Journal of American Medical Association* (for adverse drug reactions death numbers; April 14, 1998 issue of *JAMA*; 2791200-1205, 1998).

Total deaths 2,322,265

1.	Heart Disease	733,834
2.	Cancer	544,278
3.	Stroke	160,431
4.	Adverse Drug Reactions (1994) from legal drugs at doses used for prevention, diagnosis, or therapy	106,000
5.	Pulmonary disease	106,146
6.	Accidents	93,874
7.	Pneumonia/influenza	82,579
8.	Diabetes	61,559
9.	HIV/AIDS	32,665
10.	Suicide	30,862
11.	Liver disease	25,135
14.	Homicide	20,738

ILLICIT DRUG OVERDOSE . . . . 3,800 to 5,200
(Deliberate or accidental) from all illegal drugs.

Chart 9.2 (see page 253)

Number of United States Deaths per Year

TOBACCO . . . . .340,000 to 450,000

ALCOHOL . . . . .150,000+
(Not including 50% of highway deaths, 65% of all murders.)

ASPIRIN (Including deliberate overdose) . . . . 180 to 1000+

CAFFEINE . . . . 1000 to 10,000
(From stress, ulcers and triggering heartbeats, etc.)

"LEGAL" DRUG OVERDOSE . . . . .14,000 to 27,000
(Deliberate or accidental) prescribed or patent medicines
and/or mixing with alcohol, e.g. Valium/alcohol.

ILLICIT DRUG OVERDOSE
(Deliberate or accidental) from all illegal drugs . . . . 3,800 to 5,200

THEOPHYLLINE (Pharmaceutical drug legally prescribed for asthma) 50
(Theophylline is also responsible for 6,500 Emergency Room admits
and 1,000 cases of permanent brain damage per year.)

MARIJUANA 0

---

10. Gun Control Advocates—Good Guys with Blood on Their Hands

Figure 10.1 (see page 270)

State Concealed-Handgun Laws as of 1996

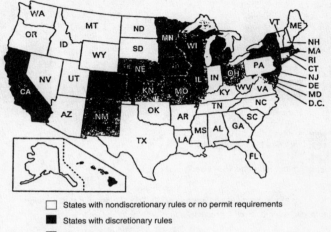

☐ States with nondiscretionary rules or no permit requirements

■ States with discretionary rules

■ States forbidding concealed handguns

Chart 10.1 (see page 294)

TV News Segments on Gun Policy

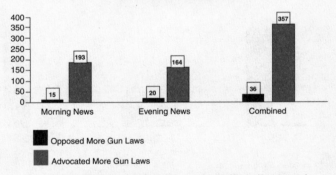

■ Opposed More Gun Laws

■ Advocated More Gun Laws

ABC, CBS, NBC, and CNN, 1997–1999 (CNN not included in Morning News category).

SOURCE: Media Research Center, Alexandria, VA.

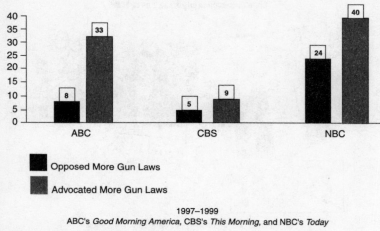

Chart 10.2 (see page 294)

A.M. News Guests on Gun Policy

Opposed More Gun Laws

Advocated More Gun Laws

1997–1999
ABC's *Good Morning America*, CBS's *This Morning*, and NBC's *Today*
SOURCE: Media Research Center, Alexandria, VA

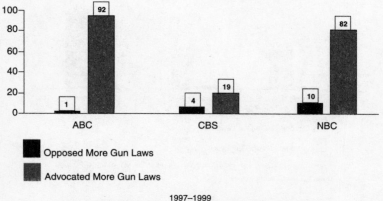

Chart 10.3 (see page 294)

A.M. News Segments on Gun Policy

Opposed More Gun Laws

Advocated More Gun Laws

1997–1999
ABC's *Good Morning America*, CBS's *This Morning*, and NBC's *Today*
SOURCE: Media Research Center, Alexandria, VA

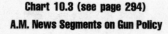

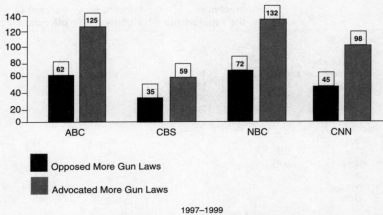

Chart 10.4 (see page 294)

P.M. News Soundbites on Gun Policy

■ Opposed More Gun Laws

■ Advocated More Gun Laws

1997–1999
ABC's *World News Tonight*, CBS's *Evening News*, NBC's *Nightly News*, and CNN's *The World Today*
SOURCE: Media Research Center, Alexandria, VA

Figure 10.2 (see page 296)
Murderers and Victims: Relationship and Characteristics

	Percent of cases involving the relationship	Percent of victims	Percent of offenders
Relationship		—	—
Family	18%		
Acquaintance (nonfriend and friend)	40		
Stranger	13		
Unknown	30		
Total	101		
Race			
Black		38%	33%
White		54	42
Hispanic		2	2
Other		5	4
Unknown		1	19
Total		100	100
Sex			
Female		29	9
Male		71	72
Unknown		0	19
Total		100	100

SOURCE: U.S. Dept. of Justice, FBI staff, *Uniform Crime Reports*, (Washington, D.C.: U.S. Govt. Printing Office, 1992).

NOTE: Nonfriend acquaintances include drug pushers and buyers, gang members, prostitutes and their clients, bar customers, gamblers, cab drivers killed by their customers, neighbors, other nonfriend acquaintances, and friends. The total equals more than 100 percent because of rounding. The average age of victims was 33; that of offenders was 30.

NOTES

1. Blacks Are More Racist than Whites

1 "Open Letter to Larry Elder and Other Idiots," *Los Angeles Sentinel* (May 16, 1996).

2 Kevin Sack, "Affirmative Action Alive and Well in Atlanta," *New York Times* (June 10, 1996).

3 Sam Fulwood III, "Rep. Waters Labels Bush 'a Racist,'" *Los Angeles Times* (July 9, 1992).

4 Robin Givhan, "Clearing the Decks at Gore Headquarters, Campaign Manager Donna Brazile Is Nothing if Not an Activist," *Washington Post* (November 16, 1999).

5 Marilyn Rauber, "Gore's Top Aide in Racial Furor," *New York Post* (January 7, 2000).

6 Alex Haley, *The Autobiography of Malcolm X* (New York: Ballantine Books, 1992) p. 468.

7 Rita Kramer, "Adoption in Black and White," *Wall Street Journal* (October 24, 1994).

8 Stephen and Abigail Thernstrom, *America in Black and White* (New York: Simon & Schuster, 1997), p. 525.

9 Kelly Ryan, "School Plaintiff: 'America is Still a Racist Nation,'" *St. Petersburg Times* (February 28, 2000).

10 "Brown, Racial Change, and the Civil Rights Movement," *Virginia Law Review* 80:7 (1994): p. 66–67; see also Jackson Draft Opinion, *Brown*

v. Board of Education 1 (March 15, 1954), Library of Congress, Jackson papers, Box 184, case file: segregation cases, on file with the Virginia Law Review Association p. 66.

11 Bill Maxwell, "Black Republicans: Self Loathers" *San Francisco Examiner* (January 3, 2000).

12 Richard Cohen, "Still Divided by Race," *Washington Post* (November 1, 1994).

13 *U.S. News* poll of 1,000 registered voters, with an oversample of 45 African-American voters conducted by Celinda Lake of Lake Research and Ed Goeas of the Tarrance Group July 25–27, 1995. Margin of error: Plus or minus 2.9, *U.S. News & World Report* (August 21, 1995)

14 William J. Moran, "Arthur Ashe: A Role Model For Young People," *Orange County Register* (July 10, 1998).

15 Amy Wallace, "Connerly, Sen. Watson Engage in Shouting Match Legislature," *Los Angeles Times* (February 21, 1996).

16 Suzanne Fields, "The Message of Clarence Thomas," *Washington Times* (November 28, 1994).

17 Jared Taylor, *Paved With Good Intentions* (New York: Carroll & Graf, 1992), p. 103.

18 Charles Krauthammer, "A Taxi Still Can't Fit Congressional Black Caucus," *Houston Chronicle* (November 17, 1996).

19 Jonathan Tilove, "House Blacks Show Strength to Outlive Overturned Districts," *Austin American-Statesman* (July 21, 1996).

20 Charles Krauthammer, "A Taxi Still Can't Fit Congressional Black Caucus," *Houston Chronicle* (November 17, 1996).

21 "Whoopi on Being Black in Movie Biz," *Cincinnati Enquirer* (March 16, 1994).

22 Bob Nightengale, "50 Years, Still Fears," *Los Angeles Times* (April 15, 1997).

23 Cindy Pearlman, "Reeves Headed to Chicago For Techno-Thriller 'Critical Path,'" *Chicago Sun-Times* (August 27, 1995).

24 Jill Stewart, "Kevin's Big Scam," *New Times* 3:25, (June 18–24 1998).

25 Maria Newman, "The Angry Insider U.S. Rep. Maxine Waters is a Combative But Effective Voice of the Disenfranchised," *Kansas City Star* (May 30, 1992).

26 Andrea Ford and Michael K. Frisby, "Maximum Effect," *Emerge* (April 1997).

27 *Washington Post*/Kaiser Family Foundation/Harvard University survey, "Worry, Frustration Build for Many in Black Middle Class," *Washington Post* (October 9, 1995).

28 *Washington Post*/Kaiser Family Foundation/Harvard University survey, "A Glass Ceiling of Misconceptions," *Washington Post* (October 10, 1995).

29 Ibid.

30 David Beard, "Barbados Kids Learn With Methods U.S. Shuns," *Sun-Sentinel, South Florida* (June 6, 1997).

31 Ibid.

32 Ibid.

33 Elizabeth Mehren, "Fire and Flair," *Los Angeles Times* (June 3, 1994).

34 Ron Studghill II, "A Train Hop to Tragedy," *Time* 150:3 (July 21, 1997).

35 Lianne Hart and Mark Fritz, "Enraged Man Kills 2, Injures 3 in Pennsylvania Gun Rampage," *Los Angeles Times* (March 2, 2000).

36 Rhonda Stewart, "Living The Dream," *Emerge* (September 1999): p. 52.

37 Ibid., p. 54.

38 Jon Jeter, "Glued to Their TV Sets," *Washington Post National Weekly Edition* (July 1–7, 1996).

39 Ibid.

40 Earl Ofari Hutchinson, *The Assassination of the Black Male Image, Kirkus Reviews*, May 1, 1991.

41 Linda and S. Robert, Lichter and Stanley Rothman, *Watching America: What Television Tells Us About Our Lives* (New Jersey: Prentice Hall Press, 1991).

42 Dave Gardetta, "Elvis Has Just Entered the Building," *Los Angeles Times Magazine* (August 15, 1999): p. 18.

43 "Capitalism: The Cure for Racism" CSPAN (October 23, 1996).

44 Mike Dodd and Dick Patrick, "Pressure Builds For Action. Fans in Cincinnati, Across USA Call For Boycott, Punishment," *USA Today* (May 9, 1996).

45 Andrea Ford and Michael K. Frisby, "Maximum Effect," *Emerge* (April 1997): p. 48.

46 "Brown, Racial Change, and the Civil Rights Movement," *Virginia Law Review* 80:7 (1994): p. 46.

47 Booker T. Washington, *Up from Slavery* (New York: Doubleday, Page and Company, 1901), p. 149.

48 Mark Gerson, "Race, O. J. and My Kids," *New Republic* (April 24, 1995): pp. 27–29.

49 *San Gabriel Valley Tribune*, "The Essential Difference," letters to the Editor section (December 3, 1996).

50 Jack Newfield, "Jesse Jackson's Mid-Life Crisis," *Penthouse* 25:12 (August 1994).

51 Jackson Toby, " 'Racial Profiling' Doesn't Prove Cops Are Racist," *Wall Street Journal* (March 11, 1999).

52 Kevin Johnson, "Florida Study Challenges Belief Police Use Force More Often Against Their Own Racial or Ethnic Groups," *USA Today* (March 13, 2000).

53 Jared Taylor, *Paved With Good Intentions* (New York: Carroll & Graf, 1992), p. 40.

54 Bureau of the Census–1998, *The World Almanac 2000* (New York: St. Martin's Press, 1999), p. 393.

55 James Q. Wilson and Richard Herrnstein, *Crime and Human Nature*, (New York: Simon and Schuster, 1986). David Rubinstein, "Don't Blame Crime on Joblessness," *Wall Street Journal* (November 11, 1992).

56 Robert J. Samuelson, "The Worthless Ivy League?" *Newsweek* (November 1, 1999).

57 Ibid.

58 Ibid.

59 Terry Eastland, *Ending Affirmative Action* (New York: Basic Books, 1996), p. 43.

60 *Ebony* 18:10 (August 1963): p. 56.

61 *Ebony* 18:12 (October 1963): p. 88.

62 *Ebony* 18:9 (July 1963): p. 82.

63 *U.S. News & World Report* 55:10 (September 2, 1963): pp. 8–9.

64 Dinesh D'Souza, *The Race Merchants* (New York: The Free Press, 1995), p. 217.

65 Stephen & Abigail Thernstrom, *America in Black and White* (New York: Simon & Schuster, 1997), pp. 184, 187.

66 Jack E. White, "Help Yourself," *Time* (July 5, 1999).

67 Joseph N. Boyce, " 'American Dream' Becomes a Reality for More Minorities," *Wall Street Journal* (October 7, 1997).

68 Thomas J. Stanley, *The Millionaire Mind* (Andrews McMeel Publishing, 2000).

69 Nancy Gibbs, "The EQ Factor," *Time* 146:14 (October 2, 1995).

70 Jonathan Wilcox, "The Willie Brown Paradox," *Daily News* (April 7, 1995).

71 Terence Monmaney, "The Upshot Is it Pays to Be Upbeat," *Los Angeles Times* (January 5, 2000).

72 Survey by Times Mirror Center for the People & the Press, 1994, "Race: Separatism, Inclusiveness Debated," *Los Angeles Times* (October 18, 1995).

73 Nancy Gibbs, "The EQ Factor," *Time* 146:14 (October 2, 1995).

2. White Condescension Is as Bad as Black Racism

1 William W. Beach and John M. Olin "Social Security's Rate of Return," *Heritage Center for Data Analysis* (January 15, 1998): pp. 10–12.

2 Christopher John Farley, "Kids and Race," *Time* (November 24, 1997).

3 "White Weight," Body Image section, *Psychology Today* (September, 1994).

4 Ibid.

5 Tim A. Auger and Patrick K. Turley, "The Female Soft Tissue Profile as Presented in Fashion Magazines During the 1900s: A Photographic Analysis," *Int J Orthod Orthognath Surg* 14:1 (1999). Robert E. Sutter, Jr. and Patrick K. Turley, "Soft Tissue Evaluation of Contemporary Caucasian and African American Female Facial Profiles," *Angle Orthod* 68:6 (1998): pp. 487–496.

6 John Leo, "On Society," *U.S. News & World Report* (May 18, 1998).

7 Lisa Bannon, "Willes Will Set Specific Goals For Featuring Minorities and Women in the Paper," *Wall Street Journal.* (May 15, 1998).

8 *Los Angeles Daily News*, Valley section, (July 7, 1996): p. V4.

9 Haya El Nasser, "Poll: Whites Increasingly Accept Blacks," *USA Today* (June 11, 1997).

10 Ibid.

11 John Balz, "Black Students Optimistic About Future, Study Finds," *Los Angeles Times* (August 11, 1999).

12 Robert Lichter and Stanley Rothman, *Environmental Cancer: A Political Disease?* (New Haven: Yale University Press, 1999).

13 David Mastio, "EPA Ignored Race Report," *Detroit News* (May 28, 1998).

14 John Leo, "Shocking, But Not True," *U.S. News & World Report* (November 22, 1999).

15 Steve Springer, "Douglas Affords Tyson Chance for Payday and Payback," *Los Angeles Times* (July 24, 1999).

16 Thomas Hauser, *Muhammad Ali, His Life and Times* (New York: Simon & Schuster, 1991): pp. 427–8.

17 Ibid., p. 173.

18 Michael A Fletcher, "NAACP Honors Don King With Its 'President's Awards,' " *The Washington Post* (July 15, 1997).

19 Rick Orlov, "Council Erupts; Hernandez Issue Leads to Name-Calling," *Daily News of Los Angeles* (October 25, 1997).

20 Robert W. Tracinski, " 'Right to Capital,' A Despotic Attack On Individual Ability," *Las Vegas Review-Journal* (May 5, 1999).

21 Jay Nordlinger, "Power Dem," *National Review* (March 20, 2000): p. 34.

22 Richard O'Brien and Hank Hersch, "Tiger: New Following, Old Stereotypes," *Sports Illustrated* (April 27, 1997).

23 Carolivia Herron, *Nappy Hair* (New York: Knopf, 1997).

24 Lynette Clemetson, "Caught in the Cross-Fire," *Newsweek* (December 14, 1998).

25 John J. Goldman, "Teacher Accused of Racial Insensitivity is Reinstated," *Los Angeles Times* (November 26, 1998).

26 Maria Alvarez and Adam Miller, " 'Nappy Hair' Teacher Gets Complaints at New School," *New York Post* (December 6, 1998).

27 Jeff Pearlman, "At Full Blast," *Sports Illustrated* (December 27, 1999).

28 "Baseball to Examine Remarks by Rocker," *Los Angeles Times* (December 23, 1999).

29 Don Greenberg and Earl Bloom, "Bird, Isiah Talk It Over, Reach Reconciliation," *Orange County Register* (June 5, 1987).

30 De Wayne Wickham, "Good Deed Goes Unnoticed," *USA Today* (February 27, 1995).

31 Jeff Benedict and Don Yaeger, *Pros and Cons* (New York: Warner Books, 1998).

32 Terry Boers, "Illegitimate Children Part of the Fabric in Today's NBA," *Chicago Daily Herald* (May 8, 1998).

3. The Media Bias—It's Real, It's Widespread, It's Destructive

1 Paul Sperry, "Old Media Ask: Bias? What Bias?" *Investor's Business Daily* (December 31, 1999).

2 Ibid.

3 Verne Gay, "The Death of Trust," *Los Angeles Times Magazine* (January 21, 1996).

4 Timothy Crouse, *Boys on the Bus* (New York: Ballantine, 1974).

5 Rowan Scarborough, "Leftist Press? You Guessed Right," *Washington Times* (April 18, 1996).

6 Phillip Michaels, "Where Does Media Bias Start?" *Investor's Business Daily* (February 2, 1998).

7 Paul Sperry, "Old Media Ask: Bias? What Bias?" *Investor's Business Daily* (December 31, 1999).

8 Rowan Scarborough, "Leftist Press? You Guessed Right," *Washington Times* (April 1996).

9 Phillip Michaels, "Where Does Media Bias Start?" *Investor's Business Daily* (February 2, 1998).

10 "Outgunned: How the Network News Media Are Spinning the Gun Control Debate," special report, Media Research Center (January 5, 2000).

11 Ibid.

12 Lily Nguyen, "Study: TV Newscasts Draw Bead on Guns; 10-to-1 Imbalance Found in Reports," *Washington Times* (January 6, 2000).

13 Ibid.

14 Lynn Rosellini, "When to Spank," *U.S. News & World Report* (April 13, 1998).

15 "Anchorman Has Temper Tantrum," *Detroit News* (November 26, 1994).

16 "The Best Notable Quotables of 1996," Media Research Center 9:26 (December 16, 1996): pp. 1–8, "Notable Quotables,"10:21 (October 20, 1997).

17 Howell Raines, *Fly Fishing Through the Midlife Crisis* (New York: Anchor Books/Doubleday, 1994).

18 James K. Glassman, "Don't Raise the Minimum Wage," *Washington Post* (February 24, 1998).

19 Editorial desk, *New York Times* (January 14, 1987).

20 "The Best Notable Quotables of 1996," Media Research Center 9:26 (December 16, 1996): p. 5.

21 Ibid.

22 Ibid.

23 Ibid.

24 Doug Bandow, "Minimum Wage, Maximum Hypocrites," *Investor's Business Daily* (October 1, 1996).

25 Bruce Bartlett, "The Minimum Wage Trap," *Wall Street Journal* (April 16, 1996).

26 Ibid.

27 Ethan Bronner, "UC Minority Enrollment Down Sharply" *Daily News* (January 14, 1998).

28 Ibid.

29 "Arson at Black Churches Echoes Bigotry of Past," *USA Today* (February 8, 1996).

30 Gary Fields, "Arson Strikes Black Churches at Record Pace," *USA Today* (August 7, 1996).

31 John Bacon, "Church Burnings Called a Provocation for Race War," *USA Today* (March 12, 1997).

32 Seymour Hersh, *The Dark Side of Camelot* (Boston: Little, Brown & Company, 1997).

33 James W. Michaels, "Black Monday and Red Faces," *Forbes* (November 3, 1997): p. 45.

34 Ibid. p. 44.

35 Michael Chapman, "Correct History For Johnny," *Investor's Business Daily* (November 27, 1998).

36 Ibid.

37 John Bartlett and Justin Kaplan, eds., *Bartlett's Quotations.* (Boston: Little, Brown & Company, 1992).

38 Dinesh D'Souza, "How Reagan Reelected Clinton," *Forbes* (November 3, 1997).

39 Jonathan Chait, "This Man is Not a Republican," *New Republic* (January 20, 2000).

40 Donald Lambro, "McCain's Compass," *Washington Times* (February 10, 2000).

41 "The Legend of Carolina," *Wall Street Journal* (February 25, 2000).

42 Kathleen Kenna, "Leading Democrat Accuses Clinton," *Toronto Star* (February 8, 1999).

43 Ibid.

44 "The Farrakhan Affair," *Washington Post* (April 4, 1984).

45 Ruth Shalit, "Race In the Newsroom," *New Republic* (October 2, 1995): p. 34.

46 Ibid.

47 Lisa Bannon, "The Publisher Plans New Type Faces For the L.A. Times," *Wall Street Journal* (May 15, 1998).

48 Sam Fulwood III and Marc Lacey, "400,000 Black Men Join in Racial Unity in Capitol March," *Los Angeles Times* (October 17, 1995).

49 Louis Freedberg, "Controversy Dogs D.C. Men's Rally," *San Francisco Chronicle* (October 3, 1997).

50 Sam Fulwood III, "Though United by Faith, Personal Quests Drew Many Commitments," *Los Angeles Times* (October 5, 1997).

4. The Glass Ceiling—Full of Holes

1 Diana Furchtgott-Roth and Christine Stolba, " 'Comparable Worth' Makes a Comeback," *Wall Street Journal* (February 5, 1998).

2 "ABA Report Finds Bias Against Women," *Los Angeles Times* (February 3, 1996).

3 "Women's Choices, Not Bias, Blamed for Lower Earnings," *Los Angeles Times* (December 15, 1995).

4 Andrea Dworkin, *Letters From a War Zone* (New York: E.P. Dutton, 1993).

5 Catharine A. MacKinnon, *Only Words* (Harvard University Press, 1993).

6 Mike Dorning, "Poll Details Global Role of Gender Bias," *Chicago Tribune* (March 27, 1996).

7 Suzanne Fields, "Women's Figures," *Washington Times* (November 25, 1996).

8 Diana Furchtgott-Roth and Christine Stolba, "American Women Aren't Really So Cheap," *Wall Street Journal* (November 20, 1998).

9 "The Shrinking Gender Gap," Perspectives column, *Investor's Business Daily* (May 9, 1995).

10 "Right Data," *National Review* (October 13, 1997): p. 16.

11 Joanne Jacobs, "Study Lets Us See Through the 'Glass Ceiling,'" *Orange County Register* (January 5, 1996).

12 "Holes in the Glass Ceiling Theory," *Newsweek* (March 27, 1995).

13 Sally Pipes, "Still Dancing On a Glass Ceiling," *Investor's Business Daily* (October 4, 1999).

14 Patricia Sellers, "The Toughest Babe in Business," *Fortune* (September 8, 1997).

15 Darla Moore, "Babes in Boy Land," *Worth* (January 1998).

16 Wendy Lee Gramm, "The Economy, a Women's Issue," *Wall Street Journal* (March 22, 1994).

17 Ibid.

18 "A Fact-Finding Report of the Federal Glass Ceiling Commission," (March 1995).

19 "Holes in the Glass Ceiling Theory," *Newsweek* (March 27, 1995).

20 "Women: Power in a Small Way," *Los Angeles Times* (October 26, 1995).

21 Cliff Edwards, "Challenging Domain of 'Pale Males,'" *Pasadena Star-News* (March 20, 2000).

22 Ibid.

23 Michael J. Sniffen, "Private Job Bias Lawsuits Tripled," *Associated Press* (January 16, 2000).

24 Ibid.

25 Ibid.

26 Harsh Luthar and Anthony Townsend, "Man Handling," *National Review* (February 6, 1995): p. 58.

27 Melissa Healy, "Vote Delay Is Day of Jubilation for Democratic Congresswomen," *Los Angeles Times* (October 10, 1991).

28 Helene R. Lee, "Watch Who You're Calling 'Trailer Trash,' " *Chicago Tribune* (April 2, 1997).

29 Marc Lacey, "NOW Condemns Leader of Its L.A. Chapter," *Los Angeles Times* (December 7, 1995).

30 Ibid.

5. America's Greatest Problem: Not Crime, Racism, or Bad Schools—It's Illegitimacy

1 Jonetta Rose Barras, "Crime and Dysfunction," *Washington Times* (February 25, 2000).

2 James Robison, *My Father's Face: A Portrait of the Perfect Father* (Multnomah Publishers, 1997).

3 Stephen and Abigail Thernstrom, *America in Black and White*, (New York: Simon & Schuster, 1997), p. 240.

4 Dale Mezzacappa, "Offered a College Dorm Room, He Sits in a Prison Cell," *Philadelphia Inquirer* (November 26, 1999).

5 Ibid.

6 Ibid.

7 Dale Mezzacappa, "Dreams Deferred," *Philadelphia Inquirer* (April 25, 1999).

8 Charles Piller and Jill Leovy, "Gates Foundation to Give $1 Billion for Scholarships," *Los Angeles Times* (September 17, 1999).

9 Matthew Robinson, "Can the U.S. Afford Illegitimacy?" *Investor's Business Daily* (October 16, 1995).

10 Ibid.

11 Herbert Gutman, *The Black Family in Slavery and Freedom* (New York: Pantheon Books, 1976).

12 Dinesh D'Souza, *The End of Racism* (New York: The Free Press, 1995), p. 97.

13 Michael Barone and Grant Ujifusa, *Almanac of American Politics, 1992*, National Journal Inc., (1991), p. 559.

14 "How Welfare Harms Kids," *Backgrounder* (June 5, 1996): p. 6.

15 R. Forste and M. Tienda, "Race and Ethnic Variation in the Schooling

Consequences of Female Adolescent Sexual Activity," *Social Science Quarterly* (March 1992).

16 Mwangi S. Kimeny, "Rational Choice, Culture of Poverty, and the Intergenerational Transmission of Welfare Dependency," *Southern Economic Journal* (April 1991).

17 Deborah A. Dawson, "Family Structure and Children's Health and Well-Being," Annual meeting of the Population Association of America, May 1990.

18 Matthew Robinson, "Can the U.S. Afford Ilegitimacy?" *Investor's Business Daily* (October 16, 1995).

19 Karl Zinsmeister, "Illegitimacy in Black and White," *Wall Street Journal* (November 16, 1987).

20 Ben Wattenberg, " 'Welfare Experts' Confirm Our Fears," *Orange County Register* (July 17, 1996).

21 Marvin Olasky, *The Tragedy of American Compassion* (Crossway Book, 1995).

22 "Mass Charity," editorial, *Investor's Business Daily* (May 5, 1995).

23 Bob Faw and Nancy Skeleton, "Thunder in America: the Impossible Campaign of the Rev. Jesse Jackson."

24 Arthur J. Magida and Julian Bond, *Prophet of Rage* (New York: HarperCollins, 1997), pp. 9–10.

25 Morgan O. Reynolds, "When More Do Time, Down Goes Crime," *Investor's Business Daily* (July 16, 1997).

26 Stephen Moore, "Despite Progress On Welfare Reform, Mission Still Far From Accomplished," *Investor's Business Daily* (March 24, 2000).

27 Ibid.

28 "Steady Drops in Teen Birth Rate Has Many 'Proud Parents,' " *USA Today* (April 30, 1999).

6. There Is No Health-Care "Crisis"

1 Janet Cawley, "First Lady Holds First Forum on U.S. Health-Care System," *Orange County Register* (February 12, 1993).

2 Ibid.

3 Angela Dire, "First Lady Returns to Healthcare Pulpit," *Colorado Springs Gazette Telegraph* (March 15, 1994).

4 Ibid.

5 Milton Friedman, "Medical Licensure," *Freedom Daily* (January 1994): p. 35.

6 Milton Friedman, *Free To Choose* (New York: Harcourt, 1980), p. 231.

7 Milton Friedman, "Gammon's Law Points to Health-Care Solution," *Wall Street Journal* (November 12, 1991).

8 Harry Browne, *Why Government Doesn't Work* (New York: St. Martin's Press, 1995), p. 15.

9 Edgar A. Suter, "Guns in the Medical Literature—A Failure of Peer Review," *Journal of the Medical Association of Georgia* (1994).

10 Lawrence D. Wilson, "The Case Against Medical Licensing," *Freedom Daily* (January 1994).

11 Associated Press, "Official says the U.S. Has Too Many Doctors," *Cleveland Plain Dealer* (July 30, 1993).

12 Shawn Tully, "America's Painful Doctor Shortage," *Fortune* (November 16, 1992).

13 Ibid.

14 Elizabeth A. Wright, "Caribbean Medical School Fights for Campus in Wyoming," Associated Press (June 10, 1999).

15 "Doctor's Income Averages $200,000," Associated Press (April 22, 1998).

16 "Tired of Socialized Medicine," *Investor's Business Daily* (January 26, 2000).

17 Ibid.

18 Regina McEnery, "Clinic Lures Canadians with Cancer-Cure Deal," *Cleveland Plain Dealer* (January 22, 2000).

19 "Tired of Socialized Medicine," *Investor's Business Daily* (January 26, 2000).

20 Sally Pipes, "Canada's Health Care Goes South," *Investor's Business Daily* (August 16, 1999).

21 Associated Press, "Warning About Clinton Healthcare Plan," *San Francisco Chronicle* (January 14, 1994).

7. America's Welfare State: The Tryanny of the Statist Quo

1 Thomas Sowell, "Facts, Stubborn Facts," *Forbes* (October 11, 1993): p. 116.

2 Ed Crane, "New Heights of Hubris," Cato Institute (January 22, 1999).

3 William H. Peterson, "Leviathan's Brood: Moral Hazards," *Investor's Business Daily* (November 1, 1999).

4 Daniel T. Oliver "Lessons From the Chicago Fire," *Alternatives in Philanthropy* (July 1999): pp. 3–4.

5 Michael Tanner, et al., "The Work Versus Welfare Trade-off," *Cato Institute Policy Analysis*, 240 (September 19, 1995).

6 Bonnie Erbe and Josette Shiner, "American Companies Giving More to Charity, But Are Individuals?" *Daily Breeze* (December 25, 1999).

7 "Wonderful Welfare," *Wall Street Journal* (March 24, 1995).

8 Bruce Upbin, "Responsibility 101," *Forbes* (May 19, 1997).

9 Lawrence M. Mead, *The New Politics of Poverty: The Nonworking Poor in America* (New York: Basic Books, 1993).

10 Walter Olson, "Three Cheers for Workfare," *Wall Street Journal* (May 6, 1992).

11 Richard Vedder and Lowell Gallaway, *Out of Work, Unemployment and Government in Twentieth-Century America*, (New York: Holmes & Meter), p. 104.

12 William H. Peterson, "Leviathan's Brood: Moral Hazards," *Investor's Business Daily* (November 1, 1999).

13 Doug Bandow (ed.) and Ian Vasquez (ed.), "Perpetuating Poverty" The Cato Institute (April 1994).

14 Doug Bandow, "A Look Behind the Marshall Plan Mythology," *Investor's Business Daily* (June 3, 1997).

15 Jeffrey Tucker, "The Marshall Plan Myth," Ludwig Von Mises Institute (September, 1997).

16 Doug Bandow, "A Look Behind the Marshall Plan Mythology," *Investor's Business Daily* (June 3, 1997).

17 "Clinton's 'Third Way' Joins Many Other Ways," *U.S. News & World Report* (July 19, 1999).

18 Randy Ludlow, "A Work in Progress, Good Times Elude Ohio's Appalachia," *Cincinnati Post* (July 6, 1999).

19 Tamar Jacoby and Fred Siegel, "Harlem's Experience With the 'Third Way' Antipoverty Approach," *New Republic* (August 23, 1999).

20 Ibid.

21 "Black America 1994—Changing Direction," The National Center For Public Policy Research (1994): p. 12.

22 Ibid.

23 Ibid.

24 Ibid.

25 Paul Craig Roberts, "Declining Power of Truth," *Investor's Business Daily* (March 15, 1999).

26 Ibid.

27 Ibid.

28 Harry Browne, *Why Government Doesn't Work* (New York: St. Martin's Press, 1995), p. 227.

29 Ann McFeatters, "Clinton Widens Access to Food Stamps Safety Net to Help Families Switching From Welfare to Work," *Pittsburgh Post-Gazette* (July 15, 1999).

30 "How Poor Are the Poor?" National Center For Policy Analysis, Brief Analysis No. 185 (October 25, 1995).

31 Ibid.

32 Robert Rector and Rea Hederman, "Report Exaggerates Income Inequality," *Los Angeles Times* (October 7, 1999).

33 "What Vouchers Can—And Can't—Solve," *Business Week* (May 10, 1999): p. 138.

34 Roy Maynard, "Voucher Kids," *CNS News Analysis* (May 10, 1999).

35 "Testimony of Darryl Scott Before the Subcommittee on Crime House Judiciary Committee," U.S. House of Representatives (May 27, 1999).

36 George H. Stein, ed., *Hitler (Great Lives Observed)*, Spectrum, p. 149.

37 Hanna Rosin, "The Fat Tax," *New Republic* (May 18, 1998): pp. 18–19.

38 Amanda Bennett and Anita Sharpe, "Health Hazard: AIDS Fight is Skewed by Federal Campaign Exaggerating Risks," *Wall Street Journal* (May 1, 1996).

39 Ibid.

40 Robert A. Levy and Rosalind B. Marimont, "Lies, Damned Lies, & 400,000 Smoking-Related Death," *Regulation* 21:4 (1998).

41 Sidney Zion, "The Data That Went Up in Smoke," *Daily News* (January 26, 1999).

42 Al Gore, *Earth in the Balance* (New York: Houghton Mifflin, 1992).

43 Ronald Baily, "Demagoguery in Green," *National Review* (March 16, 1992): p. 43.

44 John F. McManvs "Hot Topics, Cold Truth," *The New American* (January 31, 2000): p. 19.

45 Hillary Clinton, *It Takes a Village* (New York: Touchstone, 1996), p. 296.

46 Ibid., p. 297.

47 Karl Marx and Friedrich Engels, *The Communist Manifesto,* (New York: Signet, 1983).

48 Rachel Carson, *Silent Spring* (New York: Houghton Mifflin, 1994).

49 Paul R. Ehrlich, *The Population Bomb,* (Amereon 1976).

50 Jon Margolis, "A Symbol of Hope That Life Can be Nobler Than It Is," *Chicago Tribune* (November 22, 1988).

8. Republicans Versus Democrats—Maybe a Dime's Worth of Difference

1 Henry Muller and John F. Stacks, "An Interview With Clinton," *Time* (July 20, 1992): p. 25.

2 "Steel Dumping a Threat to Ohio," *Plain Dealer Cleveland* (December 1, 1998).

3 Laura Mansnerus, "Making a Case for Death," *New York Times* (May 5, 1996).

4 "Health Care Pitfalls," *Investors Business Daily* (October 1, 1999).

5 Victor Davis Hanson, "Farmers Harvest a Bumper Crop of Subsidies," *Wall Street Journal* (August 10, 1999).

6 David Lightman, "Tax Cut Debate: Anyone Smell Pork?" *Hartford Courant* (August 7, 1999).

7 Elizabeth Shogren, "Will Welfare Go the Way of Health Reform?" *Los Angeles Times* (August 10, 1995).

8 "Media Mum On Liberals' Crude Remarks," *USA Today* (April 12, 1995).

9 Ibid.

10 F. A. Hayek, *The Road to Serfdom* (Chicago: University of Chicago Press, 1994).

11 Ibid., p. xii.

12 Richard Cohen, "The Purported Power of Prayer," *Washington Post* (June 3, 1999).

9. The War Against Drugs Is Vietnam II: We're Losing This One, Too

1 Daniel Forbes, "Prime-time Propaganda," *Salon News* (January 13, 2000).

2 *New York Times* (1965), sourced on www.prdi.org.

3 Mark Thornton, "Letters to the Editor: The Destructive Power of Unenforceable Laws," *Wall Street Journal* (February 12, 1993).

4 Dirk Chase Eldridge, *Ending the War on Drugs* (Bridge Works Publishing, 1998), p. 10.

5 "Drug Addiction: Myth and Reality," *Detroit News* (May 1988).

6 Patrick McMahon, "Debate is Re-Ignited: Is Pot a 'Gateway'?" *USA Today* (March 22, 1999).

7 John P. Morgan and Lynn Zimmer, *Marijuana Myths, Marijuana Facts,* The Lindesmith Center (August 1997).

8 Eric Schlosser, "More Reefer Madness," *Atlantic Monthly* (April 1997): p. 100.

9 Dennis Cauchon, "Some Cite Drug War in Killings," *USA Today* (June 10, 1992).

10 Testimony of David Boaz, Executive Vice President of the Cato Institute, before the subcommittee on Criminal Justice, Drug Policy, and Human Resources Committee on Government Reform; U.S. House of Representatives (June 16, 1999).

11 Christine Lucassen, "U.S. Drug Official's Facts Wrong, Dutch Say," *Seattle Times* (July 14, 1998).

12 William F. Buckley, Jr., "Just Give Me The Facts, Ma'am," *Baton Rouge Morning Advocate* (October 27, 1989).

13 Peter McWilliams, *Ain't Nobody's Business If You Do* (Los Angeles: Prelude Press, 1996), p. 313.

14 John Bartlett and Justin Kaplon (eds.) *Bartlett's Familiar Quotations, 9th ed.,* (Boston: Little, Brown, & Company, 1992).

15 Daniel Forbes, "Prime-time Propaganda," *Salon News* (January 13, 2000).

16 Ibid.

17 Ibid.

18 Milton Friedman, *Seattle Post-Intelligencer* (January 15, 1998).

19 Paul Armentano, "Pot Doesn't Rot Your Brain," *High Times* (October, 1999): p. 38.

20 Ibid.

10. Gun Control Advocates—Good Guys with Blood on Their Hands

1 Mike Downey, "Thank My Sweet Lord for Gun Laws," *Los Angeles Times* (January 2, 2000).

2 John R. Lott, Jr., *More Guns, Less Crime* (Chicago: University of Chicago Press, 1998).

3 John R. Lott, Jr., and David B. Mustard, "Crime, Deterrence and Right-To-Carry Concealed Handguns," *Journal of Legal Studies,* 26 (January 1997).

4 Dr. Michael S. Brown, "Results Are In on British Gun Laws," *New York Post* (January 20, 2000).

5 Don B. Kates, Jr., "Shot Down," *National Review* (March 6, 1995): p. 52.

6 Dr. Michael S. Brown, "Results Are In on British Gun Laws," *New York Post* (January 20, 2000).

7 Ibid.

8 Rene Sanchez, "Shooting Doesn't Contradict Gun Control Stance, Rowan Says," *Washington Post* (June 16, 1988).

9 Ibid.

10 Richard Johnson "Why Sharon Laid Down Her Arms," *New York Post* (August 19, 1999).

11 John R. Lott, Jr., *More Guns, Less Crime* (Chicago: University of Chicago Press, 1998), p. 60.

12 "My Fellow Americans . . . State of Our Union is Strong," *Washington Post* (January 20, 1999).

13 John R. Lott, Jr., *More Guns, Less Crime* (Chicago: University of Chicago Press, 1998), p. 161.

14 Robert Famighetti (ed. dir.), *The World Almanac 2000* (New York: St. Martin's Press, 1999), p. 892.

15 James F. Clarity, "Suicides in Ireland, Especially Among Young, Rising Sharply," *Milwaukee Journal Sentinel* (March 14, 1999).

16 Steven Mufson and Cheryl August, "Nine Dead in Office Rampage," *Washington Post* (July 30, 1999).

17 "Hillary Clinton: Atlanta Killings Show Gun Control Need," *Dow Jones News Service* (July 30, 1999).

18 Larry Copeland, "Fears of Another Rampage Nearly Realized a Day Later," *USA Today* (August 5, 1999).

19 John Lott, *More Guns, Less Crime* (Chicago: University of Chicago Press, 1998).

20 Thomas Sowell, "When Heroism is Politically Incorrect," *Washington Times National Weekly Edition* (July 26–August 1, 1999).

21 James Q. Wilson, "Just Take Away Their Guns," *New York Times* (March 20, 1994).

22 Mike Carter and Kim Barker, "A 'Nobody' Driven by His Hatreds—Furrow Was in State Hospital," *Seattle Times* (August 12, 1999).

23 "Reno Says Gun Buyers Should Have to Pass Ownership Test," *Chicago Tribune* (August 16, 1999).

24 Michelle P. Fulcher and Sean Kelly, "Klebold Parents May Sue Sheriff," *Denver Post* (October 16, 1999).

25 Richard A. Serrano, "Tragedy in Colorado," *Los Angeles Times* (April 23, 1999).

26 John R. Lott, Jr., "More Laws Won't Cure Gun Problems," *Los Angeles Times* (June 17, 1999).

27 Ibid.

28 Testimony of Darryl Scott before the Subcommittee on Crime House Judiciary Committee; U.S. House of Representatives (May 27, 1999).

29 Melissa Healy, "Making Federal Case Out of Guns," *Los Angeles Times* (January 20, 2000).

30 *The Bill of Rights*, Amendments I to X (December 15, 1791).

31 George Skelton, "Gun Lobby Wounded by Its Own Logic," *Los Angeles Times* (February 23, 1995).

32 Collin Levey, "Liberals Have Second Thoughts on the Second Amendment," *Wall Street Journal* (November 22, 1999).

33 Don B. Cates, Jr., "Forefathers Firm on Bearing Arms," *Chicago Tribune* (December 14, 1993).

34 Ibid.

35 Ibid.

36 Laurence H. Tribe and Akhil Reed Amar, "Well-Regulated Militias, and More," *New York Times* (October 28, 1999).

37 Les Adams, *The Second Amendment Primer* (Birmingham, Alabama: Paladium Press, 1996), p. 147.

38 Edgar A. Suter, "Guns in the Medical Literature—A Failure of Peer Review," *Journal of the Medical Association of Georgia* (1994).

39 Ibid.

40 Ibid.

41 Ibid.

42 Executive Summary, "Outgunned: Now The Network News Media Are Spinning the Gun Control Debate," Media Research Center (January 5, 2000).

43 John R. Lott, Jr., "Gun Control Advocates Purvey Deadly Myths," *Wall Street Journal* (November 11, 1998).

44 John R. Lott, Jr., *More Guns, Less Crime* (Chicago: University of Chicago Press, 1998), p. 8.

45 David P. Kopel, "Rowan Case and the Need to Bear Arms," *Wall Street Journal* (June 24, 1988).

46 John J. Goldman, "NAACP Plans Class-Action Suit Against Gun Makers' Violence," *Wall Street Journal* (July 7, 1999).

47 "Paul M. Barrett NAACP Suit Puts Race on the Table in Gun Debate," *Wall Street Journal* (August 13, 1999).

48 Roy Innes, "Gun Control Sprouts From Racist Soil," *Wall Street Journal* (November 11, 1991).

11. The Last Word on the "Stolen" 2000 Election and the New Administration—Will Everybody Please Quit Whining?

1 Transcribed from an audio recording of a twenty-two-minute address by Jesse Jackson during a rally held December 6, 2000, at the State Capitol in Tallahassee, Florida.

2 Nick Anderson, "Black Leaders to Protest Tally of Electors," *Los Angeles Times* (January 6, 2001).

3 Michael Barone and Grant Ujifusa, *The Almanac of American Politics, 1998* (Washington, D.C.: National Journal Inc., 1997), p. 395.

4 Transcribed from an audio recording of an address by Patricia Ireland during a rally held December 6, 2000, at the State Capitol in Tallahassee, Florida.

5 Frank Keating, *Crossfire*, CNN (November 13, 2000).

6 *Good Morning America*, ABC (November 27, 2000).

7 Palm Beach County Supervisor of Elections website, Sample Ballot Voting Instruction page, http://www.pbcelections.org/Sample%20Ballots/instruct.jpg

8 Transcribed from an audio recording of a news conference, held outside the Palm Beach Emergency Operations Center, November 24, 2000.

9 "The Decision: Text of the U.S. Supreme Court Ruling on the Recounts," *Los Angeles Times* (December 13, 2000).

10 *60 Minutes*, CBS (December 3, 2000).

11 Lisa Snell with Lindsay Anderson, "Remedial Education Reform: Private Alternatives to Traditional Title I," Reason Public Policy Institute, *Policy Study* 266 (January 2000).

12 "A Curriculum of Indoctrination," *Issues & Views* (I & V, Fall 1992).

13 "NAACP Accuses Bush of Dividing Nation," *Los Angeles Times* (February 18, 2001).

14 William M. Welch, "Ashcroft Vows to Enforce U.S. Laws," *USA Today* (January 17, 2001).

15 Ellen Futterman, "Black Republicans a Contradiction, or the Wave of the Future?" *St. Louis Post-Dispatch* (September 22, 1991).

16 Sandra Sobieraj, "Democrats Debate Profiling," *Chicago Sun-Times* (February 20, 2000).

17 "Campaign 2000: Former Secretary Cheney and Senator Lieberman Participate in Presidential Debate Commission Debate," Federal Document Clearing House, Inc., (October 5, 2000).

18 "Ashcroft Hits Clinton on Pardon, Drug War," Dow Jones International News (February 8, 2001).

19 "Too Little Too Late: President Clinton's Prison Legacy," Justice Policy Institute (February 19, 2001).

20 Eric Lichtblau, "Ashcroft to Target Gun Crime, but Without New Laws Policy," *Los Angeles Times* (February 8, 2001).

21 " 'Controversial' Abortion Order; But Eight Years Ago Clinton Just Fulfilling 'Promise,' " *CyberAlert* 6:13 (vol. 6; no. 13), Media Research Center (January 23, 2001).

22 Ibid.

23 Ibid.

24 Ibid.

25 Ibid.

26 Ibid.

27 "Sidelights," *The American Enterprise* (October/November 2000).

28 Debra J. Saunders, "Medicare Bonanza," *Orange County Register* (February 11, 2000).

29 Tom E. McClusky, "Risky Schemes and Squandered Opportunities: A Comparison of Al Gore's and George W. Bush's Spending Proposals," National Taxpayers Union Foundation, *Issue Brief* 127 (August 18, 2000).

30 John Lancaster and Helen Dewar, "Tax Cut Votes Still Lacking, Bush Told," *Washington Post* (February 16, 2001).

31 Ibid.

32 "Urban Delinquency and Substance Abuse, Initial Findings," Office of Juvenile Justice and Delinquency Prevention, U.S. Department of Justice (March 1994).

INDEX